The Annual Report of Butterflies and Moths in Yorkshire 2019
Argus 87

This edition has been published by Butterfly Conservation (BC) under the imprint of Butterfly Conservation Yorkshire (BCY) and the Yorkshire Naturalists' Union (YNU).
ISBN 978-1-9160879-2-7
Copyright ©2019 BCY/YNU

This booklet has been written to share information on Yorkshire's moths and butterflies in the interests of conservation and scientific learning. The publishers will be happy to see that information utilised for the benefit of our Lepidoptera on the condition that any written or published use by whatever means, is fully referenced to this publication.

British Library-in-Publication Data: A catalogue record for this booklet is available from the British Library.

Images should be submitted in digital format and original high (300dpi) resolution and size, with your name, species, picture details, date and place incorporated into the file name. Unless otherwise requested it will be assumed we may retain pictures on file for future use in Argus or in publicising the work of BCY/YNU. The owner retains copyright and will always be acknowledged in any further use. Design and layout are undertaken by the editors.

B
co
in
ter
25
He
Ma
Dorset, BH20 5QP
Tel.: 01929 400209
Email: info@butterfly-conservation.org
www.butterfly-conservation.org

Butterfly Conservation Yorkshire (BCY) is a regional branch of the national organisation, with a website detailing activities at:
www.yorkshirebutterflies.org.uk

The Yorkshire Naturalists' Union (YNU) is both an individual membership organisation and a federation of Yorkshire Natural History Societies and conservation groups.
Registered Charity: 224 018.
Registered office:
YNU c/o NEYEDC,
10a Minster Gates, York, YO17JF
Tel: 01904 636952
More information at: www.ynu.org.uk

Data protection policies can be found at www.butterfly-conservation.org

Front Cover Clockwise from top right:
Painted Lady Skelton Cleveland, Damian Money
Small Elephant + Elephant Hawk-Moth North Cliffe Wood, Mike Pearson.
Brown Argus Paul Simmons.
Drinker Skelton Cleveland, Damian Money.

Back Cover Anti-clockwise from top left:
Dusky Sallow 3rd August 2019 Kirk Smeaton, Dave Williamson.
Green-veined Whites 9th May 2019 Calley Heath, Steve Relf.
Tansy Plume *Gillmeria ochrodactyla* 16th July 2019 Treeton Dyke, Mike Smethurst.
Silver Hook 16th June 2019 Strensall Common, Peter Mayhew.
Black Arches 23rd July 2019 Rotherham, Mike Smethurst.
Purple Hairstreak Rolf Farrell.

YORKSHIRE BUTTERFLIES AND MOTHS 2019 ARGUS 87

EDITORS
Micro-moths - Harry E Beaumont
Macro-moths - Charles H Fletcher
Butterflies - David RR Smith
General Editor - Penny A Relf

VICE-COUNTY CO-ORDINATORS OF RECORDING AND CONTRIBUTORY EDITORS
(BUTTERFLIES 1ST, MOTHS 2ND)
VC 61: Sean Clough, Ian Marshall
VC 62: Dave O'Brien, Robert Woods
VC 63: David R R Smith, Mike Couling
VC 64: Dave Ramsden, Charles Fletcher
VC 65: Paul Millard, Charles Fletcher

WRITERS AND COMPILERS
Harry E Beaumont, Philip Brook
Nyree Fearnley, Charles H Fletcher
Paul Fletcher, Mark Hasson
Dave Hatton, Lizzie Ingram
Callum MacGregor, Steve Mattock
Peter Mayhew, Ron Moat
Dave O'Brien, Robert Parks
Martin Partridge, Dave Ramsden
Paul and Joyce Simmons, David R R
Smith, Jennifer A Smith, Andrew Suggitt
Emily Summer, Dave Wainwright
Jennifer Watts, Jax Westmoreland
Lee Westmoreland
Terry Whitaker, David Woodmansey

Small Scallop Askham Bog 8 July 2019
Terry Crawford VC64 record

Buff Arches
20 July 2019 Dave Williamson

Orange-tip female *Anthocharis cardamines*
John Money

CONTENTS

INTRODUCTION

This is the 24th Yorkshire Butterfly and Moth Report in the current series and the 15th new-format report produced jointly between Butterfly Conservation Yorkshire (BCY) and the Yorkshire Naturalists' Union (YNU) Lepidoptera Group. For BC Yorkshire members it is also Argus 87.

Penny Relf (PR) has undertaken the general editing and design work. David Smith (DRRS) has edited the Butterfly Sections and the introductory comments.
The Butterfly Vice-county Recorders and Species Co-ordinators provide considerable assistance in that process by sending contributions already typed up in a suitable format.
The introductory comments and reports relating to the moths have been assembled, edited and typed up by Charles Fletcher (CHF) and Harry E. Beaumont (HEB), with assistance from the Moth Vice-county Recorders.

Oak Lutestring New Laithe Farm Mark Breaks
24 Aug 2019 first in Yorkshire since 1996

We have integrated the butterfly and moth records into a combined Annual Lepidoptera Report. Our Report opens with introductory comments on 2019 followed by the detailed species reports, the Systematic List. As there are too many moths to include in one report we have to be selective, favouring species with fewer than 20 records in the year, plus those whose distributions have changed, together with any interesting migrants. We have included all Yorkshire's butterflies with the addition of some exotics and rare migrants.

Large White in flight, Rolf Farrell.

As always, a huge thank you to everyone who has helped with this year's Report, especially the photographers, recorders and proof readers, it's a massive team effort and we hope that you enjoy reading the results.
PAR/DRRS/CHF/HEB

Early Thorn Rotherham 6 Aug 19 Mike Smethurst
This is a very pale form.

Yorkshire Weather Overview 2019
Dave Ramsden

Weather extremes continued this year. We recorded the highest February temperature and there was the first of several wildfires on Marsden Moor. We recorded the highest all-time temperature in July and heavy rain caused flash floods in the Dales and further heavy rain in December resulted in flooding in parts of south Yorkshire. Rainfall for the year was the 2nd highest (2012) I have on record.

January
The mean temperature was similar to the long-term average at 4.6°C. The month started dry, but this changed for the second half when rain was recorded most days, although finishing with rainfall of only 50% of the norm.

February
The month started with a sprinkling of snow, but ended being the 2nd warmest on record with a mean temperature of 7°C and the highest February temperature on record of 17.7°C on the 26th. It was a sunny month and rainfall was again lower than the mean.

March
Storms Freya and Gareth influenced our weather for the first half of the month, bringing wet and windy weather with rain most days, becoming more settled for the second half. Rainfall was 150% of the norm. Temperatures for the month were above the mean and the highest minimum temperature for March was recorded at 1°C.

April
A relatively dry month with only 40% of the long-term rainfall recorded. Whilst the mean temperature for the month was around the long-term average, we did enjoy a warm sunny period during the 3rd quarter which coincided with the Easter period.

May
The month was slightly cooler than the long-term average with the lowest day maximum temperaturefor May at 8.6°C being recorded on the 9th.

June
Generally unsettled and cool, becoming warmer for the latter part. It was wetter than average with rainfall 160 % of the norm. We had the longest wet period for June with rain recorded for 14 consecutive days up to the 17th.

July
The mean temperature for the month was 18.1°C, 1.2°C above the average. An exceptionally hot spell towards the end of the month saw the highest temperature for July being recorded at 34.1°C and also the highest minimum of 18.7°C. Rainfall was above the mean, but as is typical at this time of year, can vary widely between locations.

August
The mean temperature was above the long-term average at 17.4°C with the highest minimum also being recorded at 9.8°C and rainfall above the mean. The month recorded the highest rainfall recorded in an hour at 24.4mm on the 24th.

September
The first half of the month was relatively settled, with some pleasant warm sunny days and low rainfall. The last third of the month became much more unsettled with a few days of heavy rainfall which finished well above the mean.

October
A wet, cloudy and cool month, with rainfall recorded on 21 continuous days and finishing with the highest recorded rainfall for October at 138.8mm. The mean temperature was 1°C lower than the long-term average.

November
An unsettled cloudy month with little sunshine. The mean temperature was lower than the long-term average and like the past few months, rainfall was much higher than the norm with rain being recorded on 25 days of the month.

December
Overall a mild month with the mean temperature 1.2°C above the long-term average, with few frosty mornings. A brief spell of Snow in North Yorks in the middle of the month caused some roads to be closed. Rainfall was average for the month.

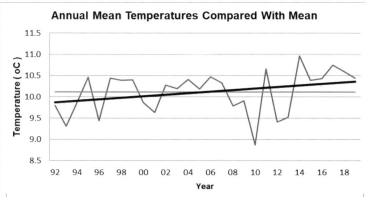

Annual Mean Temperatures Compared With Mean

Monthly Mean Max / Min Temperatures

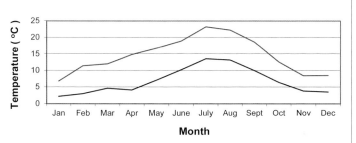

Temperature Difference From Mean

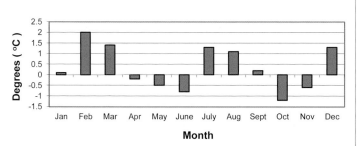

Monthly Rainfall

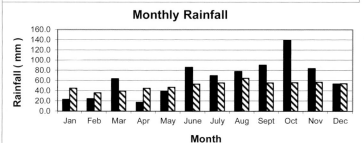

■2019 ▨27 Year Mean

WEATHER STATISTICS FOR WETHERBY 2019

These statistics are based on readings taken by Dave Ramsden who runs a meteorological station at Wetherby North Yorkshire VC 64.
Elevation 54m.
Latitude -53° 55′ N.
Longitude -1° 24′ 16′ W.
This point is roughly in the centre of the county.
We have published similar tables in our Annual Reports since 1997.
As Yorkshire is such a large county, with many variations in relief, these figures will not represent the whole situation. They simply provide a sample which may help to indicate the changes taking place over a longer period of years. In the accompanying tables and graphs the 'variation' or 'difference', is that compared to the mean over 27 years of collecting statistics near this site.
In previous Annual Reports, similar comparisons are made but for mean figures covering the relevant number of years from 1997.

Annual Climatological Summary for 2019

Wetherby
Elevation: 54 Metres Latitude : 53 55' 58" N

West Yorkshire
Longitude: 1 24' 16" W

Month	Temperature ($^{\circ}$C)								Rain (mm)				Wind (mph)			
	Mean Max	Mean Min	Mean	From Mean	Max	Date	Min	Date	Rain	From Mean	Max Obs	Date	Mean	High	Date	Dom Dir
Jan	6.8	2.2	4.6	0.1	11.8	7	-4.4	31	23.0	-21.9	4.0	27	5.8	45	13	W
Feb	11.4	3	7.0	2	17.7	26	-4.0	3	24.2	-11.7	7.8	7	5.3	56	9	S
Mar	12	4.6	8.0	1.4	18.4	20	1.0	8	63.0	23.8	16.6	16	8.4	49	13	W
Apr	14.8	4.1	8.9	-0.2	23.3	20	-0.6	14	17.2	-27.7	7.2	27	4.5	31	5	E
May	16.7	7.1	11.6	-0.5	22.7	30	2.4	12	38.8	-8.2	10.0	8	4.8	33	30	W
June	18.9	10.2	14.2	-0.8	28.6	29	6.8	27	85.6	32.5	14.0	4	4.8	28	3	W
July	23.2	13.6	18.1	1.3	34.1	25	8.3	3	69.6	14.1	23.9	27	4.6	35	20	W
Aug	22.2	13.2	17.4	1.1	30.1	25	9.8	29	77.4	12.8	26.2	4	5.7	39	10	SW
Sept	18.6	10	14.0	0.2	23.6	21	4.7	8	89.8	34.5	23.0	29	5	35	2	W
Oct	12.6	6.4	9.3	-1.2	16.1	8	1.1	28	138.8	83.0	26.0	25	4.4	35	9	SW
Nov	8.4	3.8	6.3	-0.6	12.8	2	-2.3	19	83.4	26.7	9.6	1	3.6	37	11	N
Dec	8.5	3.5	5.9	1.3	12.9	6	-1.1	18	53.0	-0.8	6.2	12	5.2	43	10	SW
Year	14.5	6.8	10.5	0.3	34.1	JUL	-4.4	JAN	763.8	157.3	26.2	AUG	5.2	56	FEB	W

A selection of autumn moths Dave Williamson 29 9 2019 Kirk Smeaton VC63
including Angle Shades, Pink-barred Sallow, Lunar Underwing, Black Rustic, Brown-spot Pinion

BUTTERFLIES 2019. Highlights and Summaries

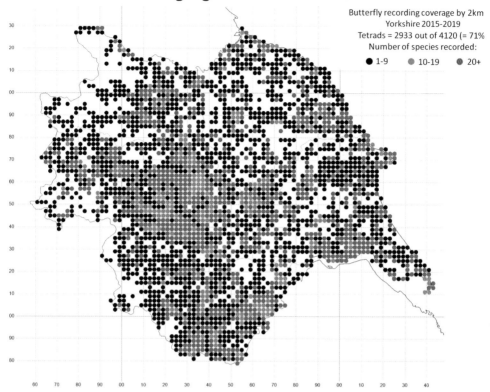

Butterfly recording coverage by 2km
Yorkshire 2015-2019
Tetrads = 2933 out of 4120 (= 71%
Number of species recorded:

● 1-9   ● 10-19   ● 20+

This map shows butterfly recording coverage by tetrad (i.e., 2x2km squares on the OS grid) for 2015-2019. Butterfly Conservation organises butterfly recording nationally in 5-year blocks and produces a summary report every five years. The current cycle started in 2015, so this map summarises our coverage in Yorkshire over the complete 5-year national survey. The dots are colour-coded at three levels allowing us to judge species richness: black means between 1-9 different species were seen in the tetrad over the five years of the recording cycle; bluish green means between 10-19 species were seen in the tetrad; and vermilion means 20+ species were seen in the tetrad over the recording cycle. The last five years' weather has made achieving our goal of maximising coverage interesting: with the poor erratic weather in 2015, the wet spring with a cold April in 2016, the mixed summer of 2017, the exceptionally long, hot and dry summer of 2018, and finally a quixotic 2019 which was marked by long periods of rain interspersed with record high temperatures. Yet I am delighted to say that we have finished the five-year recording cycle having managed to cover 71% of the county (2933 out of 4120 tetrads), with an average number of 8.9 butterfly species per tetrad. This represents a great achievement and I thank all the recorders who have sent in their butterfly records over the last five years. The five-year (2015-19) coverage is considerably better than the previous five-year cycle (2010-14, 62%, average 7.7 species per tetrad) and just beats the five-cycle before that (2005-09, 71%, average 8.4 butterfly species per tetrad).

Flight Patterns

A summary of the first and last butterfly sightings for the whole of Yorkshire

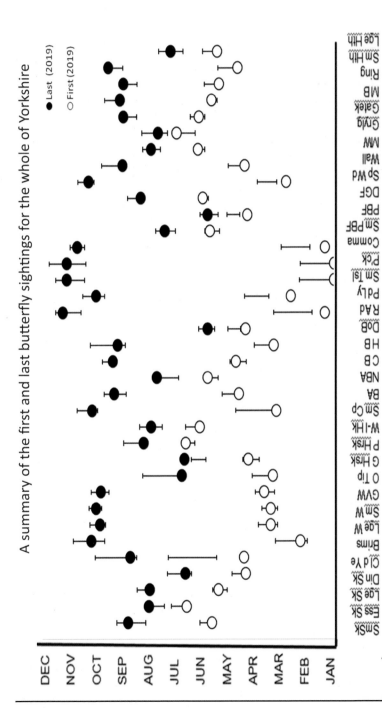

Legend: Summary of first and last sightings butterfly records for the whole of Yorkshire. The errors bars are ± 1 standard deviations of the last ten years' (2009-2018) first and last sightings for each butterfly species. The length of the error bars indicate the variability of first (or last) sightings over those ten years – short error bars indicating little variation and long errors bars indicating greater variation. Roughly speaking you might expect two-thirds of the time for a first (or last) sighting to be within the error bars. The open circles are the 2019 season day of first sighting and solid circles are the 2019 season day of last sighting. The graph tells us, at a glance, whether a particular butterfly species appeared earlier or later in the year than usual (or finished earlier or later in the year than usual for last sightings). It also shows us the length of the flying season for each butterfly. For instance, the migrant Clouded Yellow appeared in Yorkshire much earlier than most years (its first sighting is well before the lower bracket of the ten-year error bars) and finished the season early but not unusually early (last sighting is just inside the lower bracket of the error bars).

Our next five-year cycle starts this year but the global covid-19 pandemic has effectively stopped all butterfly recording other than from our gardens or what we see on our daily exercise. We are very grateful for those records so please keep sending them in to your vice-county butterfly recorder. Keep a look out for the Butterfly Conservation Yorkshire Branch website http://www.yorkshirebutterflies.org. uk/ where I shall be updating the GoogleEarth map of Yorkshire butterfly sightings so as to incorporate the sightings from 2019. Zoom into your area of Yorkshire to see where *locally* you could fill in the recording gaps (**we do not wish to have records other than from your garden or those you have seen on your daily exercise** – this will be the case until restrictions on movement are relaxed by the government sufficiently to allow butterfly recording from further afield). Look out for the dots you have added in next year's Report. Record sheets are available from the VC Butterfly Recorders listed at the back of this Report (see also the Butterfly Conservation Yorkshire Branch website). Garden recording is really important especially if it is done regularly throughout the season. If you usually take part in the national Garden Butterfly Survey (GBS) please note that now BC encourage you to enter these records online (www.gardenbutterflysurvey.org). We should get these online records repatriated to us but if you submit records on paper to the GBS then please send us the information as well.

Butterflies Countywide 2019   David Smith

The global average temperature in the last five years 2015-2019 has been +1.1°C above the pre-industrial period (1850-1900)[1], accelerating beyond even the elevation of +0.2°C in 2011-2015 (World Health Organization (WHO), Sept 2019, 2019 data set based at publication on six months available data). These numbers may seem at first glance small (and putting aside the choice of a pre-industrial base line that is clearly not 'pre-industrial') but represent vast amounts of extra heat energy retained within the earth's biosphere. This leads to increased volatility and systematic departures in our climate which are heavily felt by us on the ground. In 2019, though we were spared the extended heat wave of 2018, we nevertheless experienced a variable year with record amounts of rain
interspersed with some record high temperatures. A strikingly warm day on February 26th with the highest ever February temperature of 17.7°C remains in memory. Think back to the year before that to the 27th February, 2018 and reflect that marked the start of the severe late-winter storm the 'Beast from the East'! February and March were both drier and much warmer than average (2°C and 1.4°C warmer respectively). This caused a few notably early but isolated spring emergences (Small Copper 13/03 by Lee & Jax Westmoreland, Scarborough VC62 which is still later than the earliest ever Yorkshire sighting of 08/03/2011 by Mick Townsend, Thorpe Marsh VC63) and Speckled Wood (01/03 by Richard Laverack on Cudworth Marsh). We also received a few very early migrant Painted Lady towards the end of February and Clouded Yellow at RSPB St Aidan's on 22/04. But overall the spring emergences were not particularly early. The temperatures in the early summer (May and June) were lower than average but the late summer months of July and August were notably warmer than average (1.3°C and 1.1°C respectively). We had a record July temperature of 34°C – a day I spent filling a recording hole in Cottingham moving leadenly across a baking landscape. The last half of the year was also characterised by a lot of rain especially towards the end of the year (Sept-Nov). No species lingered long and last sightings were all fairly normal.

As usual it has been a varied year for our butterflies in Yorkshire. **Painted Lady** had an exceptional '*cardui*' year – the best year since 2009. They arrived early in April but the main arrival was in the more typical month of June. The conditions appear to have been good for breeding in eastern parts of North Africa from where there was extensive migration into the eastern southern Mediterranean and beyond. I have heard accounts of mass migrations moving westwards from Armenia so the large numbers that moved into the UK in June were presumably mainly from an intermediate generation in continental Europe as well as direct from Africa. Like everyone I saw them everywhere. On top

1. Different parts of the world experienced their Industrial Revolutions at different points of time. In northern Europe pre-1750 would be a more accurate date for the 'pre-industrial' period. Within Europe industrial pollution was clearly a major issue in the 19th century: for instance, Porritt (born 1848 in Huddersfield) noted the decline of Lepidoptera in his birth place attributable to the rapid industrialisation in VC63 towns leading to atmospheric smoke haze, sulphur dioxide (SO_2), and soot deposition; as well as the rise of the melanic (darkened) form (Porritt, 1907) in more than 40 species of moths in the area (see fascinating chapters in Frost (2005) and Frost et al. (2011) by Geoffrey Fryer).

of a mountain in the Lake District in early July I could see Painted Lady moving towards me flying a couple of metres above the ground as they engaged in hill-topping – a method of meeting up with other butterflies to mate by converging on higher ground (locating points of local maxima). Insects don't have night clubs so where do they meet partners? Keep following the terrain upwards and you will end up on a hill or other high point. **Red Admiral** with a ranking of 4th most widely-distributed butterfly reflects the good year it was for immigrant butterflies.

Peacock did very well and posted its second highest total in the millennium. **Small Tortoiseshell** had a very good year in 2019. This was a relief because this species has been traditionally our most widely distributed species but numbers have been half of what we would expect during the years 2018-2016 (~7,500). The pre-2016 summers were around the ~15,000 mark. I am pleased to announce that numbers have improved to ~13,000 in 2019 which is a huge improvement. Unfortunately, **Small White** and **Large White** both had a very poor year. Since the collapse in numbers seen in 2014, these two *Pieridae* (The Whites') had made some improvement, but the collapse this year (distribution 16% down for Small White and 20% down for Large White) has undone all the improvements of the last four years. One suspicion is that parasitic braconid wasps such as *Cotesia glomerata* are responsible for these periodic collapses. But another *Pieridae*, the **Orange-tip**, has done remarkably well over the last few years. In 2019 Orange-tip has further improved its fortunes by increasing its numbers by half from 2018 (a year which in itself had been the best season for a decade). Orange-tip is now our 6th most widely distributed butterfly species. The Lycaenid ('Blues & Hairstreaks') **Holly Blue** appears to have entered the waning part of the cycle in its numbers. There is a well-known host-parasitoid cycle between the parasitic ichneumon wasp *Listrodomus nycthemerus* and its sole host the Holly Blue. The wasp lays its eggs in the early instar caterpillars of Holly Blue which periodically drives Holly Blue numbers down. Holly Blue numbers peaked in 2018 and now in 2019 we have seen their first decline. For the next few years we should expect Holly Blue numbers to decline substantially. My favourite *Lycaenidae*, the **Small Copper**, having done so well in the heat wave summer of 2018 (remember its strong partial 3rd brood in late October and early November of that year!), has reverted back to its usual ranking in 2019.

The **Speckled Wood** season was typical of the post-expansion years which I would mark as being from 2007 to now. There has not been a repeat of 2018's possible third brood for **Brown Argus** with the season ending on the 30th September, slightly earlier than usual. The sightings of Brown Argus from across the extent of the Spurn NNR reflect the new drive by Howard and Chris Frost to improve coverage here. There has been little change in **Northern Brown Argus**. The **Small Pearl-bordered Fritillary** had reports to the end of July on the North York Moors; somewhat unusual and indicative of an attempted second brood. However, nothing compared to the 2018 second brood where there were five reports in August (5th to the 21st).

Our four skippers all fared well. **Essex Skipper** continues to spread in VC61 and VC63. It is still rare in VC62 and VC64 and is yet to be seen in VC65. The sighting of Essex Skipper in Langdale Forest (VC62) by Ian and Pauline Popely is unexpected and represents a new 10-km square (SE99). Again there was no repeat of the highly unusual partial second brood in **Dingy Skipper** seen in 2017. The Dingy Skipper season finished early in 2019 possibly due to the extended periods of rain in June; in 2018 the early curtailment of the season was attributed to burn-out from the heat wave.

Wall status remains pretty stable in Yorkshire. It is nationally a species of concern with low-lying inland colonies being at risk of failing due to global warming. Looking at the maps there is a loss from southern and lowland parts of Yorkshire. Populations are stronger on the coast and in the north-west at intermediate altitudes where populations have some relief from rising temperatures. There is no indication currently that Yorkshire Wall is attempting a third brood in October which has been suggested is a 'development trap' (van Dyck et al., 2014). The idea is that having a third late brood does not allow enough time for larvae to reach the overwintering third instar stage before winter hits. Any third brood is thus a waste of investment. However, targeted searching for this under-recorded species can often reveal their presence. It would be instructive to monitor the phenology of inland Wall populations compared to coastal or higher altitude populations.

Silver-washed Fritillary was seen in all five VCs of Yorkshire for the first time. The Silver-washed Fritillary populations in Yorkshire are a mixture of unofficial introductions, populations breeding from previous introductions (Bishop Wood is extensively colonised now from unofficial introductions released in 2017 for instance), and naturally occurring wandering individuals that have been moving northwards. This was given a powerful boost in the long hot summer of 2018. I have provided a map and flight period chart for the first time this year acknowledging the established position of this species in Yorkshire.

Dark Green Fritillary continues its expansion with some natural dispersal from VC64 into VC61 (Naburn, 18/08 by Mike Hayes). Overall VC64 had a very good year with upland areas reporting a doubling of butterflies across both known and new locations in the Dales. **Marbled White** has registered its third consecutive year of decline in abundance and now sits at around two-thirds of the pre-boom average of around 4,000 adults. However, there are still very strong numbers in Brockadale LNR in VC63. Walks in the Wolds of VC61 are also frequently graced by this distinctive Nymphalid, rather confusingly belonging to the subgroup Satyrinae (the 'Browns').

Our three Hairstreaks had a varied year: **Purple Hairstreak** and **White-letter Hairstreak** both had poor years. However, **Green Hairstreak** had an excellent year, probably its best in a decade – and it is good to see that the Spurn NNR populations have done remarkably well.

There was another excellent year for the **Duke of Burgundy**. Known sites produced strong numbers and there were extinct sites in Gundale and Pexton where butterflies were recorded from after many years of absence. The news for **Pearl Bordered Fritillary** was also very positive; both the Valley and Common sites produced numbers that were the best for many years. Grayling was again not seen in VC61, but was present in known locations in VC62 and VC63. Dispersal into new sites in VC63 appears to have been successful.

Gatekeeper fortunes improved this year. The numbers in 2018 were the worst in 13 years – thankfully numbers doubled compared to that year in 2019. This makes it the best year since 2009 – talk about yo-yoing. However, its distribution is still stalled with signs of retraction. Those butterflies which we generally have large populations (our 'big hitters') like the **Meadow Brown** and **Ringlet** have both shown improvements: there was a 50% increase on 2018 numbers for Meadow Brown meaning that the species had its best year since 2014; and Ringlet numbers increased by ~10% compared to 2018 meaning that numbers returned to almost their 2016 level.

It has been yet another interesting Yorkshire butterfly year. Many of us had gloomily expected a poor year in 2019 because that is what happened after the heat wave summer of 1976. A great butterfly year in 1976 was followed by a terrible butterfly year in 1977. The prolonged summer clearly took its toll on many of the larval food plants – many of the butterfly species prematurely ended their season in 2018. However, we ended up having a rather good year in 2019. Many of our less showy but high abundance species rallied. Nationally, we have yet to learn how 2019 ranked out of the 44 years the UKBMS (butterfly monitoring scheme) has been running.

Butterfly Statistics

In 2019, 37 naturally wild species were recorded countywide, plus a further 3 species [Scotch Argus, Small Blue, and Silver-studded Blue] which have been introduced. The Silver-washed Fritillary now appears in all VCs of Yorkshire – it is a mixture of unofficial introductions, progeny of those introductions, and widely distributed naturally occurring populations representing a general northwards expansion. Other rare and exotic species are listed in the appropriate section – there have been three interesting species not counting obvious escapees from Butterfly Houses. An astounding 50,191 butterfly records were submitted with 245,349 individual adult butterflies counted. As well as the usual Butterflies for the New Millennium (BNM) counts, these numbers include entries for iRecord for some vice-counties (if live verified) but BC HQ were later than usual in repatriating iRecord in batch mode as well as other scheme records such as from the Wider Countryside Survey, Migrant Watch, Big Butterfly Count *etc*, so we were unable to incorporate these datasets into our numbers and maps for publication.

Ringlet *Aphantopus hyperantus* Damian Money

VC61 South-east Yorkshire -
Sean Clough

There were definite signs of recovery in 2019 after the two worst consecutive years of our recording program. This suggests that while the very hot summer of 2018 depressed adult numbers it did not overly impact the success of the larval stages as might have been feared. One of the very few butterflies to have had a good 2018, the **Orange-tip**, continued to prosper almost equalling its highest ever total of 794 in 2004 with 792 individual butterflies. Most other species picked up in numbers. Two notable exceptions were the **Speckled Wood** and **Marbled White**. While the Speckled Wood remains widespread in VC61 its numbers are now below those of 2005 when it

Wolds view - looking back towards Wharram lost village

was still colonising the area (850 against 1,599 respectively). Speckled Wood numbers rose to a peak of 3,229 in 2009 after which they settled at around 1,500 to 2,000. It is tempting to speculate that its unique over-lapping broods left it somehow more vulnerable to the extreme heat of last summer? The Marbled White's number tumbled to its lowest ever (326) this century (barring 2001 when the Foot and Mouth crisis closed access to most of its sites). We can reasonably assume that the exposed chalk grassland that forms its habitats in VC61 will have been amongst the worst affected by the heat of 2018. The **Silver-washed Fritillary** was seen again in VC61 with two sightings at Tophill Low Reserve (Phil Morgan & David Smith). **Dark Green Fritillary** was seen again on the Wolds (David Smith) along with a wanderer near Naburn (Mike Hayes). We have now completed 20 years of recording since 2000. Thanks to the efforts of Howard and Christine Frost we now have detailed records being collected from the Spurn Point NNR once again and what a time to start. There was an explosion of the **Green Hairstreak** colony there with 296 individuals recorded all along the peninsula. Whether this represents an influx of migrants, or a response to the summer of 2018, remains unknown. Whilst the collection of our records is *ad hoc*, meaning it is difficult to make definitive statements using it, a couple of statistics from VC61 are worth considering. First the average number of butterflies counted for each species record, i.e., how many of each species were counted at one site on one visit by a single recorder. This gives an indication of overall abundance of butterflies. The average for VC61 for the five years 2000-2004 was 6.7; 2008-2012 was 5.0; and 2015-2019 was 4.1. This suggests we may be seeing a decline in overall abundance. The other statistic is the number of species per recorded 1km square. For 2000-2004 it was 5.3; for 2008-2012 it was 5.2; and for 2015-2019 it was 5.0. This suggests the diversity of species remains relatively constant.

VC62 North-east Yorkshire - **Dave O'Brien**

Mild weather in March meant an early emergence for **Orange-tip**, **Small Copper**, and surprisingly,

Yorkshire Wildlife Trust's Fen Bog VC62 in June P Relf

Holly Blue, which went on to have an excellent year. **Duke of Burgundy** continued to do well in 2019, with an early emergence, further signs of colonisation of new sites, and a positive response to habitat management work. **Pearl-bordered Fritillary** was recorded in good numbers at one of its sites. As in 2018, there was a 2nd brood of **Small Pearl-bordered Fritillary** in August. **White-letter Hairstreak** numbers were low, and there were worrying signs of Dutch Elm Disease at some sites, which could have a long-term impact on this species. **Large Heath** was only seen in low numbers, and it's been several years since it was recorded away from the well-known Fen Bog locality. Probably the highlight of 2019 was the influx of **Painted Lady**, with many accounts coming in of 100s of butterflies seen in June and July. **Silver-washed Fritillary** was more widespread than in previous years, with many seen away from the core areas around Dalby Forest. **Essex Skipper** was recorded from new sites in 2019; it will be worth double-checking any **Small Skipper** sightings in 2020. Dry conditions in 2018 led to fears that some species (especially our rarities) might suffer in 2019 due to desiccation of their larval food-plants. Fortunately this doesn't appear to have been the case.

VC63 South-west Yorkshire – David Smith

Butterfly species largely did very well or very poorly. A comparison between 2019 and 2018 showed increases (>30%) in total number of individuals recorded in **Essex Skipper, Small Skipper, Brimstone, Meadow Brown, Gatekeeper, Red Admiral** (nearly five times more numerous), **Painted Lady** (nearly 40 times more numerous), **Peacock** (nearly three times more numerous), **Small Tortoiseshell, Comma** and **Green Hairstreak**. Declines (>30%) were seen in **Dingy Skipper, Large Skipper, Large White, Small White, Green-veined White, Wall, Small Copper, White-letter Hairstreak, Holly Blue, Brown Argus** and **Common Blue**. It was nice to see **Clouded Yellow** back again. There were 19 reports totalling 32 individual **Silver-washed Fritillary** (by far the most Silver-washed Fritillary VC63 has experienced in one year even if some of these were double counted). There was an interesting arrival in Doncaster sometime between the 2nd and 9th September. Please see the Exotic and Rare Species section at the end of the systematic list for butterflies to see what it was.

VC64 Mid-west Yorkshire - Dave Ramsden

The hot summer of 2018 had us all wondering about what effect this might have on the butterfly populations this year. As it turns out, we need not have feared as generally the good numbers experienced last year have continued. The total number of butterflies seen has been more than in last year's record-breaking year and there is still the Big Butterfly Count and Garden Butterfly Survey data to be received. In fact, several species had a record year in one way or another and none could be classed as having a bad year. The **Dingy Skipper** is only recorded in 25 monads (1km squares) in VC64, so two new locations at Lea Green near Grassington and York were particularly pleasing. Dingy Skipper is an easy species to overlook and one to look out for when in the right habitat. Reports were received again for **Essex Skipper** at Fairburn Ings, with new records from Bishop Wood and St Aidan's, all of singles. I don't think this an easy species to ID, so again one to keep an eye out for, and please take a picture if possible to help with the identification. The **Orange-tip** is probably one of everyone's favourites. It has shown an increase in numbers for three years and enjoyed the best year in VC64 I have on record, with almost double the numbers seen last year. Similarly, the **Brimstone** posted its best ever results. **Marbled White** also had its best year, but without being seen in any new locations. This is a species which does appear to be on the increase in the VC. **Clouded yellow** turned up very early with three records in spring fairly close to each other in the Aire Valley. This was followed by a number at Ripon City Wetlands in late August, which from the comments received, many recorders were clearly pleased to see. Maybe these were the offspring from an earlier un-noticed migrant? The **Wall** has shown signs of improvement over the past two years (2018 and 2019 being

Woodthorpe Roundabout York VC64 June Peter Mayhew

the best years since 2006). There were sightings in 25 new monads this year. Other Nymphalids also did well. It was certainly a **Painted Lady** year with records turning up as early as February. The total number of butterflies seen was twice the previous record. Interestingly most of the high peak counts came from the NW of the VC. **Peacock** had its best summer on record and **Small Tortoiseshell** its best year since 2015. The **Silver-washed Fritillary** continued where it left off last year, with more sightings from more locations, although Bramham and Bishop Wood remain the strongholds. The **Dark Green Fritillary** also had its best year since 2006, with two particularly high counts near Arncliffe. In my Autumn Newsletter sent out to those who contribute records to me I commented that I felt the Blues were well down. I spoke too soon. **Common Blue** numbers were in the main typical and there were two very high counts at Duck Street Quarry. **Holly Blue** had another good year although not quite as good as last year. **Brown Argus** had its best year both in terms of numbers seen and observations. I wonder if we are all becoming more aware of this species? **Green Hairstreak** is another species that did well, with records approaching those seen in 2014. Last but not least, the Browns. **Gatekeeper** had its best year since 2006 with numbers up 300% compared to 2018 and **Meadow Brown** was seen more times and recorded its highest number on record. No species did poorly, certainly not enough to comment. Maybe my summary should just have been "it was a very good year".

VC65 North-west Yorkshire — Paul Millard

2019 was of course a **Painted Lady** year. In VC65 it was the most commonly recorded butterfly with over 900 records of over 6,000 individuals. It is amazing to think that it cannot survive our winters. The **Peacock** came a close second also having a record year 847 records of 5,900 individuals, followed by **Small Tortoiseshell** which merely doubled its previous maximum count to 2,800 insects seen. The **Orange-tip** also had record numbers but reassuringly there was no confusing second generation this year. The **Silver-washed Fritillary** has arrived with four individuals seen at Thorp Perrow Arboretum. Three were seen in July and one was still present a month later. Thirty species of butterfly were seen in the Vice County this year. Sadly there were no Clouded Yellow even though it showed so well just over the border in Ripon. There were also no Marbled White or Small Pearl-bordered Fritillary. New sites were discovered for **Purple Hairstreak** and **White-letter Hairstreak** in Wensleydale. It was also good to see that a strong colony of **Northern Brown Argus** is still present at Morpeth Scar where it has not been recorded since 2008. The details in this annual report for VC65 have been based on data before the inclusion of the highly popular Big Butterfly Count (BBC). If we also include verified BBC data then VC65 had a record 8,067 records representing thirty species and 35,544 individual insects. This is the highest ever number of records in one year; 2018 being the year with the previous highest number of records of 5,164. I expect there will be yet more late records to come. A large number of BBC records had to be rejected simply because the grid reference did not match the location description. Please take great care to get the grid reference right and use a local village name or feature for the description. Try and avoid using a postcode or house name as with GDPR we have to manually alter these records to anonymise them. 77% of records arrived electronically having originated from records entered online. iRecord including the smartphone app accounts for 1,381 records (17%), BBC 2,058 records (26%), WCS and UKBMS transects 2,288 records (28%). The remaining 23% have arrived as they always used to by email in spreadsheets or in the post. These traditional routes have not reduced – the growth in recording activity is all online.

Rockrose on Morpeth Scar Swinithwaite Paul Millard

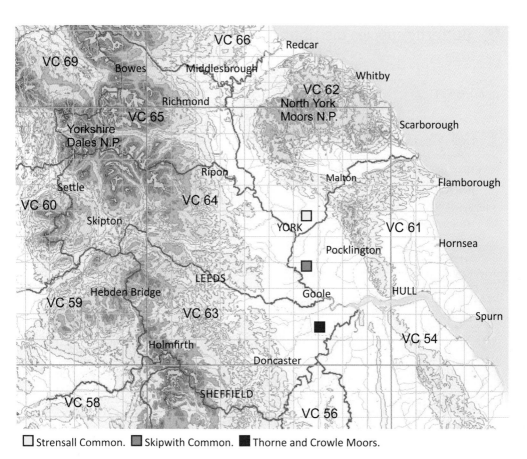

☐ Strensall Common. ◼ (grey) Skipwith Common. ◼ Thorne and Crowle Moors.

VICE COUNTIES - an explanation

The Map above shows Vice-counties in Yorkshire and the bordering Vice-counties which are still used by butterfly and moth recorders (as well as people recording other wildlife such as plants) because they provide historical stability. The borders of Vice-counties do not change, whereas those of political counties have changed dramatically and continue to do so. County Recorders typically work to Vice-county boundaries. In Britain, butterfly and moth recording is generally organised in accordance with the system of Vice-counties. This system was devised by the botanist H.C. Watson in the mid-nineteenth century. Large traditional counties were split into several Vice-counties to produce units of approximately equal size across the country. Thus large counties such as Devon and Lincolnshire each comprise two Vice-counties, whereas smaller counties such as Bedfordshire and Monmouthshire are each single Vice-counties. YORKSHIRE CONTAINS FIVE VICE-COUNTIES: VCS 61 - 65.

How do you find out which Vice-county you are living and recording in?

The Botanical Society of the British Isles has an online tool that will assign a grid reference to a Vice-county, http://herbariaunited.org/gridrefVC/
The Biological Records Centre website has a useful feature which lists Ordnance Survey grid squares in each Vice-county, http://www.brc.ac.uk vcgrid
Another easy to use site is Cucaera, http://www.cucaera.co.uk/grp/

Butterfly species distribution in Yorkshire - comparing the 2019-2016 seasons

Species	% tetrads 2019 (tet. #) records from 1510	% diff 2018 to 2019	% diff 2018 to 2017	% diff. 2017 to 2016	2019 Rank	2018 Rank	2017 Rank	2016 Rank
Painted Lady	53.4 (807)	+31.5	-1.2	-5.7	1	15	11	10
Peacock	49.7 (751)	+2.5	+3.5	+2.1	2	3	5	8
S. Tortoiseshell	48.8 (737)	+3.7	-1.9	-4.1	3	5	4	3
Red Admiral	45.0 (679)	+6.6	-24.1	+20.2	4	7	1	5
Small White	44.6 (674)	-16.2	+7.4	-4.1	5	1	2	1
Orange-tip	40.4 (610)	+6.4	+13.3	-0.4	6	11	13	13
Green-vein. W.	40.3 (608)	-6.7	+7.9	-3.0	7	4	7	7
Speckled Wd	38.9 (587)	-5.0	+9.8	-4.1	8	6	9	9
Meadow Brown	34.9 (527)	-2.6	-2.6	-5.5	9	8	6	4
Ringlet	33.4 (504)	-0.8	-2.2	-5.8	10	10	8	6
Large White	32.8 (495)	-19.5	+4.1	-6.1	11	2	3	2
Comma	28.7 (434)	-6.4	+1.2	+11.3	12	9	10	12
Brimstone	22.1 (333)	+2.7	+3.9	-0.6	13	16	14	17
Holly Blue	21.1 (318)	-5.2	+13.7	+0.3	14	12	19	18
Small Skipper	20.6 (311)	+2.4	+3.4	-1.5	15	18	15	16
Common Blue	17.4 (262)	-5.5	+8.9	-2.5	16	14	16	15
Gatekeeper	16.8 (253)	-1.5	-3.8	-1.3	17	17	12	11
Small Copper	16.6 (250)	-7.6	+11.2	+2.7	18	13	18	20
Large Skipper	15.9 (240)	+1.4	+1.3	-5.4	19	19	17	14
Small Heath	14.9 (225)	+0.8	+4.1	-2.2	20	20	20	19
Wall	10.5 (159)	-0.3	+4.0	+1.2	21	21	21	21
Green Hairstr.	6.2 (94)	+1.4	+1.3	-0.6	22	26	24	26
Brown Argus	5.6 (85)	-2.6	+5.1	+0.6	23	22	25	28
Dark Gr. Frit.	5.6 (85)	-0.8	+2.3	-1.3	24	25	26	24
Purple Hairstr.	5.0 (75)	-1.6	+4.4	-0.5	25	24	29	27
Dingy Skipper	4.6 (69)	+0.1	+1.0	-0.5	26	27	23	23
White-l Hairstr.	4.1 (62)	-3.7	+5.5	-1.3	27	23	28	25
Marbled White	3.5 (53)	0.0	-0.3	-1.3	28	28	22	22
Essex Skipper	2.3 (35)	+0.7	-0.7	+1.3	29	29	27	30
Small P-b Frit.	1.3 (19)	-0.1	+0.4	+0.2	30	30	30	31
Northern BA	1.1 (17)	-0.2	+0.3	-0.2	31	31	31	29
Clouded Yell.	0.9 (14)	+0.6	0.0	+0.2	32	35	34	36
Duke of Burg.	0.8 (12)	+0.2	-0.2	-0.3	33	33	32	32
Large Health	0.7 (11)	-0.1	+0.5	-0.2	34	32	33	33
Grayling	0.4 (6)	+0.1	-0.1	-0.1	35	34	36	34
Pearl-b. Frit.	0.2 (3)	+0.1	-0.1	+0.1	36	36	35	35

The table on page 16 shows how the thirty-six resident butterflies of Yorkshire compare against each other in terms of distribution. Where there was the same distribution in tetrads, we ranked according to numbers of reports provided. The distribution measure is expressed as a percentage of the number of tetrads recorded in the reporting year so it is a relative metric; comparison between years when arguing absolute change is problematic to the degree by which the number of recorded tetrads between years varies.

We can immediately see that **Painted Lady** was the mostly widely distributed butterfly in Yorkshire in 2019. This is no surprise – the 2019 season was the best year for this immigrant butterfly species since 2009. The healthy positioning of **Red Admiral** with a ranking of 4th reflects the good year it was for immigrant butterflies. **Peacock** and **Small Tortoiseshell** continue their slow movement up the table. **Small White** and **Large White** both had a very poor year – after four years spent recovering from the collapse in numbers of these two species experienced in 2014 – we are back to square one for both species. The suspicion is that parasites of these butterfly species depress numbers in a similar fashion as occurs in the well-known cycle observed in **Holly Blue**. But another Pieridae ('White') the **Orange-tip** has done remarkably well over the last few years. In 2018 Orange-tip had the best season in a decade but just missed out on a top-10 position. In 2019 Orange-tip has further improved its fortunes and has hurtled up the table to the 6th most widely distributed of our butterfly species. Holly Blue numbers peaked in 2018; for the next few years as the parasitic ichneumon wasp Listrodomus nycthemerus numbers build we should expect reduced numbers of Holly Blue. The first initial drop in numbers has been confirmed by a small drop in Holly Blue's distribution ranking in 2019. **Small Copper**, having done so well in the heat wave summer of 2018 (remember its strong partial 3rd brood that year!), has reverted back to its usual ranking in 2019. **Pearl-bordered Fritillary** once again had the most restricted of distributions of Yorkshire's butterflies in 2019. Please study the chart to see what patterns you can discern.

Butterflies: the small print

Please read this section if you want to understand what we have done in presenting these records for you and why we have done it, especially if you are using this Lepidoptera Report for research.

KEY to the BUTTERFLY REPORTS

The statistical information in our butterfly section is based on records received by November 2019. Maps are based on 50,191 records in Levana. Records sent in later than November will not generally make it into the Annual Report listings, though they should eventually end up in our databases. We encourage all butterfly recorders to send in their records at regular intervals through the year so that the VC Recorders can keep on top of the work of verifying and entering the data in order to have it ready for the end of the year. For newcomers to our recording project we urge you to use our special recording forms available from the VC Recorders or the BC Yorkshire Branch website (http://www.yorkshirebutterflies.org.uk/). Once you have enrolled with a VC Recorder you should automatically receive replacement forms in the spring, and whenever you request them, as well as regional recording newsletters.

The definition of '**a record**', as used in this Report, is a sighting of one or more butterflies (or moths) of a single species observed on a single site usually no bigger than a 1km grid square as used on Ordnance Survey (OS) maps; more than one independent observation of the same species/site/date combination will yield more than one record. This Report publishes butterfly distribution maps based on tetrads (2x2km squares on the OS grid). Unless otherwise indicated, our species maps show the recorded presence in the year of the Report. We started to do this in 2015 so be aware that in years previous to that date what was shown was the accumulated records for the current recording cycle. Annual Reports have been produced as separate booklets since 1996, and in the present thicker booklet format, since 2005.

For all our regular species, and some of those which are less common, we have produced a set of statistics mainly intended to clarify the size of the sample we are using for our comments. We emphasise this because of the dangers of reading too much into the figures. Readers should always remember that such statistics are directly related to the number of observers and the number of visits they make. However, we also consider that the number of records we are now receiving from all five VCs (20,000 to 40,000+ records per year) represents a large enough sample to have some validity in enabling us to make reasonably objective comparisons from year to year. Nevertheless, the large size of the county and the difficulties associated with covering our higher and more remote regions means that our generalisations may not hold for every corner of the county. There are also a few anomalies in our recording system. Spurn NNR is a linear nature reserve covering 14x1km squares in two different 10km squares, records are usually submitted on a 10km basis and from one of those 10km squares (TA41). As our butterfly maps are tetrad based this means that many Spurn records are not mapped. The published maps in our Report will thus underestimate the amount of recording that goes on at Spurn. However, please note that from 2018 Howard and Chris Frost have set up a new system of butterfly recording at Spurn NNR such that now many of the records from Spurn will be reported down to the monad level (1km square). There may also be a small lack of agreement in the number of dots shown on a map and the figures in the statistics for that species. This is because the maps are based on records sent in after Christmas which may include repatriated data from national recording schemes (iRecord, Migrant Watch, Big Butterfly Count *etc*), whilst the statistics are based largely on data received before Christmas though augmented by significant late records. Figures for each species may change considerably when late batches of records are received, therefore any comparisons drawn from statistics given in our Annual Reports should be made with due caution.

The butterfly statistics – definitions: **Monthly flight days** refers to the number of days the species has been recorded flying in each month and is compared to the total number of butterflies (i.e., the sum of all counts made) seen countywide in that month.

Total flight days is the number of different days on which our observers have recorded the butterfly in the year. Whilst many observers only record during the weekends, there are daily counts made in a number of nature reserves and gardens, which help to make this assessment realistic, although it should still be seen as a broad generalisation. More regular garden counts would help to make this statistic even more valuable.

Flight season length is measured as the number of days from the first sighting to the last sighting and in most cases this is taken through all broods.

In **total reports** a 'report' is almost the same as a 'record', but where a record may be of say 60 butterflies, the report associated with it counts as one, irrespective of the number of butterflies seen. By dividing the number of reports into the number of butterflies counted we get the mean number of butterflies seen in an observation. Though this may seem a rather artificial number (possibly inflated by occasional large counts), it gives us some measure of the success of a species from year to year irrespective of annual variations in the number of observers. We encourage observers to make actual counts of the number of butterflies they see unless those numbers are so big that an estimate is the only way to give some idea of the number present. In the figures we give in our reports, round numbers such as 50, 100, 150 and upwards are taken to be estimates, whilst other exact figures are taken to be actual counts.

Maps: This year's Report has retained the use of maps from Butterfly Conservation's Levana software. This offers better resolution dot (2x2km tetrads) distributions with a three-colour code of abundance. However, there is no terrain map option in Levana as there is in MapMate (used in some earlier Reports). We use a colour palette for the dots which should be equally visually distinctive for all readers including those with varying degrees of colour blindness. This is the second year we have used this colour palette.

Flight period graphs: The graphs work by dividing the year into weeks (starting on 1st Jan) and then for each week counting the number of records we receive in that week for a given species. If we receive 35 records, which in total might represent for instance 789 individual butterflies, then the bar height will be 35. These charts have been created for all butterfly species where the number of reports is high enough to be meaningful. We hope that they provide a good indication of when to expect a butterfly to be flying (though flight periods change somewhat from year to year).

Arrangement: We follow the *Checklist of the Lepidoptera of the British Isles* (2013) by Agassiz, DJL, Beavan, SD, & Heckford, RJ. We no longer (since the 2017 season Report) include the old Bradley numbers.

MOTHS 2019

Highlights

A warm winter and an early spring meant that the year started quite differently to 2018 when we had to suffer the "beast from the east". This meant that the season started with a flurry of unusual early records. The weather in general was good for moth trapping and there were some impressive catches during some warm spells in the summer. The final total of 173,055 records received was 15,000 fewer than in 2018 but still the second highest total ever. The number of species recorded in the county with last year's figures in brackets was as follows: 1246 (1238) species comprising 703 (709) species of microlepidoptera and 543 (529) species of macrolepidoptera. This was just short of the record total of 1250 in 2017. Microlepidoptera comprised 26.6% of all records – a similar proportion to the previous year. We received records from 484 contributors, a slight drop from the record of 509 in 2018.

Macro Moths

Charles Fletcher

There were three new macro moths for the county recorded in 2019. The first one looks as if we had a crystal ball, as in this section last year we wrote "perhaps we can expect a Scarlet Tiger in Leeds sometime soon". It duly arrived on 22nd June when a single Scarlet Tiger moth was photographed in Leeds and posted on iRecord. Unfortunately, we could not find out more details – one of the many problems of iRecord! This species has been gradually moving north and we are likely to see more. The second new moth was far more unexpected. A Nine-spotted was seen and photographed near Wentbridge on 14th July. The photograph was good and enabled us to eliminate other confusion species. This is the third record of this day-flying moth for the UK following records in 1872 and 2000. It is not usually known to be a migrant so its provenance must remain a mystery. The third new addition to the county list was a more conventional rare migrant – Shining Marbled was first seen in the country in 2006 and there have only been a handful of records since. One was trapped at Spurn on 28th July.

There were a good number of vice-county records this year. In VC61, a larval web of Oak Processionary Moth was found on a newly planted oak at Hull University on 16th July. This was reported to the Forestry Commission and the tree was destroyed. This is the third record for the county. Beautiful Snout also reached VC61 for the first time with one at Muston on 13th July. This is not surprising as it has been spreading rapidly across the county and we now have records for all five VCs. VC62 had two new moths. Marsh Oblique-barred is only known from the west of VC64 so it was a surprise when one was seen at Strensall Common on 28th July. This tiny macro is such an easy moth to overlook that it may have been resident there for many years escaping detection. Least Carpet had an outstanding year and spread widely across the county. The first for VC62 reached Skelton on 31st July and it also reached VC64 with one at Burley-in-Wharfedale on 1st August. In VC63, Yorkshire's second Beautiful Marbled was trapped at Cudworth on 25th July; the first having been seen at Spurn in 2017. This is another migrant moth which is fairly new to the country, the first having been seen in 2001. Tree-lichen Beauty is a recent colonist to south-east England and has been spreading north west. Extra-limital moths are usually assumed to be migrants. It had a remarkable year with 12 at Spurn and one up the coast at Flamborough. One at Swinefleet on 25th July was the first for VC63. This species may soon become resident in Yorkshire. The last new moth for VC63 was a White-point at Austerfield on 9th July. This is another species moving slowly north and west and has been seen regularly in VC61 since 1997. VC64 had three new species in addition to the Least Carpet already mentioned. There has been some regular trapping at Askham Bog this year and a Small Scallop was found there on 8th July. It is an overdue addition to the VC64 list and may have been lurking there for some time. There was a small influx of Small Marbled into the county this year; three were seen in VC61 and one at Tadcaster on 13th July was the first for VC64. The last new moth was Marbled Clover which was seen by day and photographed in Ripon on 2nd August. This is a migrant species in our area and was the fifth county record; the fourth having been trapped at Beverley in VC61 the previous night. Surprisingly there were no new species for VC65 which remains very unexplored compared to the other VCs. There are 28 species which have been seen in all VCs except for VC65, so perhaps the most likely contenders to cross the border in 2020 might be Varied Coronet, Devon Carpet or even Small Ranunculus.

There were so many other highlights that it is difficult to know where to begin as it was a good year for rare moths. Cypress Carpet was new to the county in 2018 and two moths were seen nearby at Little

Preston in July, so it is evidently established in this area. Yarrow Pug was also new to the county in 2018 and it is good to see that it is still present at Austerfield along with Shaded Pug which was also found there last year. Our third and fourth records of Bilberry Pug came from Guisecliffe near Pateley Bridge and from Wadsley and Loxley Common near Sheffield. It is likely to occur at several other sites in the county if actively searched for. Several species not seen in the county for several years put in an appearance in 2019. Peacock Moth has not been seen since 2008 and can be tricky to separate from Sharp-angled Peacock; moths were found at Spurn and Wykeham Causeway in July and August. There were only eight previous records of Waved Black so it was surprising that four were trapped at three sites in the south of the county. Another rarity, Oak Lutestring is occasionally seen in the very western parts of the county where it shares its distribution with the population in Cumbria and north Lancashire. Our first record since 1996 was found in the Bowland area, a part of Yorkshire which would repay more trapping as several other rarities might occur here. Healthy numbers of Dentated Pug were found at Askham Bog – the first records since 2013. Other highlights included a record total of 25 Purple-bordered Gold flying by day at Thorne Moors, two Goat Moth larvae at Potteric Carr, a new site for this rare and spectacular moth, and healthy numbers of Chalk Carpet at Flamborough where it is flying much earlier than the books tell us it should do. The Yorkshire Dales has some rare moths; Heath Rivulet and Least Minor were found in the Littondale/Upper Wharfedale area again, Tissue continues to do well with good populations over-wintering in caves, whilst Thyme Pug was found at Greenhow, well to the east of its usual sites. Privet and Pine Hawk-moths were found at a lot of new sites across the county, and a major survey of Small Eggar larval webs found them at an amazing 80 sites in the Pickering/Malton area. Several species which have invaded the county in recent years continue to do well. Devon Carpet has extended its range considerably and was found at eight new sites in the centre and north of the county. Chocolate-tip continues to expand its range in the south east, and Black Arches was found at six sites in VC61, 63 and 64. Beautiful Hook-tip continues to do well and was found at a surprising 85 sites, and numbers of Vine's Rustic increased considerably. Small Ranunculus expanded westwards this year rather than northwards, but numbers of Red-necked Footman fell for the first time. Perhaps its parasitoids have caught up with it after a period of expansion. Numbers of Maiden's Blush also fell slightly after its recent dramatic expansion.

It was a good year for unusual migrants. In addition to the county and vice-county records listed above, there were two records of adult Death's-head Hawk-moth plus a larva, the first Clifden Nonpareil since 2007 was found at Flamborough, and our second Dark Crimson Underwing turned up at Spurn, two years after the first. A Golden Twin-spot at Catwick was the first since 2011, a Pale-lemon Sallow at North Ferriby was the third for the county, and some unusual lowland records of Light Knot-grass were probably part of a migrant wave which was also noticed in counties to our south.

Not all species did well, and there were no records at all of Large Ranunculus or Small White Wave. There have been no records of Manchester Treble-bar or Northern Drab for two years, and no Netted Pugs for three years. There was only one Barred Rivulet, and four records of Figure of Eight is the lowest number of records ever received. Dark Spinach numbers were the worst for many years. The status of Dark Bordered Beauty at Strensall Common is worrying with very low counts this year. A lot of woodland species flying in late spring and early summer did particularly badly in 2019, perhaps due to over-wintering factors. On a more positive note, 237 species at High Batts NR on the YNU VC64 outing on 12th July is the biggest total ever recorded at light on one night in the county. What is perhaps rather unusual for a VC64 outing, all were caught just over the rather convoluted border in VC65! So, despite having an impoverished fauna, 240 fewer species than the next poorest vice-county, a very small number of moth trappers and fewer than 10,000 records per year, VC65 can still hold its head high with this record.

Micro Moths
Harry Beaumont

Moths found for the first time within the county in 2019 numbered five which is similar to annual additions in recent years. Four of these were in VC63; as the most southerly of Yorkshire vice-counties it is well placed to receive species that are extending their range northwards. That is the case with *Ectoedemia heringella*, the larvae of which mine the leaves of holm oak, which was found near Doncaster in August and then shortly afterwards at Hessle in VC61 indicating that it may occur more widely in the extreme south of the county. The same can be said of *Phyllocnistis saligna* whose larvae mine the bark of willows; it was identified at four localities in the Doncaster district in early September and then at Cottingham in VC61 the following week. It will be interesting to see how rapidly these two moths extend their range in Yorkshire in the future. More than twenty-five years ago *Cochylis molliculana* was first found in Britain since when it has slowly extended its range northwards. Even so when one occurred at Kirk Smeaton in August it was an unexpected find, some way to the north of any other British record. The remaining two additions are likely to be the result of immigration; that is certainly the case with the plume moth *Oxyptilus laetus* which was recorded quite widely in Britain during the year. One occurred at Austerfield in July while a moth suspected of being this species turned up at Swillington in VC64 but unfortunately it was not retained and a photograph remained inconclusive despite being submitted to the national expert for appraisal. The final addition is the distinctive pyralid moth *Oncocera semirubella*, this is a resident moth in southern England but is also believed to be an occasional immigrant. Two moths found on the same date, at Semerwater in VC64 and at York in VC62 on 26 July, could be indicative of immigration; the first Nottinghamshire record occurred about the same time and there were also extra-limital occurrences elsewhere in Britain.

The number of new vice-county records has reduced slightly but this was always to be expected as the more widespread species are finally located in each of Yorkshire's five vice-counties. Nevertheless there was a total of 38 such records spread between VC61 (5), VC62 (6), VC63 (5), VC64 (11) and VC65 (11); these totals exclude those that provided the new county occurrences in VC63 (4) and VC64 (1) but include two records dating from 2018. The recording of leaf mining moths has continued and has resulted in *Ectoedemia heringi* being found in two additional vice-counties 62 and 65, well north of previous occurrences in the south of the county. An adult of the alder feeding *Bohemannia quadrimaculella* was found at Ellington Banks in VC64, the few previous records are all of adults and the precise detail of its life history is yet to be established. Mines of *Perittia obscurepunctella* on honeysuckle were located at three localities in VC63; all other recent occurrences have been in VC64 although there are old records from vice-counties 61 and 62. Leaf cones made by larvae of *Caloptilia semifascia*, a scarce moth in the county with only four earlier records, were found on field maple in vice-counties 64 and 65; cones on this foodplant can be accepted but not those on Norway maple which may involve other species, however no moths have yet been reared from any cones in Yorkshire. The distinctive alder feeding moth *Stathmopoda pedella* is now well established in the south of the county and had been recorded as far north as Askham Bog. In 2019 it has made a small step into VC62 to the north of York although it has been found further north elsewhere in England. One of the most rapid range expansions among the tortricoid moths has been by *Epinotia signatana* which was first found in Yorkshire in VC61 as recently as 2014 and rapidly gained a foothold in that vice-county from where the majority of county records now occur. It spread northwards into VC62 in 2016 and has now occurred, albeit as single examples, in vice-counties 63 and 65. A moth that seems surprisingly scarce in the county is the pine feeding *Pseudococcyx posticana* which had been seen on only four occasions in vice-counties 62 and 63. Thus one at Stainburn Forest at the end of May provided the first in VC64; perhaps more outings to coniferous woodland early in the year will show it to be more widespread. Some species are consistently under-recorded and this applies to members of the genus *Dichrorampha*. During the year the presence of *D. vancouverana* was confirmed in VC64 at Alwoodley; almost all previous records are from the south of the county in vice-counties 61 and 63 with only a single record in VC65 coming from the more northern districts. The pyralid *Sitochroa verticalis* is mainly a southern moth in Britain and there was only a single previous county record from Millington (VC61) as long ago as 1939 so one at West Melton in VC63 in late June was unexpected. Whether it originated from the resident population in the south or arrived as an immigrant is uncertain.

One of the highlights of the year resulted from the identification of two examples of *Nematopogon magna* taken a day apart and in adjacent 10km squares either side of the VC64 and VC65 boundary. The distribution of this moth was thought to be restricted to central Scotland and the west of Ireland until a specimen from Wadworth Wood in VC63 dating from 1904 was identified in the collections at Doncaster Museum in 1985. This remained the only English record until 2018 when moths captured near Kirkby Malzeard (VC64) and Bellflask (VC65) were recognised early in 2019. With records now from three vice-counties there can be little doubt that this moth is resident in Yorkshire at very low density.

One problem that besets county recorders is that species are sometimes shown as occurring within a vice-county on published distribution maps without any data being provided to substantiate the records and confirmation is often difficult or impossible to obtain. We have a number of such 'records' in Yorkshire and that is why some occurrences are referred to as being the first confirmed records. Three species that fall into this category are included in the present report and these are *Pseudopostega crepusculella*, *Adela cuprella* and *Depressaria pimpinellae*.

Whilst new vice-county occurrences highlight any increasing distributions of our moths, whether real or due to under-recording in the past, many significant records do not involve a presence in a new vice-county. Two *Nephopterix angustella* made an appearance in VC61 during the year following on from two earlier records in 2010 and 2017. This spindle feeding moth is resident from East Anglia southwards; are our Yorkshire moths wanderers from this resident population of are they immigrants from the continent? The second county *Vitula serratilineella* occurred at Easington at the end of August, not far from Spurn where the first British example was found in 1997. This moth, the larvae of which live in bumble bee nests, was later found to have a resident population to the north of Yorkshire in Northumberland. A number of tortricoid moths that have been recorded for the first time in Yorkshire in recent years are showing welcome signs of a more permanent presence; these include *Spatalistis bifasciana* that provided the fifth occurrence since the first in 2014. All have been in the south of the county in vice-counties 61 and 63 and are presently the most northerly in Britain. Others have had a presence in Yorkshire for some time but are very infrequently encountered, *Thiodia citrana* is an example with three occurrences in the Spurn area in 1953, 1995 and 2014. It is a distinctive moth that is unlikely to have been overlooked; it was found further up the coast at Hunmanby Gap at the end of July. In contrast our fourth *Bactra lacteana* and the first since 2008 at Coniston Cold in September is a moth that would be easy to overlook and which requires dissection to confirm its identity.

Among the undoubted immigrants were three examples of *Ancylosis oblitella* at Easington on 25th August with moths also being recorded on the following two nights; some or all of these could have resulted from the re-trapping of the original moths. There is only a single earlier occurrence at Spurn in 1996. We have four records of *Euchromius ocellea*, the last in 2014. Moths were seen at Kilnsea on 10th July and at nearby Easington the following night leading to speculation as to whether or not the records related to the same individual.

Finally, mention must be made of *Cydalima perspectalis*, the Box Moth, a large and spectacular Asian pyralid moth that first turned up in Europe in 2006 having been introduced as larvae with infected plants. It has since expanded its range explosively, no doubt aided by the horticultural trade and is now widespread, sometimes occurring in plague proportions throughout much of mainland Europe. It had found its way to Britain by 2007 and already in southern England the larvae occur is such numbers as to defoliate box plants. Despite the considerable increase in records of this moth in Yorkshire in 2019, involving vice-counties 61 to 64, there has so far not been any report of larval damage. It can only be a matter of time!

Migrants

The migrant season started early in 2019 as the winter was warm and there was no "beast from the east" to delay proceedings. A number of Diamond-back Moths in January were probably left over from the small influx at the end of 2018, and a Small Mottled Willow inside a supermarket pepper in January cannot be classed as a proper migrant, so the first real migrants arrived during a very warm spell with southerly winds starting in mid-February. This brought extremely early records of Small Mottled Willows to Lund and Ingleton, Silver Y at Sheffield, Humming-bird Hawk-moth at Seamer and

Bordered Straw at Asenby in a quite remarkable period of two weeks. Most migrants appeared earlier than usual. The first Dark Sword-grass was found in March and more Humming-bird Hawk-moths arrived, though the main influx of this species was in June and July as usual.

The first of the rarer migrants appeared in June with two Death's-head Hawk-moths at Spurn. A larva at Guisborough in September probably stemmed from this small influx. It was July however when the real excitement started. A Small Marbled arrived at Spurn on 9th, closely followed by more at Hunmanby Gap, Spurn again, then inland at Tadcaster over a period of four days. There have only been five previous county records and the Tadcaster moth was the first for VC64. A

73.008 Golden Twin-spot Catwick a very rare migrant in VC61. Jim Morgan.

nationwide influx of the scarce plume moth *Oxyptilus laetus* brought one to Austerfield on 16th July, the first for Yorkshire. Two more probable examples were trapped but unfortunately were not retained so could not be verified although one was photographed. Tree-lichen Beauty was first found in the county in 2018 and the first of a major influx of this moth arrived at Spurn on 23rd July. Over the next month, a remarkable 11 more arrived at Spurn, one was up the coast at Flamborough, and the first for VC63 arrived at Swinefleet. More excitement was to follow with Yorkshire's second Beautiful Marbled at Cudworth on 25th July and a small influx of the tortricid *Cydia amplana* further up the coast over a period of three days with two at Skelton and a remarkable three on one night at Hunmanby Gap. We have only five previous county records of this species. Two *Euchromius ocellea* arrived at Spurn in July, our fifth and sixth records. The last excitement for July was Yorkshire's first Shining Marbled at Spurn on 28th. There have only been a handful of national records since the first in 2006. August started with a bang. Yorkshire's second Dark Crimson Underwing was found at Spurn on 1st August and on the same day a Marbled Clover was trapped at Beverley, the fourth county record and the first since 1968. Remarkably one was seen and photographed the following day at Ripon, and more moths were seen in Northumberland soon afterwards. Also on 1st August, Yorkshire's first Golden Twin-spot since 2011 turned up at Catwick. Later in the year, the other migrant Hawk-moths had a mixed year. Bedstraw Hawk-moths appeared in good numbers with five of the eight records well inland, but Convolvulus Hawk-moth appeared in smaller numbers than usual; all being coastal apart from one in Masham. At the end of August, Yorkshire's 12th Clifden Nonpareil was found at Flamborough. This was the first record of this spectacular moth in the county since 2007. The main influx of *Udea ferrugalis* arrived at the end of August bringing the biggest totals seen since 2006, but *Nomophila noctuella* had a much poorer year than usual with a small influx arriving in August and September.

Other micro moths arriving at this time included a single *Loxostege sticticalis* at Stillingfleet and just two *Palpita vitrealis* at Sharow and Hollym Carrs. Late summer and early autumn also brought good numbers of Vestals to all five vice-counties and a Bordered Straw to Flamborough, whilst a reasonable influx of Scarce Bordered Straw arrived in September. A number of Delicates left it until October to arrive and a scattering of Pearly Underwings were mostly late in the year. The only regular migrant not to appear at all was Gem. This was its first blank year since 2012.

Diamond-back Moths arrived in large numbers; the main influxes being in May, June and July, but the biggest totals were all in mid-June in coastal areas where there were several counts of up to 2000 moths seen by day and counts of up to 400 in moth traps. This species provided the final migrants of the year with the last one being seen at North Frodingham on 19th December.

Several other species not normally known as migrants appeared in unusual places in 2019 and are worth mentioning here. Yorkshire's third Pale Lemon Sallow arrived at North Ferriby on 5th October. Records away from the core area are generally thought to be migrants. There were two very strange records of Light Knot-grass in VC61 and one at Austerfield in VC63. The latter could possibly have been a wanderer from Thorne or Hatfield Moors, but one of the VC61 moths, the Austerfield moth, one out of area at Great Smeaton in VC62, and moths in Nottinghamshire and Leicestershire, all arrived on 24th or 25th May so this sounds like a coordinated arrival. Two examples of the attractive pyralid moth *Oncocera semirubella* arrived on the night of 25th July at two widely separated sites, Semerwater and Haxby. This was a new species for Yorkshire and it coincided with other examples arriving unexpectedly in other parts of the country.

A very unusual record of Nine-spotted came from a site near Wentbridge on 14th July may have been a migrant, and finally, it is worth noting that Willow Ermine, *Yponomeuta rorrella,* was found at 15 sites, including seven where it had not been seen before. There was an apparent influx of this species in 2018 and this could have been a new influx or perhaps moths staying on to breed from 2018.

63.031 Rusty-dot Pearl 30 Aug 19 Kirk Smeaton VC63
Dave Williamson

The following table shows the number of records (not individuals) for each migrant species in 2019 compared with numbers in the five previous years (ie 2014 – 15 – 16 – 17 – 18). This enables readers to check how many of each species might have been expected in a typical year.

Plutella xylostella (Diamond-back Moth)	1752	(872 – 293 – 1952 – 377 - 1172)
Ostrinia nubilalis (European Corn Borer)	1	(3 – 1 – 4 – 0 - 3)
Oxyptilus laetus (Scarce Light Plume)	1	(0 – 0 – 0 – 0 – 0)
Cydia amplana	3	(0 – 0 – 0 – 0 – 0)
Loxostege sticticalis	1	(0 – 0 – 0 – 0 – 0)
Udea ferrugalis (Rusty-dot Pearl)	92	(75 – 47 – 52 – 87 - 17)
Palpita vitrealis	2	(4 – 4 – 0 – 4 - 5)
Nomophila noctuella (Rush Veneer)	27	(46 – 128 – 71 – 64 - 35)
Euchromius ocellea	2	(0 – 0 – 0 – 0 – 0)
Convolvulus Hawk-moth	8	(7 – 45 – 17 – 12 - 9)
Death's-head Hawk-moth	3	(3 – 1 – 1 – 0 - 1)
Humming-bird Hawk-moth	148	(112 – 709 – 59 – 177 - 198)
Bedstraw Hawk-moth	8	(3 – 4 – 0 – 4 – 0)
Vestal	13	(3 – 10 – 7 – 38 – 0)
Small Marbled	4	(0 – 4 – 0 – 0 – 0)
Beautiful Marbled	1	(0 – 0 – 0 – 1 – 0)
Clifden Nonpareil	1	(0 – 0 – 0 – 0 – 0)
Dark Crimson Underwing	1	(0 – 0 – 0 – 0 – 1)
Golden Twin-spot	1	(0 – 0 – 0 – 0 – 0)
Silver Y	1895	(1168 -2489 -1670 -1742 - 3681)
Marbled Clover	2	(0 – 0 – 0 – 0 – 0)
Bordered Straw	2	(0 – 62 – 0 – 0 - 1)
Scarce Bordered Straw	10	(2 – 8 – 4 – 30 - 3)
Tree-lichen Beauty	13	(0 – 0 – 0 – 0 – 4)
Shining Marbled	1	(0 – 0 – 0 – 0 – 0)
Small Mottled Willow	5	(2 – 28 – 2 – 4 - 1)
Delicate	7	(0 – 0 – 3 – 7 - 9)
Pearly Underwing	9	(7 – 16 – 2 – 11 - 2)
Dark Sword-grass	149	(122 – 244 – 104 – 260 - 339)

Cydia amplana Skelton Cleveland July 2019 Damian Money

The Yorkshire Moth database – what happened in 2019?

The total of 173,055 records received in 2019 was a little down on the huge number of 188,710 in 2018, but is still the second highest total we have had. 4,000 records were added from previous years, so the database now contains 2,875,907 records of over 10.8 million moths. This is now becoming a serious amount of records, and as long as Access databases continue to be supported, MapMate will cope for a little longer. The final total will be a little higher as we do receive some records very late in the day, for example from some of the on-line schemes and from Rothamsted traps. Now that the NMRS have completed the Atlas, they are a bit more up to date with data repatriation, so some of these records are coming to us a little faster. There is not much advantage of using any of the on-line schemes for your records as they all have to be sent to us for verification before being sent back to the NMRS which just delays the process, so you are not saving us any work. A much better idea is to send them to us directly and you are likely to get prompter and better feedback. It also means that we don't have to spend hours verifying records in February when we should be writing this report!

All of your records have been examined thoroughly and anything looking dodgy weeded out. This is particularly important when we send them through to the NMRS, as they are (quite rightly) quick to tell us if any records look wrong, if any gridrefs are in the wrong vice-county and if any records appear to be well out in the North Sea when they construct the national maps. They then forward the records to other national schemes. Many of these have their own web sites such as British Leafminers at www. leafmines.co.uk and the National Gelechiid Scheme at www.gelechiid.co.uk so you can see how your records "fit in" with the national picture. As most of you know, our own Yorkshire Moths web site at www.yorkshiremoths.info has distribution maps and lots of information for each species. We apologise that this is only complete up to the end of 2015 for some rather tricky technical reasons which are proving difficult to solve.

The maps displayed here as usual show the total numbers of macro and micro moths recorded in each of Yorkshire's 200 x 10K squares. If you like figures like these, you might want to compare them with the maps on page 37 of the 2018 report. To give you an idea of the amount of recording which has taken place across the county this year, a bit of number crunching shows that there have been 2,355 x 10K square records. 934 for macros and 1421 for micros. The prize for the macro moth with the largest numbers of new squares is shared by Beautiful Hook-tip and Scarce Footman, each with ten squares. The equivalent prize for micros is shared by *Ectoedemia occultella* and *Parornix devoniella*, each with 11 squares and an indication of what some wandering leaf-mining enthusiasts were up to in the autumn. This now means that the average square now has 268 macros and 183 micros. Looking back five years, this is a 13% rise for macros and 31% rise for micros. This year's winning squares are:

1. TA24: 125 new species. Some old records from 2014 and 2018 were submitted from a trap at Hornsea, a very under-recorded part of VC61.
2. SE03: 109 new species. A new enthusiast has started trapping at Thornton, west of Bradford. This area is so under-recorded that the majority of his macros were new to the square. Once we get him started on micros, the maps will look even better.
3. SD85: 63 new species. The Coniston Cold trap has led the field for the last two years and despite relegation to third place, is still pulling in a lot of new species.
4. SE86: 53 new species. This is the square which includes Wharram Quarry. This just shows how many species can be added in a day looking for leaf mines in an under-recorded area. One or two more were added light trapping at the quarry.
5. SD94: 47 new species. Another new enthusiast trapping at Thornton-in-Craven, south-west of Skipton has discovered a lot of new species for the area.

Micro Moths
Species per 10K square

As you can see from the maps, coverage is still very patchy across the county. We still have the same six squares which have recorded fewer than 100 species of macro and it would be lovely if some of these could be targeted in 2020. Who knows what is waiting there to be discovered! These in area of importance are:

1. NY90: This is not an easy square. Arkengarthdale above Langthwaite runs across the centre. We need someone with enthusiasm and enterprise for this one.

2. SD75: Stocks Reservoir area. This is an easy square with plenty of accessible woodland. Some light trapping took place in 2005 but none since. There are bound to be some seriously good moths to be discovered here.

3. SD87: Horton-in-Ribblesdale and the area over to Halton Gill in upper Littondale. There are accessible areas particularly at the Ribblesdale end.

4. NZ00: The areas to the east of NY90, so lower Arkengarthdale and the area north of Swaledale. Stang Forest is accessible and has hardly been trapped although for a very short period of time there was a Rothamsted trap there.

5. SE73: East of Selby and west of Holme-on-Spalding-Moor. An ignored area. There was limited light trapping for a while at Bubwith but nothing else. An easy square to target. We don't even have a Large Yellow Underwing here.

6. TA22: This was the infamous "Holderness Hole". Recent trapping has got the macro list up to 95 but we need a few more.

Another way of looking at the figures is to see how many species have been logged in more than 100 squares. This has risen significantly from 337 to 348. Ten years ago, the figure was 123 which shows what we have managed to achieve. The leader is still Silver Y which has been found in 186 of our 200 squares. It is closely followed by Silver-ground Carpet with 183 and Large Yellow Underwing with 180. Catching up fast is Humming-bird Hawk-moth which has been seen in a surprising 178 different squares! The leading micros are Anthophila fabriciana (175), Agriphila straminella (171) and Stigmella aurella (169).

Map figure with species-per-10K-square counts:

0 102 153 6   92 230 361 114
3 120 290 8 12 0 155 357 472 308 288 52
62 46 74 303 222 347 114 326 122 360 393 213 1
115 41 183 207 197 363 296 295 218 197 134 220 346 398 184
77 170 107 228 218 352 277 125 276 311 283 243 390 440 486 174
291 318 58 183 235 215 483 469 334 405 135 304 164 183 445 367 335
357 316 430 311 311 312 373 391 250 280 371 245 261 192 413 396 306
3 128 58 326 266 307 319 424 489 190 370 524 233 101 289 236 344 1
0 258 292 25 169 307 463 348 299 438 466 409 442 381 404 392 373 230
0   109 212 421 439 439 372 379 464 70 391 328 430 131 165 4
324 386 391 315 334 425 248 317 246 279 212 399 125 95 309 4
11 258 407 354 411 250 416 321 403 9   67 389 529
17 89 290 260 394 427 480 432 278
59 211 351 388 398 433
269 468 294 342
6 1

Macro Moths
Species per 10K square

You can see the results of all this "square bashing" in the new *Atlas of Britain and Ireland's Larger Moths* and it is nice to see Yorkshire looking well represented on all the maps. You can also see what we can do to improve the situation to make it look even better when the next edition is published. At some stage there is likely to be an atlas of the smaller moths though this may be some years off, and as you can see, we have a lot of work to fill in some of the gaps, as micro coverage is much patchier. Whilst it is convenient and fun to trap at home, it is even more interesting to trap away from the garden. Try to target some new areas in 2020, especially in under-recorded parts of the county. If you want to target your own 10K square a bit better, you might wonder which species have been found there already. If so, drop your VC recorder an email and he can send you a list of species already on the database for your area. There are still some really unexplored parts of Yorkshire and some major discoveries to be made. Particularly amongst the micros, it is highly likely that there are some resident species still to be discovered. So, persuade your better half that a portable generator would be a really sensible investment for power cuts (especially a nice new Honda Eu10i which will run a moth trap for over eight hours), and target some of the blanks on the maps.

Early records

If we exclude those species with fewer than ten records on the database, 43 species flew on their earliest ever date in 2019, mostly in April and May. This was not surprising as we had a mild winter and early spring. Here is a selection of some of the most interesting:

Mottled Grey	6th January	Coniston Cold (ARh)
Shoulder Stripe	24th February	Grewelthorpe (MH)
Bordered Straw	3rd March	Asenby (K&DH)
Muslin Mot	18th March	Barmby Moor (PRe)
V-Pug	25th March	Potteric Carr (RI&JCH)
Chinse Character	29th March	Spurn (JHF)
Motled Pug	5th April	Spofforth (AD)
Red Twin-spot Carpet	7th April	Bellflask (BM)
Spruce Carpet	7th April	Cotherstone (PWe)
Small Yellow Underwing	19th April	Rodley NR (PM)
Latticed Heath	20th April	Turkey Carpet (AR, JHo)
May Highflier	21st April	North Ferriby (IM)
Glaucous Shears	21st April	Keighley Moor (IHa)
Vine's Rustic	22nd April	North Ferriby (IM)
Orange Footman	23rd April	Great Smeaton (JE)
Coronet	30th April	Hawkswick (PMi et al.)
Treble Lines	30th April	Austerfield (SB)
Flame	1st May	Spurn (JHF)
Chalk Carpet	23rd May	Flamborough (AAl)
Slender Brindle	30th May	Sutherbruff Rigg (JW)

Late records

At the other end of the year, just 21 species flew on their latest ever date. Several of these were species which are expanding their numbers and range in the county and it is interesting that Vine's Rustic appears in both lists. Here again are some of the most interesting:

Satyr Pug	25th July	Askham Bog (AF et al.)
Red-necked Footman	15th August	Lindholme (P&JS)
Scorched Carpet	27th August	Balby (PG)
Annulet	11th September	Flamborough (AAl)
Eyed Hawk-moth	21st Septmber	Askham Bryan (DL)
Elephant Hawk-moth	21st September	Guisborough (RWo)
Common Footman	21st September	Low Dalby (JW)
Small Ranunculus	22nd September	Wombwell (HBe)
Least Carpet	27th September	Luddenden (MHy)
Waved Umber	5th October	Pateley Bridge (T&PB)
Spectacle	11th October	Austerfield (SB)
Vine's Rustic	21st October	Spurn (MFS)
Square-spot Rustic	20th November	Flamborough (AAl)
Juniper Carpet	24th November	West Bradford (BH)

Moths to look out for in 2020 – invaders from the south-west

72.029 Scarlet Tiger Shaun Poland

Scarlet Tiger *Callimorpha dominula*

On page 18 of the 2018 report we wrote "perhaps we can expect a Scarlet Tiger in Leeds sometime soon", and hey presto, a Scarlet Tiger appeared in Leeds in 2019. We hope you are suitably impressed with the calibre of our crystal ball. Originally confined to the south and west of the country, climatic change has brought an expansion of this species to the north and east in recent years. Adults are usually seen flying by day, especially in the late afternoon and early evening, but will also come to light. The distinctive black larvae with a yellow and white dorsal stripe will feed on various herbaceous plants but have a particular liking for comfrey. The attractive, almost tropical-looking adults with spotted forewings and red hindwings are quite unlike any other species and should be   looked for in June and July in fens, marshes and along river banks.

Cypress Pug *Eupithecia phoeniceata*

This is another conifer-feeding species which is rapidly expanding its range. It was first found in the UK in 1959 in Cornwall and has been slowly spreading. The rate of spread seems to have accelerated in the last few years and there have been recent records in Cheshire. It is only a matter of time before we will be able to claim it on our Yorkshire list. The scientific name refers to its continental food plant, *Juniperus phoenicea* whereas in the UK the larvae feed on non-native species, Monterey, Lawson's and Leyland cypresses. Whereas many Pugs are tricky to identify, Cypress Pug is easy. The oblique cross-lines and black stripes make confusion with any other species unlikely. It should be looked for in August and September. Our first record is likely to come from a garden light trap.

70.159 Cypress Pug Les J Finch

Hoary Footman *Eilema caniola*

Like the previous two species, this moth has always been confined to the south west of the country but in recent years has been moving quite rapidly north and east. This pattern has been seen with several other "Footman" species since 2000 and it is now the turn of Hoary. It rests with its wings wrapped around the body in a manner reminiscent of Scarce Footman but not quite so extreme, and this is probably the main confusion species, especially if worn. Its wings however are silky and pale grey and the orangey-yellow costal stripe of Scarce Footman is replaced with a much more subdued pale-yellow stripe. The hindwing is strikingly different being very pale grey instead of the straw colour of Scarce Footman. Like its relatives it is a lichen-feeder. It used to be confined to rocky coastlines and shingle beaches but this is not the case with the recent expansion and it could turn up anywhere. It is just the sort of species which is likely to appear at Spurn.

72.047 Hoary Footman. Les J Finch

Rarities

As you will all see from your shiny new Atlas of Britain and Ireland's Larger Moths, submission of records to the NMRS must be as accurate as is reasonably possible to avoid strange dots appearing on the maps. If we send in dodgy records, it is only a matter of time before a sceptical email appears and we have to justify it. This is our excuse for our disbelieving attitude when assessing some of your records. Unlike the birding community we do not have a formal rarities committee, but instead, records are first assessed by the vice-county or county recorders and in the majority of cases verification is fairly easy, especially when we receive a good photograph or specimen. Some moths however are much trickier and we may have to obtain further opinions from those who are more learned and wiser than we are. For any new species to be added to the county or vice-county list we really must see the evidence, no matter how convinced you are. We're not going to claim one ourselves without a photograph or specimen so we have to treat you the same. Those moths which are new to a 10K square will also attract a lot more scrutiny, and this year we have had over 2,000 to assess. None of this of course means that we are going to reject the new species you have had in your garden, especially when the chap at the other end of the village catches it regularly. Also, your reed-feeding species become a lot more likely when we realise there are some nice wetlands a mile or so away, but your moorland species will attract a more critical eye when the nearest expanses of heather are 20 miles away. As we say every year, if there is any doubt at all KEEP THE SPECIMEN until you have heard back from us. Two or three really exciting moths this year could not be verified. If you disagree with our decision, that's fine. We're happy to canvas more opinions. We must however have the final say, as no records are accepted onto national schemes without going through the bottleneck of the county recorder.

The situation with micro moths is even harder as a higher proportion can not be identified from a photograph and more need to be dissected. It's even more important to keep the specimen if there is any doubt. The national moth recording scheme has both regional and national panels for microlepidoptera to help county recorders with tricky records and we do sometimes use these to help adjudicate on difficult decisions. Harry Beaumont and Charles Fletcher are both members of the northern regional panel so often liaise with other panel members. The scheme has also issued verification guidelines for microlepidoptera showing the level of evidence required for each species. These can be viewed on-line on the Moths Count web site at http://www.mothscount.org/text/73/guidance_notes.html and are extremely useful. These are of course just guidelines and not rigid rules to be slavishly obeyed at all times. In particular they are national guidelines which in some cases may not be quite so relevant in a regional or local context. They are however extremely useful to let you know which species need dissection and which can be identified from a photograph.

63.045 *Cydalima perspectalis*, the Box-tree Moth, a large and spectacular Asian pyralid moth, two of the three different forms are shown here, Intermediate morph on the left and Melanistic morph right. Both were caught in a garden light trap in York by Alastair Fitter.

Top Mothing Misidentifications

Unless you are superhuman, you are not going to correctly identify every moth in your trap. Don't think that you have to. If you're not sure, then ask someone or just don't record it. There is no disgrace in letting the odd moth "accidentally" fly away before you manage to pot it. The hardest thing for new moth trappers is to get an idea of which moths are likely and which are unlikely to appear in their garden. Faced with hundreds of pictures in a field guide, it can all be a bit daunting. There are however various aids to help you. A very useful tool which has recently been produced is a smartphone app called "What's Flying Tonight" produced by the Centre for Ecology and Hydrology. Google it and download it to your phone. Once it knows your location it gives you a list of the commonest moths in your 10K square in that particular week by looking at NMRS data. This is for macros only. The Yorkshire Moths web site at http://www.yorkshiremoths.info/ has a similar idea on its pages "Flying Tonight" and "Common Species out now" which also list the commonest species on the wing at that time of the year in Yorkshire. For micros, it is useful to look at the Micro Moth Grading Guidelines which can be downloaded from the Moths Count website at http://www.mothscount.org/text/73/guidance_notes.html - look for "Micro-moth grading guidelines" and "Micro-moth Verification Guidance Notes" at the bottom of the page and these will tell you which records you can sneak under the county recorders nose when his back is turned.

Identifying moths is a learning curve and it can be pretty steep at times. We're all somewhere on it and none of us can claim to be on the uppermost reaches where life is plain sailing. If you've matched your moth to a picture in a field guide do read the small print. Does it occur in your area? Does it fly at the correct time of year? Is the food plant in the area? Be aware that Sterling, Parsons and Lewington's excellent field guide to micro moths only illustrates 1033 out of over 1600 species, and Manley's excellent photographic field guide cannot show every variation of every species so confusion species are not always obvious.

If you manage to send 2000 records without a typo or a misidentification then you can award yourself something nice as you are quite an unusual person. Before you click "send", have a final look at the list. Was that Chimney Sweeper really in the light trap or did you see it in the field next door? Was the Satellite in July really an adult or was it a larva? Those *Stigmella aurella* mines that you found; were they really on apple? This is why we like your records early as we often find quite a few of this type of error. I'm sorry that we're a bit pernickety at times but we want the NMRS to think that we Yorkshire folk can tell our Treble-bars from our Lesser Treble-bars and that they can trust our records. They are quite quick to get back to us if we make mistakes! One advantage of using MapMate is to be able to use its inbuilt validation checks which you can activate under Date Entry/Records/Properties/Validation. It is very good at pointing out in a supercilious manner that your Slender Pug is unlikely to be flying in April and that your Figure of Eighty is unlikely to be the Figure of Eight you have just typed in as it is only July.

The commonest errors as usual turn out to be typos, and the common ones keep turning up every year: Spinach is rare and most are typos for Northern Spinach (or misidentifications of Barred Straw). In fact, we get so sceptical about Spinach nowadays that our default position is to assume it is an error unless proven otherwise.
Bordered Straw can occasionally be Bordered Straw. Two this year were. The other six or seven were typos for Barred Straw.
Lunar Yellow Underwing – we can tell this is a typo for Lunar Underwing as the records come in late in the year. If they are in July they are misidentifications for one of the other "Yellow Underwings". The nearest colonies that we know about are in Norfolk.
Small Yellow Underwing in the garden trap in August is a typo for one of the other "Yellow Underwings".
Hebrew Character after the first week June is nearly always Setaceous Hebrew Character. Just once in a blue moon it isn't so if you catch one in July, please can you take a photo.
Five-spot Burnet. Lots of these recorded every year. It's Narrow-bordered Five-spot which is a different species.
Common Fan-foot. A misnomer as it isn't. The common Fan-foot is Fan-foot.
Common misidentifications which turned up this year included:
White-point – occasionally correct but the majority turn out to be Clay.
Plain Wave is quite a rare beast unless you are trapping on heathland. Most are worn Riband Waves.

Northern Winter Moth – just because you have a fairly big pale Winter Moth, it doesn't mean it's automatically Northern Winter Moth which is not common in gardens and is most often found in birch woodland.

Pale Pinion. This should be easy to identify but we get lots of records in July when it shouldn't be flying. We rarely get a photo. We've seen it misidentified as Light Arches. If you catch one in July, please photograph it.

Garden Dart. No it isn't. Really. Unless you are incredibly lucky in which case we need to see a really good photo or preferably a specimen.

Triple-spotted Clay. Lots of records. It's Double Square-spot unless you live in the western fringes of the county and have won the lottery.

Orange Footman in August is the orange form of Buff Footman or occasionally Dingy Footman.

Late Common Quakers are Vine's Rustic.

Late Muslin Moths – lots this year! Most were typos for Muslin Footman but some were caused by putting in "mendica" which is also Ingrailed Clay.

Lead-coloured Drab – a large number turn out to be "lead-coloured" forms of Clouded Drab. Look for the feathery antennae!

Micros

If it's easy to misidentify a macro, it's a real piece of cake to misidentify a micro. The possibilities for looking daft are endless, and we have all done it. The trick is to start with the easy ones with distinctive markings before you get carried away with looking at rare poorly-marked ones. Use the "what's flying tonight" ideas that we have listed above, and get to know the moths that ought to be common in your garden. Get to know the ones that can be identified by sight and those that need dissection by looking at the verification guidelines. You will certainly need the Field Guide to Micro Moths and Manley's guide that we have mentioned above, but do be aware that not all species are illustrated, not all forms of common species are illustrated, and there is a little bit of a bias towards moths that appear in the south of the country. The introductory sections are important and if you can use the key to narrow it down to a family then that is half the battle done. To do this you need to pay far more attention to palps, head scales, antennae and shape of hindwing than you do with macros. Here are some of this year's mistakes. These are uncannily similar to the year before!

Coleophora species cause huge problems. There are really very few that can be identified by sight. The grading guidelines will tell you. If you are claiming them without dissection, we really need to know how you have reached your conclusion. Of course if you are recording larval cases, that is often (but not always) an easier proposition.

Yponomeuta (Small Ermine) species cause a lot of anguish. We'll let you have Bird-cherry Ermine and you are allowed Orchard Ermine if it's the totally grey form. You can have Willow Ermine if you are completely sure but you really need to be certain. You can have Apple and Spindle Ermines if you disturb them from the relevant food plant or if you record them as larvae. Otherwise, forget them.

Parornix sp. We get a lot of records of these identified to species level. People often assume they have caught *anglicella* because it is reputed to be the commonest, but when you start dissecting them, it's amazing how often you are wrong. Only extremely clever people can identify them without dissection and we're not that clever. We don't think you are too.

Dichrorampha is another genus which causes a lot of headaches. Some can be identified by sight. Get to know which ones by looking at the guidelines and make sure you have noticed whether there is a costal fold. This is really important. Just because books say *acuminatana* is the commonest at light, people think that they are all this species. Several other species, in particular *montanana* appear in light traps on a regular basis.

Wax Moth and Lesser Wax Moth continue to fool people, particularly the former as looks a bit like a macro. At least the orange nose of Lesser Wax Moth gives the game away.

Eudonia/Scoparia species are worse than Pugs to identify and many people don't try. Many that do send in records of real rarities and we had a lot of claims this year for *Eudonia delunella* and *Scoparia basistrigalis*. Both are vanishingly unlikely and we would need the specimen. We can't identify them all ourselves and often find ourselves conveniently losing all the worn ones.

Acleris species cause more trouble than they should. Don't forget *ferrugana* and *notana* are only separable by dissection and this is also the case for *laterana* and *comariana*. People often claim *shepherdana* or

schalleriana on the basis that it looks like the picture in the book. They are very rarely correct.
Oegoconia sp. A lot of people think they can identify these to species level. We can't and we're pretty sure you can't.
Little tiny hairy "micros" that scuttle about the bottom of your trap should all be sent to Sharon Flint at flintsentomologists@btinternet.com as they are all micro caddis and she loves them.
Leaf mines – heck this is a minefield (sorry!) so we've written a separate section.

Leaf mines

The number of people sending in records of leaf mines has rocketed in recent years so we thought that it might be a good idea to lay down some simple rules, guidelines and general advice on the subject. The best resources for identifying leaf mines are all on-line. There are three of them. They are:
1. British Leafminers at http://www.leafmines.co.uk/ is an excellent resource. There are pages for all invertebrates that mine leaves and the keys are excellent but they will only key out lepidopterous miners.
2. Plant Parasites of Europe at https://bladmineerders.nl/ is a Dutch site so you need to click on "English" on the home page. The keys include all miners, so are in some cases a little more clunky. It does also include a lot of species which are not known to occur in the UK and mention some food plants which are not utilised here. The information here however is excellent and it often includes diagnostic features not mentioned by the first site.
3. The leaf and stem mines of British flies and other insects at http://www.ukflymines.co.uk/ is not just concerned with diptera. The keys include all invertebrate miners and although to some extent it draws on information from the first two sites, it has quite a bit of unique information.
There are some basic rules:
1. You MUST identify the plant properly. If you can't, then you will make mistakes. This is by far the biggest rule and should be in flashing lights. If you don't know what the plant is, forget it.
2. Beware of and get to know the polyphagous miners which fool people every year. These are:

- *Lyonetia clerkella* which mines cherry, apple, hawthorn, birch, rowan, blackthorn, etc. A dirty narrow mine winding all across the leaf with no egg at the start and a deeply-segmented larva which is "belly up" in the mine. Extremely common.

- *Phyllonorycter leucographella* which mines *Pyracantha* (firethorn), hawthorn, apple, rowan, whitebeam, cherry etc. Can be confused with the much less common *Phyllonorycter corylifoliella* which has multiple dark flecks.

- *Phyllonorycter messaniella* which mines oak (especially holm oak), hornbeam, beech, sweet chestnut etc. Difficult to identify on deciduous oaks and on beech where it is not as common as people think – most mines are old *maestingella* mines pretending to be *messaniella*.

3. Beware of non-lepidopterous miners which fool many people. The commonest culprits are the beetles *Rhamphus oxyacanthae* on hawthorn and *Orchestes fagi* on beech. Get to know the appearance of dipterous mines which often have two sparse lines of frass and sawfly mines which are often dirty brown blisters.
4. Oak – all *Phyllonorycter* mines must be bred out with the possible exception of *lautella* which is allowable if you are really confident. *Stigmella* species are tricky. *S. basiguttella* should be easy but some people confuse it with thick mines of *samiatella* though the frass here never completely fills the gallery. Most of the rest are identifiable if bred through and also (with care) if a larva is present though we need to know the site of the egg and details of the larval head. *S. samiatella* is best bred through. Examining the pupal cremaster can also help identification of *Phyllonorycter* species.
5. Willow/Sallow – all *Phyllonorycter* mines should be bred through. If you are recording *Stigmella salicis*, please make a note of the position of the egg, as "*salicis*" with an upperside egg appears to be a different (so far unnamed) species.
6. Alder – *Stigmella* mines are not identifiable unless tenanted. The larval head is diagnostic.
7. The golden rule elsewhere in this report is "keep the specimen". The golden rule for leaf mines is "if in doubt, breed it out!" You may well be surprised what emerges.

Top Macro-moths in 2019
Based on number of records

Code	Vernacular	Records	Individuals
73.342	Large Yellow Underwing	4895	111784
73.317	Heart and Dart	2887	22739
73.162	Dark Arches	2824	32370
73.359	Setaceous Hebrew Character	2448	22053
73.345	Lesser Yellow Underwing	2185	8734
73.249	Hebrew Character	2116	12886
73.015	Silver Y	1898	4958
73.325	Shuttle-shaped Dart	1821	5406
70.016	Riband Wave	1737	8153
73.329	Flame Shoulder	1677	4505
73.244	Common Quaker	1612	13055
72.045	Common Footman	1596	13447
73.357	Square-spot Rustic	1454	11555
70.258	Willow Beauty	1436	3076
73.348	Lesser Broad-bordered Yellow Underwing	1362	5036
73.293	Smoky Wainscot	1362	7838
70.226	Brimstone Moth	1361	2546
73.242	Clouded Drab	1244	6081
73.096	Uncertain	1232	12971
72.003	Snout	1151	2284
69.003	Poplar Hawk-moth	1151	2143
72.002	Straw Dot	1100	3795
70.011	Single-dotted Wave	1039	2310
73.084	Marbled Beauty	1033	2630
72.044	Dingy Footman	1004	7702

Riband Wave Stephen Relf

Top Micro-moths in 2019
Based on number of records

Code	Taxon	Vernacular	Records	Individuals
49.039	*Epiphyas postvittana*	Light Brown Apple Moth	2543	8410
18.001	*Plutella xylostella*	Diamond-back Moth	1755	27612
63.080	*Chrysoteuchia culmella*	Garden Grass-veneer	1735	29634
49.166	*Celypha lacunana*		1157	3730
63.038	*Patania ruralis*	Mother of Pearl	1129	7741
63.089	*Agriphila tristella*		1087	7896
63.093	*Agriphila straminella*		1077	13844
41.002	*Blastobasis adustella*		1065	14349
63.025	*Anania hortulata*	Small Magpie	1064	2451
62.001	*Aphomia sociella*	Bee Moth	917	1572
28.010	*Hofmannophila pseudospretella*	Brown House-moth	805	1278
49.109	*Agapeta hamana*		796	2744
63.067	*Eudonia lacustrata*		674	3456
63.064	*Scoparia ambigualis*		669	2060
63.074	*Eudonia mercurella*		665	2453
45.044	*Emmelina monodactyla*	Common Plume	572	841
49.161	*Celypha striana*		544	948
16.001	*Yponomeuta evonymella*	Bird-cherry Ermine	529	6770
49.156	*Hedya nubiferana*	Marbled Orchard Tortrix	520	1328
41.003	*Blastobasis lacticolella*		497	1047
28.009	*Endrosis sarcitrella*	White-shouldered House-moth	493	646
49.091	*Pseudargyrotoza conwagana*		450	824
49.077	*Acleris variegana*	Garden Rose Tortrix	426	531
62.077	*Endotricha flammealis*		404	1906
63.033	*Udea lutealis*		361	719

Bee Moth Jesika Bone

Small Magpie Yves Bouvet

Winners and Losers in 2019

Which species did well in 2019 and which came out in lower numbers than usual? Which species over-wintered well in the relatively mild winter and came out in big numbers in the warm early spring weather and in the hot summer weather? Several species relatively new to the county made big gains in distribution but was this accompanied by big numbers? The following figures are derived in the same way as usual by comparing the number of records in 2019 with the average of the five previous years and applying a correction factor to compensate for differences in recording effort from year to year. The figures are all for those resident macro moths which are fairly widespread in the county and which have a significant number of records. Migrants, rarities and very local species are omitted.

Winners	Change	Losers	Change
Least Carpet	+302%	Bordered Sallow	-75%
Spring Usher	+291%	May Highflyer	-68%
Vine's Rustic	+244%	Alder Moth	-66%
Beautiful Snout	+221%	Figure of Eighty	-66%
Devon Carpet	+216%	Small Square-spot	-65%
Oak-tree Pug	+155%	Common Lutestring	-64%
Lunar Marbled Brown	+145%	Dark Spinach	-59%
Treble Lines	+140%	Small Angle Shades	-59%
Twin-spotted Quaker	+128%	Currant Pug	-56%
Pale Brindled Beauty	+119%	Broken-barred Carpet	-55%
Pine Hawk-moth	+119%	Gold Spangle	-55%
Mullein	+116%	Green Silver-lines	-54%
Dotted Border	+107%	Dusky-lemon Sallow	-53%
March Moth	+105%	Wormwood Pug	-53%
Mottled Grey	+100%	Peach Blossom	-51%
Turnip Moth	+97%	Broom Moth	-50%
Broad-bordered Yellow Underwing	+94%	Red-necked Footman	-50%
Early Moth	+87%	Cabbage Moth	-49%
Narrow-winged Pug	+84%	Puss Moth	-49%
Privet Hawk-moth	+79%	Small Fan-foot	-46%

Looking first at the list of winners, it is evident that some recent invaders took advantage of the warm summer and rapidly increased their numbers and range. Foremost amongst these were Least Carpet, Devon Carpet and Beautiful Snout which are all now appearing in significant numbers. Beautiful Hook-tip and Maiden's Blush continue to do well but did not quite make the top 20. An older invader, Vine's Rustic, has really started to increase again following a drop in numbers a few years ago and is undergoing a second phase of expansion. This is often seen with new colonists and may be due to fluctuations in parasitoid numbers. Warm February weather resulted in increased numbers of Spring Usher, Pale Brindled Beauty, Dotted Border and Early Moth and this increase carried on into spring where most species did well, especially March Moth and Mottled Grey which appeared in unprecedented numbers. All the *Orthosia* species did well though only Twin-spotted Quaker made the top 20. Lunar Marbled Brown is another spring species which had an exceptional year, and Chestnut, Dark Chestnut and Orange Underwing also enjoyed a big increase in numbers. Unexpected numbers of Privet and Pine Hawk-moths were accompanied by some range expansion and appearance at several new sites. Increases in some other species are harder to explain. Treble Lines appeared in quite astonishing numbers especially at Austerfield where the catch went into three figures on several occasions. Narrow-winged Pug numbers often seem to fluctuate wildly for no apparent reason. Reasons for the increase in Turnip Moth and Broad-bordered Yellow Underwing numbers are not obvious.

Looking at the list of losers, it is immediately apparent that it is largely populated by moths whose flight time is in May and June, many of which are woodland species. Looking at over-wintering stages, a surprising 17 out of the 20 species listed here over-winter as pupae. To put this into perspective, 43% of macro moths which are resident in the county over-winter as pupae, so this is a far higher percentage than expected. As usual this prompts more questions than it answers. The best moth trapping weather in 2019 was in early spring and late summer, and the early summer period might not have been quite so productive, so this might have been a factor. More likely however, winter conditions might provide the answer. There is some evidence that over-wintering as a pupa is particularly successful in cold weather. In 2018 we had the "beast from the east" and this certainly did no harm to over-wintering pupae, in fact as we noticed last year, almost all Pug species did extremely well and all (with the exception of Slender Pug) over-winter as pupae. The winter of 2018/9 however was a different affair and much warmer. Do warmer conditions lead to more fungal attacks on pupae? Do predators find it easier to locate pupae when they are not under snow and ice? So many questions. Not all the losers however fit into this category. The decline in numbers of Bordered Sallow is largely due to a dramatic collapse at Spurn. Dark Spinach and Dusky-lemon Sallow are in long-term decline across the whole country. The fall in numbers of Red-necked Footman may be due to fluctuations in the predator/prey cycle as its parasitoids catch up with it after its recent expansion. The dramatic fall in numbers of Small Square-spot has been remarked upon all across the country and this affected both generations. The reasons are not known. Gold Spangle does not fall into any of these categories and is also a bit of a mystery.

Advice to MapMate Users

We realise that MapMate isn't everyone's cup of tea, but most people find it the most useful and easy way to store, retrieve and submit their records.

The biggest problem by a country mile is the sync process. Don't feel that you have to send us your records via a MapMate sync as it's often easier (and in fact often better for us) if you copy your MapMate records onto Excel. We can then import them directly back into MapMate at our end. If you are just sending your own records, this is a really good way. If you have other people's records on MapMate, for example if you hold some or all of the county database, then we must receive records via a MapMate sync file, otherwise it will result in duplication at your end if we sync back. Currently only nine of you fall into this category so for the rest, do consider sending via Excel. To do this is really really easy:
Open the data entry box, "2020" in the date field, "Enter", "Query/Records in Export Format", "Select all" (the red tick at the top), "Copy Selection" (the icon to the left of the red tick), open Excel and paste in. Don't try to fiddle with the columns and don't worry that there are no vernacular names etc. All will be well.

If you are sending a sync and it just isn't working, it's normally due to a failure to upload to the server. If you've done it correctly, a box pops up telling you the recipient has been informed. If you don't get this message, you haven't uploaded it. Often this is due to firewall issues so you may need to turn it off for a minute whilst the file uploads. It's often a lot easier to send the file by email. The file you are looking for will be in Documents/My MapMate/Data/Cache/Upload and will be called "xxxtoyyy.sqz" where "xxx" is your cuk and "yyy" is your sync partner's cuk.

The other major problem that we have is with users not downloading patches. Most people now realise that about 10% of the old scientific names in the Bradley and Fletcher list were changed with the adoption of the new AB&H list. Many people however, didn't realise this year that there was a further revision which resulted in several more name changes. It is a good idea to download all new patches, whether you think you need them or not. Those who haven't downloaded the recent patches have been sending us records of *Pleuroptya ruralis* which should now be *Patania ruralis*, *Aphelia paleana* which should be *Zelotherses paleana* and several more. If the records come via a sync, we can't change them for you. Perhaps this is another reason to send records via Excel!

A few other general words of advice are worth repeating as the same problems crop up every year.

- Do pay your yearly subscriptions or else you won't be able to download patches. Don't forget we have a Yorkshire MapMate group which enables us to make substantial savings on annual subscriptions. Please contact Penny Relf (details at the back of this publication) for more details.

- Please back up your database and keep one or preferably two copies in a safe place. We are regularly asked to "send back" someone's records as their computer has crashed and they have no records. This is extremely difficult via MapMate and takes a lot of time and effort.

- Please use the comments field a bit more – it is really useful for us to know that you realise that the record is unusual/late/early or that you've dissected it. If the moth is reared, or is of a leaf mine then please record the foodplant. It makes us less likely to query the record.

- The reference field is not for where you've looked it up (eg in Waring or Manley) but is designed to provide traceability back to the source of the record you are entering. It's like a literary reference with author, year and title for example "Joe Smith, records, 2019".

- Do use the validation functions on MapMate (from Data Entry – records/properties/validation). These prevent a lot of errors like entering Lunar Yellow Underwing when you meant to type Lunar Underwing.

- When sending moth records please use the filter "Lepidoptera: Moths" as we don't really want all your butterfly records. Also, please set the site filter to V61-5 as we don't really want the records from your holiday in Devon.

- Please make sure you use the correct stage. If you find a dead moth, the stage should be "dead". If you find a larva in August and breed out the adult in the following March, log the stage as "larval" and the date as August rather than when the adult moth appears. The NMRS are very hot on this as it improves their flight time phenograms and removes records of moths appearing very early in the year indoors.

- Please do not just put "garden" for site as we have to get the map out every time. "Huddersfield (garden)" makes it a lot easier for us when writing the report. "Huddersfield – 5 Hill Top Road" is even better.

- It can be surprisingly easy to enter duplicate records. Everyone should check by running "Analysis/Database info/Show duplicated Records entered here".

- We receive a lot of records with strange subspecies, for example only forms seen in the Outer Hebrides. Only use subspecies if you are quite sure you are correct.

- Do make sure that your gridrefs are correct. It is only too easy to put SD instead of SE or to transpose northings and eastings. Also, please ensure that the site is in the correct VC. MapMate will do this automatically for you if you create the site by putting (for example) Rotherham@SE123456. This year we have again had quite a few records which mapped in the North Sea and in neighbouring counties. Please use four figures for country walks (SE1234) and six figures for your garden trap (SE123456) and other sites where you need to be accurate. Please don't use ten-figure gridrefs as we don't need the record to the nearest metre. You're dealing with moths which are mobile things which fly around. You wouldn't log a Sparrowhawk to the nearest metre.

Making the best use of your County or Vice-County Recorder

The postman has certainly been busy this year and the number of parcels in the post shows no signs of slowing down. At times, the volume of photographs to identify and specimens to dissect can seem overwhelming so please do try to keep our workload to a minimum. A look at the back of this publication shows that there are almost 500 people sending in records of moths. If each person sent us half a dozen photographs and two or three moths to dissect, we would barely have time to sleep. One county recorder was asked recently at a meeting how much money he earned in the role and the enquirer was surprised to hear the answer. If you were to get your moths dissected by a commercial service you would pay about ten pounds per slide. We however do this in our "spare" time for no reward at all.

The basic equation with sending in specimens and photos is that information in is proportional to information out, in other words, the more details we get, the more we can give back to you. A blurry badly composed photograph or a moth with no scales is unlikely to leave you with an accurate identification.

Photographs

Some of you take wonderful photos, sharp and close up with shots from the side and from above, so keep up the good work. Some of you don't. Some photos are so big and the moth so small that we have great difficulty telling that it is actually a moth! Some photographs pixelate so much when we blow them up that we can't see any detail. Buy a decent camera. They really aren't too expensive. Think about colour balance. Don't photograph it in the dark. Use a tripod if you can. We can't identify moths from underneath (a common request) or from looking at them face-on.

Identifying moths is a steep learning curve and we are all somewhere on the curve. We're really happy to facilitate your journey up the curve but do try to progress a little. Don't become stuck in the place where we have to tell you for the fifth year in a row that it's the *combusta* form of Clouded-bordered Brindle and that your Common Rustic agg. in May is Small Clouded Brindle. Have a stab at identification yourself. The worst that can happen is that we tell you that you're wrong, which isn't so terrible. Please don't say "I think I know what it is but I thought I would ask you". Stick your head above the parapet and have a go.

Size as they say is everything. If we know the length of the forewing it makes it much easier for us. It's all about narrowing down the possibilities, so date and site can also be vital pieces of information. Some species just can't be identified from photographs. It's a good idea to keep the specimen until you've heard back from us in case it needs dissecting.

Do consider other sources of information for example Twitter and Facebook. Do be aware however that not all those who offer an identification will be accurate. On Twitter your request may well be answered by someone with a good general knowledge of moths but without the knowledge of which species occur in Yorkshire and which specimens should be retained for further examination. Be aware that there are tens of thousands of inaccurately labelled photographs of moths on the internet. Misidentification is staggeringly common. One of the best internet resources is the German site http://www.lepiforum.de/ which has multiple photographs of each species. It is not perfect and some photographs show continental forms but the number of errors is extremely low.

We have stopped offering to identify photographs and specimens of moths from outside the county. We do have a thin volume titled "*The Moths of the Faroe Islands*" but it's gathering dust at the back of the shelf and we would like it to stay there.

A CD with 300 photographs on it is the very last thing we will look at, after we have done everything else.

Specimens

Some people have the idea that when they send us a specimen, we detach the abdomen, put it on a slide and the answer just pops out like DNA barcoding from a computer. Wrong! First of all, we try to narrow the field down to two or three species before we start dissection. This is made a lot easier if the moth is in perfect condition, missing few scales, and with palps and antennae attached. The only way of doing this is to kill the moth quickly rather than let it languish in the fridge for a fortnight, then individually pack it in a small container in (for example) cotton wool so it doesn't get knocked about. A dozen specimens rattling around in a pot is not a good idea. Postage costs may be cheaper if the moth is ironed flat but it is not to be recommended.

We have had several instances again this year where the moth was still alive. This startles us somewhat when we take the top off the container and it flies out. This is particularly the case with moths that fly in the colder months of the year as they seem to positively enjoy ten minutes in the freezer which usually kills their summer-flying cousins.

Please think about postal charges. Don't forget that a letter more than 5mm thick is a large letter, and any sort of tube is likely to make the envelope more than 25mm thick which makes it a packet. So, if you package your moths correctly, you are almost never going to get away with just a first-class stamp. Every year we have to trek down to the post office on at least one occasion and pay a surcharge to collect the packet, and this year was no exception.

Moths can look very different alive, and as you've seen the beast, you have a certain advantage, so it's a good idea to have a stab at identification yourself. To be fair, most of you are pretty good at this, but it would be nice to drag some of you outside your comfort zones to have a guess. It's all part of the learning process. We're going to award extra brownie points for "this looks like *Acleris ferrugana* or *notana*, I would be grateful if you could dissect it for me as neither have been recorded in this area" and remove points for "tortrix, please identify".

It takes about 15 minutes to dissect a moth, though really tricky ones can have us scratching our heads for half the afternoon. It's quite possible for three or four packages to arrive in a single day. A packet of scaleless unlabelled micros can take over a week to identify so please try to keep your requests down to manageable levels. A good rule of thumb might be to send anything suspected of being a county or vice-county record or moths with less than ten county records to be checked. Better still, have a go at dissection yourself and send us a photo of the slide if in doubt.

32.037 *Depressaria pimpinellae*
Hutton Conyers 22 8 19 Charles Fletcher
First VC65 confirmed record

The good news is that more people are dissecting moths which is great, and we're happy to look at photos of genitalia, but do try to take a decent photo down the microscope with adequate lighting, spread the valvae out flat and let us have a look at all the information such as the aedeagus.

It is helpful to know whether you would like your photos, specimens and tubes returned to you. We have masses of your pots at home and don't know what to do with them. If you would like them back, please enclose an SAE. Please enclose an email address if you would like us to reply by email. We will always try to reply but on occasions when we have no phone number or email address it can be a bit tricky!

4.088 *Ectoedemia heringella* 8 Sept 19 Hessle, Andy D Nunn mine on Holm oak 1st VC 61 record

Advice to iRecord users

If you meet a county recorder and he seems to be unusually tetchy, it's probably because he has been dealing with thousands of moth records on iRecord. We don't like it. For all the reasons we don't like it, please refer to last year's report. By all means use it for all of your other natural history records. The Myriapoda recorder gets two records a year and will be delighted. The Bristletail recorder will bite your hand off to get any records at all. We however have to process over 10,000 moth records from iRecord each year and it gives us a bit of a headache.

If you still have the overwhelming urge to make life difficult for us and a strange compunction to put all your moth records onto iRecord rather than send them to your friendly VC recorder, there are a few basic rules:

1. Tell us who you are. We had a photograph of a moth new for the county this year. We don't know any details. We don't know who the heck found it. We can't get in touch with him/her as he doesn't reply when we try to verify it.

2. Enter an email address. Then we just might be able to contact you to get more details.

3. Don't use pseudonyms. Do you really want us to attribute your records to "Megabirder" or "Mothguru"? GorillaPete - help us, who the heck are you? Is it your real name?

4. Don't duplicate. Some people upload to iRecord, send records to the NMRS on-line recording scheme (another bad idea, don't get us started on that), and also send records to their VC recorder and to other people in the county. At the end of the year we realise we've got five copies of all your records and weeding them out takes a lot of time. Another duplication error is when a group of you record the same moths at the same session, often using subtly different gridrefs. Please make sure that just one of you enters the records. We have to remove lots of these duplicates and it's surprisingly tricky.

5. Use sensible gridrefs. If you're walking across a moor counting Common Heaths, we don't need each one to a one metre gridref. For country walks, use 4-figure gridrefs, for your garden use 6-figure gridrefs. Never use 10-figure gridrefs under any circumstances. Moths are mobile things that fly about. They are not plants.

6. Hardly any of you use the taxon-specific input forms which can be found under Record/Taxon-specific Forms/Moths. This means that in the majority of cases we haven't a clue about the life stage or the method. "Pre-adult" can mean any one of a number of things, and it's nice to know whether you caught it at light or found it in your bedroom.

7. Please make sure that the gridref matches the site name. Sometimes the two are several miles apart and we don't know which to believe.

THE SYSTEMATIC LIST

The systematic list follows the usual format with species order in line with the Checklist of the Lepidoptera of the British Isles by David Agassiz, Stella Beavan and Robert Heckford including the recent revisions. Most people are now familiar with the numbers and scientific names of the new checklist so we have not included the old Bradley numbers in this and will not in future lists.

It is always tricky to know which species to include. We have limited space and it is not possible to include all of the 1246 species recorded in the county in 2019. As usual we have chosen to include those which we think will be of most interest to the reader. Amongst the microlepidoptera, species are selected for their rarity, spread into an area or vice-county or those showing major changes in distribution or abundance. There have again been a large number of species new for a vice-county this year and these must all be properly documented. Amongst the macrolepidoptera we have listed a much larger selection as these are usually of greater interest to the majority of our readers. These include all species with fewer than thirty records in the year, all new vice-county records, most species of migrant moth and others of interest, for example those with a limited distribution but which are locally common such as some of our coastal species. If you do not find a macro species in the list, you can assume that it is either common and widespread or it has not been recorded in the county in 2019. If readers are not sure whether a particular species is "common and widespread" or unrecorded, a glance at the Yorkshire Moths web site at www.yorkshiremoths.info or a look at the Atlas of Britain and Ireland's Larger Moths will in most cases provide the answer.

Because of GDPR regulations, Butterfly Conservation advise us that initials of recorders should only be added to records with the recorders' agreement, and this should be on an "opt-in" basis. We have therefore tried to contact all recorders whose initials we would like to include, but this has not always been possible, particularly with some records on iRecord and on social media. If we have no contact details, have received no reply or if the recorder has indicated they do not wish to be attributed, the initials have been replaced by "UR" (Unattributed Record). Permission given will be assumed to be valid for future years. We apologise if this causes any disappointment. Initials of recorders can be cross-referenced to the list of contributors at the end of the report. Whilst we can only document the less common species here, all records are extremely valuable and records of the commoner species provide important data on abundance, flight times and distribution, so we really are grateful for all records which are submitted. One or two records from previous years are included because of either late submission or identification in retrospect. Records are of adult moths unless otherwise stated.

4.024 *Stigmella magdalenae* mines on rowan, Yearsley 26 Sept 19 Charles Fletcher VC62 record.

SECTION 1. MICRO MOTHS
(mainly the smaller and primitive moths)
HEPIALOIDEA
HEPIALIDAE

3.004 Gold Swift *Phymatopus hecta* (Linnaeus)

All records except one were of adults at light though this species is usually seen at dusk especially in open woodland areas with bracken. Numbers seem to have declined in recent years and this fits in with the national picture. There have been no records in VC63 since 2016.

61. North Cliffe Wood, 29.6 & 28.7.2019 (DA, ADN, JMon).

62. Low Dalby, 30.5.2019 (JW); Wykeham Causeway, 28.7.2019 (AR, JHo).

64. Hackfall Woods, 1.6.2019 (CHF); New Laithe Farm, 4.7.2019 (MB); Colt Park, 10.7.2019 (KA, JP); Guisecliffe (Yorke's Folly), 19.7.2019 (CHF, JCW); Ellington Banks (MOD), 22.7.2019 (CHF, JCW, SMP, AWh); Dob Park, 22.7.2019 (CGH); Malham Tarn, 22.7.2019 (DCGB).

65. Beverley Wood, Great Smeaton, 30.5.2019 (JE); Cotherstone, 28.7.2019 (PWe).

NEPTICULOIDEA
NEPTICULIDAE

4.006 *Stigmella sakhalinella* Puplesis

Found quite widely since the first record in 2010 but it has not yet reached the far north-west in VC65.

61. Skipwith Common, mine on birch 11.11.2019 (ADN).

62. Mulgrave Woods, 17.9.2019; Yearsley Woods, 26.9.2019; Hovingham High Wood, 23.10.2019 (CHF).

64. Ledston Luck, mines on birch 19.11.2019 (CHF). NEW VC RECORD.

4.024 *S. magdalenae* (Klimesch)

First seen in the county in 1978 since when it has been recorded thinly in vice-counties 62 to 65.

62. Sutton Bank, mines on rowan 12.9.2019; Gormire Lake and Garbutt Wood, 12.9.2019; near Yearsley, mines on rowan 26.9.2019 (CHF). NEW VC RECORD.

65. Hag Wood, Gunnerside, mines on rowan 11.9.2019 (CHF).

4.053 *S. incognitella* (Herrich-Schäffer)

Larval mines have been found occasionally since 2005; most records coming from VC63 but it now lacks records only from VC64.

61. North Cave wetlands, mines on apple 3.9.2019 (ADN). NEW VC RECORD.

4.072 *Bohemannia quadrimaculella* (Boheman)

There are only six previous records, all in vice-counties 62 & 63.

64. Ellington Banks MOD, 22.7.2019 gen. det. CHF (CHF, JCW *et al.*). NEW VC RECORD.

4.088 *Ectoedemia heringella* (Mariani)

First found in Britain in London in 2001 these are presently the most northerly British records.

61. Humberfield Quarry, Hessle, mines on holm oak 8.9.2019 (ADN). NEW VC RECORD.

63. Hatfield Woodhouse, mines on holm oak 21.8 & 3.9.2019 (UR). NEW COUNTY RECORD.

4.091 *E. heringi* (Toll)

Previous county records are all from VC63 except for a single one in VC64.

62. Sutton-on-the-Forest, tenanted mines on oak 31.10.2019 (CHF). NEW VC RECORD.

63. Potteric Carr NR, mines 29.11.2019 (RI&JCH).

65. Leighton, tenanted mine on oak 24.10.2019 (ADN). NEW VC RECORD.

OPOSTEGIDAE

5.004 *Pseudopostega crepusculella* (Zeller)

Although occurring very thinly in all five vice-counties only VC64 has more than two records in total. This moth is shown as occurring in VC65 on map 116 in MBGBI vol. 1, (1976) but the record below is the only one for which we have data.

65. Semerwater, three 26.7.2019 (CHF, JCW, DMS, TMW). FIRST CONFIRMED VC RECORD.

ADELOIDEA
ADELIDAE

7.007 *Adela cuprella* ([Denis & Schiffermüller])
There are two records from the 1940s in the York area of VC62. There are indications of its occurrence in other Yorkshire vice-counties on distribution maps (in MBGBI vol. 1 & *A Field Guide to the Smaller Moths of Great Britain and Ireland* (2018)) but we have no details of any of these.
63. Thrybergh C.P., 8.4.2019 (DSh). FIRST CONFIRMED VC RECORD.

7.008 *A. croesella* (Scopoli)
Thinly distributed in vice-counties 61 to 64 but with fewer than twenty previous records.
61. Cali Heath, 23.6.2019 (UR).
62. Ashberry Pastures, 9.6.2019 (TAB).
63. Austerfield, 25.5.2019 (SB).

7.013 *Nematopogon magna* (Zeller)
These two moths, taken a day apart in 2018 are the second and third Yorkshire (and indeed English) records. Otherwise it is known only from Scotland and the west of Ireland. The only previous county occurrence was in VC63 in 1904 but its identity was not recognised until 1985.
64. Westfield, Kirkby Malzeard, 28.5.2018 gen. det HEB (CHF). NEW VC RECORD.
65. Bog Wood, Bellflask, Ripon, 29.5.2018 gen. det. HEB (BM). NEW VC RECORD.

7.013 *Nematopogon magna*, 29 May 2018, Bellflask, Brian Morland, first for VC65 and third for Yorkshire.

TINEOIDEA
PSYCHIDAE

11.003 *Dahlica triquetrella* (Hübner)
The few previous county records were in VC63.
62. Burton Riggs NR, case on fence 21.10.2019 (DSh). NEW VC RECORD.

TINEIDAE

12.011 *Triaxomera fulvimitrella* (Sodoffsky)
Although widespread with records in all five vice-counties it is nowhere numerous. No VC has more than seven occurrences.
61. East Cottingwith, 2.6.2019 (JOHS).
64. Hackfall Woods, 1.6.2019 (CHF).

12.017 *Nemapogon koenigi* Capuşe
An uncommon moth but it has appeared more frequently during the past five years. Now only VC64 is without a record.
61. Lund, 28.7 & 8.8.2019 (MCo).
65. Hutton Conyers, 4.7.2019 gen. det. (CHF). NEW VC RECORD.

12.021 *N. clematella* (Fabricius)
There are only nine previous county records but these involve all five vice-counties.
65. High Batts NR, 12.7.2019 (CHF, TMW, DMS).

12.026 Common Clothes Moth *Tineola bisselliella* (Hummel)
This moth was formerly a common household pest but became scarce from the mid-20th century due to central heating and the use of artificial fabrics. The last few years has seen an increase with some considerable infestations.

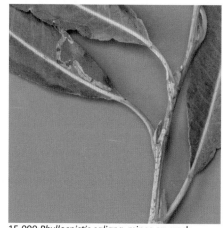

15.090 *Phyllocnistis saligna*, mines on crack willow, Hatfield Moors, photographer anonymous, 7th September 2019, new for Yorkshire.

61. Beverley, infestation in carpet shop 21.7.2019 (ADN).

62. Heworth, York, 29.3 & 24.5.2019, gen. det. RWo (BB).

64. Little Preston, frequent 27.2 - 22.10.2018 (JMa); Coniston Cold, 15 & 23.3.2019 (ARh.); Menston, 14.6.2019 (CGH).

12.039 *Monopis crocicapitella* (Clemens)

We have fewer than ten records, all in vice-counties 61 & 64.

61. Catwick, 1.6.2019 (JM).

64. Little Preston, 31.8 & 1.9.2019 gen. det. CHF (JMa).

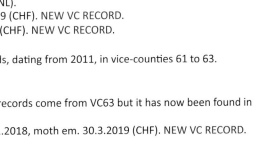

15.012 *Caloptilia semifascia*, leaf rolls on field maple Richmond 6 Sept 19 Charles Fletcher VC65 record.

GRACILLARIOIDEA
GRACILLARIIDAE

15.012 *Caloptilia semifascia* (Haworth)

Despite only four previous county records the wide distribution indicates that it may have been overlooked in the past.

63. Went Hills, mine on field maple 22.7.2019 (NL).

64. Skipton, larval cone on field maple 3.10.2019 (CHF). NEW VC RECORD.

65. Ripon, larval cones on field maple 7.9.2019 (CHF). NEW VC RECORD.

15.026 *Parornix fagivora* (Frey)

We have three widely scattered previous records, dating from 2011, in vice-counties 61 to 63.

62. Burton Riggs NR, mine 21.10.2019 (DSh).

15.036 *Phyllonorycter heegeriella* (Zeller)

A widespread moth but under-recorded. Most records come from VC63 but it has now been found in all five vice-counties.

65. Well (House Close Wood), mine on oak 3.11.2018, moth em. 30.3.2019 (CHF). NEW VC RECORD.

15.074 *P. schreberella* (Fabricius)

Frequent in the south of the county but scarcer towards the north. Our VC62 & 65 records are the most northerly in Britain.

62. Bell Bottom, 23.10.2019 (CHF).

65. Middleton Tyas, mines on elm 5.11.2019 (CHF). NEW VC RECORD.

15.076 *P. emberizaepenella* (Bouché)

Quite widespread in vice-counties 61 & 63 but evidently scarce in the north of the county with few records from VC62 and none from VC65.

64. Fountains Abbey, mines on snowberry 25.10.2018 em.17.3.2019; near Wetherby, mine with pupa 27.10.2019 (CHF). NEW VC RECORD.

15.090 *Phyllocnistis saligna* (Zeller)

A moth that is evidently extending its distribution northwards; these are the most northerly British records.

61. Cottingham, mines on white willow 13.9.2019 (ADN). NEW VC RECORD.

63. Hatfield Moors, mines on crack willow 7 & 10.9.2019; Brick Hill Carr Common & Lindholme, 10.9.2019; Thorne, pupa 13.9.2019, moth emerged same day (UR). NEW COUNTY RECORD.

YPONOMEUTOIDEA
YPSOLOPHIDAE

17.006 *Ypsolopha horridella* (Treitschke)

A recent arrival in Yorkshire with records from vice-counties 61 to 64. All 2019 occurrences were in VC61.

61. Lund, 3.8.2019; Hollym Carrs, 4.8.2019 (MCo); Catwick, 4.8.2019 (JM); Kilnwick, 7.8.2019 (MCo); Newton-upon-Derwent, 26.8.2019 (IRH).

ARGYRESTHIIDAE

20.017 *Argyresthia glaucinella* Zeller
A scarce or under-recorded moth. There are a few recent records in vice-counties 62 to 64, a single occurrence in VC61 in 1951 and it remains unrecorded in VC65.
62. Duncombe Park, 14.6.2019 (JOHS).
63. Potteric Carr NR, 5.7.2019 (RI&JCH, HEB).

PRAYDIDAE

22.003 *Prays ruficeps* (Heinemann)
Since it was recognised as a taxon distinct from *P. fraxinella* it has been found quite widely in vice-counties 61 & 63. VC64 records are few and there are currently none from VC65.
62. Seamer, 4.6.2019 (DLo); Skelton, 4.8.2019 (DM). NEW VC RECORD.
64. Hackfall Woods, 1.6.2019 (CHF).

GELECHIOIDEA
OECOPHORIDAE

28.024 *Tachystola acroxantha* (Meyrick)
Now well established and often locally common in vice-counties 63 & 64. There are two records in VC61 but none from VC65.
62. Huntington, York, 25.8.2019 gen. det. RWo (AF). NEW VC RECORD.
63. Pudsey, 20.4-19.7.2019 (DH); Halifax, 14.5-26.10.2019 (DSu); Farsley, 25.5-18.7.2019; Bramley, 23.8.2019 (JWC).
64. Ilkley, 30.4.2019 det. CHF (P&JB); Alwoodley, Leeds, 31.5-10.10.2019 (PRM).

28.024 Tachystola acroxantha York 25 Aug 19 A Fitter First VC 62 Record

LYPUSIDAE

30.004 *Amphisbatis incongruella* (Stainton)
This is a scarce or overlooked moth with fewer than ten records from heathland and moorland localities in vice-counties 61 to 63, that in VC63 dating from the 19th century. An unpublished record from 2010 is included below.
62. Fen Bog, 13.4.2010; Lealholm Moor, 30.3.2019 (GF).

DEPRESSARIIDAE

32.009 *Agonopterix purpurea* (Haworth)
We have two previous records of single moths in 2017 & 2018. Three examples in 2019 suggest that it is now resident in the south of the county in the Doncaster and Rotherham districts.
63. Potteric Carr NR, 19.2 & 18.4.2019 (RI&JCH); Austerfield, 20.4.2019 (SB).

32.011 *A. scopariella* (Heinemann)
With fewer than ten records this moth may well be overlooked; all occurrences have been in VC63.
63. Wintersett CP, 27.8.2019 det. HEB (PSm).

32.029 *A. umbellana* (Fabricius)
An infrequently recorded moth with records in vice-counties 61 to 64.
61. Hunmanby Gap, 25.4.2019 (KC).
62. Strensall Common, 20.4.2019 (YB).

32.035 *A. yeatiana* (Fabricius)
A rarely recorded moth with some ten records in vice-counties 61 to 64 but the majority are from the Spurn area of VC61.
61. Easington, 8 & 15.9.2019 (MFS).

32.037 *Depressaria pimpinellae* Zeller
Although shown as occurring in vice-counties 61, 62, 64 & 65 on map 44 in MBGBI 4(1) we have no data from elsewhere than VC62 from where we have three previous records.
65. Hutton Conyers, 22.8.2019 (CHF). FIRST CONFIRMED VC RECORD.

32.039 *D. daucella* ([Denis & Schiffermüller])
Thinly distributed in vice-counties 61 to 64 but usually occurring as single moths.
61. St. Aiden's NR, 13.9.2019 gen. det. CHF (PRM).

ETHMIIDAE
33.002 *Ethmia quadrillella* (Goeze)
All previous county records are from vice-counties 62, 64 & 65 where it occurs regularly.
63. Stannington, Sheffield, 5.6.2018 (UR). NEW VC RECORD.

GELECHIIDAE
35.003 *Aproaerema larseniella* (Gozmány)
Recorded occasionally in vice-counties 61 to 64; there is only one previous occurrence in VC64.
62. Huntington, York, 16 & 18.7.2019 gen. det. RWo (AF).
64. Askham Bog, 25.7.2019 gen. det. CHF (AF, TJC).

35.042 *Bryotropha boreella* (Douglas)
We have ten previous records in vice-counties 63 to 65 of this moth of boggy moorland; Semerwater is a new locality.
65. Semerwater, 26.7.2019 (CHF, JCW, DMS, TMC).

35.050 *Aristotelia ericinella* (Zeller)
Widely recorded in heathery areas in vice-counties 61 to 64, surprisingly this is the first occurrence in VC65.
65. Foxglove Covert MOD, 23.8.2019 (CHF, JCW). NEW VC RECORD.

35.050 *Aristotelia ericinella* Foxglove Covert 23 Aug 19 first for VC65 Charles Fletcher

35.107 *Psoricoptera gibbosella* (Zeller)
There are five previous records in vice-counties 63 to 65; they are the most northerly in Britain.
63. Potteric Carr N.R. 24.7.2019 gen. det. HEB (HEB, RI&JCH); Haw Park, Wintersett C.P., 27.8.19 det. HEB (PSm).

35.127 *Tuta absoluta* (Meyrick)
An adventive moth occasionally found among imported tomatoes.
61. Cottingham, indoors 12.4.2019 conf. (gen. det.) SMP (HW).

COLEOPHORIDAE
37.013 *Coleophora siccifolia* Stainton
We have five previous records covering all five vice-counties although three of them date from over a hundred years ago.
61. Tophill Low NR, 27.6.2019 gen. det. DF (MHo, GF).

37.019 *C. trigeminella* Fuchs
A local moth with ten previous records but it has been found in all five vice-counties.
61. Tophill Low NR, 5.7.2019 gen. det. DF (MHo, GF).

37.107 *C. clypeiferella* Hofmann
The two previous records are from Spurn (VC61) in 2010 and Blaxton (VC63) in 2014.
61. Skidby, 24.7.2019 (ADN).

37.108 *C. salicorniae* Heinemann & Wocke
These are the first records away from the coast in the Spurn area where it has been found regularly in recent years.
61. Skidby, 24 & 25.7.2019 gen.det. (ADN); Tophill Low NR, 25.7.2019 gen. det. DF (MHo, GF).

ELACHISTIDAE
38.001 *Perittia obscurepunctella* (Stainton)
The few modern records have all been in VC64; it was formerly found in VC61 in the 19th century and in VC62 before 1950.
63. Kirk Sandall, mines on honeysuckle 21.7.2019; River Torne banks, mines 22.7.2019; Hatfield Moors, mines 15.8.2019 (UR). NEW VC RECORD.

38.007 *Elachista subocellea* (Stephens)
Recorded occasionally in vice-counties 62 to 65, most frequently in VC64. There is only a single previous VC63 occurrence.
63. Brockadale NR, 5.6.2019; Went Hills, 20.7.2019 (DWi).
64. Ellington Banks MOD, 8 & 22.7.2019 (CHF, JCW *et al.*).
65. High Batts NR, 12.7.2019 (CHF, TMW, DMS *et al.*).
38.016 *E. subalbidella* Schläger
An uncommon moth with about eight records distributed quite widely. Previous occurrences cover the remaining vice-counties although the only one listed from VC62 at 'York' in the 19th century cannot be guaranteed to be from that vice-county.
64. Askham Bog, 1.6.2019 gen.det. CHF (LFM). NEW VC RECORD.

BLASTOBASIDAE
42.002 *Stathmopoda pedella* (Linnaeus)
Has occurred quite frequently in vice-counties 61 & 63 following the first Yorkshire occurrence in 1983. Scarce in VC64 with four previous records dating from 2004 and presently unrecorded in VC65.
62. Huntington, York, 24.7.2019 det. RWo (AF). NEW VC RECORD.
64. Ellington Banks MOD, 22.7.2019 (CHF, JCW *et al.*); Askham Bog, 25.7.2019 (AF, TJC *et al.*).

PTEROPHOROIDEA
PTEROPHORIDAE
45.023 *Marasmarcha lunaedactyla* (Haworth)
Widespread in vice-counties 61 & 63 and more infrequent in VC62. There is presently no VC65 record.
61. Wharram Quarry, 9 & 23.7.2019 (JG, IM, ADN); Kilnwick, 25.7.2019 (MCo).
62. Ellerburn Bank, 18.7.2019 (GF).
63. Thorne Colliery site, 9 & 10.7.2019 (HRK, MWa); Went Hills, 13.7.2019 (LD); Kirk Smeaton, 25 & 26.7.2019 (P&JS).
64. Tadcaster, 14 & 15.7.2019 (DBa). NEW VC RECORD.

45.023 Marasmarcha lunaedactyla Tadcaster
David Baker First for VC 64

45.027 *Oxyptilus laetus* (Zeller)
An infrequent immigrant moth that occurred quite widely in Britain during 2019.
63. Austerfield, 16.7.2019 conf. (gen. det.) HEB (SB). NEW COUNTY RECORD.
[64. Swillington, 9.7.2019 (DN). Specimen not retained; a photo was inconclusive but may be of *laetus* (Colin Hart, *pers. comm.*)].

EPERMENIOIDEA
EPERMENIIDAE
47.006 *Epermenia falciformis* (Haworth)
Since the first Yorkshire occurrence in 1999 this moth has spread rapidly and is now seen regularly throughout the county although much scarcer in the north. The record below is only the second in VC65.
65. Ainderby Steeple, 1.6.2019 (JE).

TORTRICOIDEA
TORTRICIDAE
49.005 *Epagoge grotiana* (Fabricius)
There are three pre 21st century records in vice-counties 62 (2) and 64 (1). Since 2008 it has occurred sparsely in VC63 from where all but one modern record has come, the exception being one in VC64 in 2009.
63. Potteric Carr NR, 1.6 & 5.7.2019 (RI&JCH, HEB); Austerfield, 5.7.2019 (SB); Lindholme, Hatfield Moors, 16.7.2019 (DWi, P&JS).
49.008 *Philedone gerningana* ([Denis & Schiffermüller])
Formerly recorded quite regularly, particularly in the north and west of the county. Recent records are few and **these are the first since 2016.**

64. Moughton, 23.7.2019 (TMW).

65. Semerwater, 26.7.2019 (CHF, JCW, TMW, DMS).

49.048 *Eana penziana* (Thunberg) *ssp. bellana* (Curtis)
All records come from the higher ground in the west of VC64 where it is seen occasionally. That from Duck Street Quarry is some 30 km. further east than previous records and the first from the Harrogate district.

64. Duck Street Quarry, 17.7.2019 (PMi, ARh *et al.*); Ribblehead Quarry NR, 18.7.2019; Moughton, 23.7.2019 (TMW).

49.058 *Spatalistis bifasciana* (Hübner)
This moth was added to the Yorkshire list in 2014; there are four previous occurrences in vice-counties 61 & 63.

61. North Cliffe Wood, 29.6.2019 (DA).

49.076 *Acleris cristana* ([Denis & Schiffermüller])
Except for two records in the mid-19th century this moth has only occurred since 2006 but in increasing numbers; only VC65 lacks records.

61. Kilnwick, 15.2.2019; Lund, 16.2 & 24.9.2019 (MCo); Skidby, 14 & 23.3.2019 (ADN); Tophill Low NR, 8.8.2019 (MHo, GF); North Ferriby, 23.8.2019 (IM); Cali Heath, 28.12.2019 (IA).

62. Wykeham Causeway, 22.2.2019 (AR, JHo); Haxby, 9 & 19.3.2019 (TJC).

63. Austerfield, 8 & 22.2, 20.3 & 7.4.2019 (SB); West Melton, 7.12.2019 (HEB).

64. Tadcaster, 1 & 16.3.2019 (DBa); Little Preston, 1 & 29.9.2019 (JMa).

49.086 *A. logiana* (Clerck)
First seen in the county in 2010 it has since occurred thinly but widely and has been found in all five vice-counties.

62. Haxby, 12.2.2019 (TJC); Wykeham Causeway, 13.2.2019 (AR, JHo).

63. Austerfield, 21.3 & 6.7.2019 (SB); Cromwell Bottom, 30.6.2019 (CS); Farsley, 20.7.2019 (JWC); Thorne Moors, 16.10.2019 (MWa *et al.*).

64. Ellington Banks MOD, 22.7.2019 (CHF, JCW *et al.*); Askham Bryan, 23.11.2019 (DL).

49.138 *Cochylis molliculana* Zeller
First found in Britain in 1991 since when it has spread slowly northwards. This is currently the most northerly British record.

63. Kirk Smeaton, 24.8.2019 gen. det. (DWi.) NEW COUNTY RECORD.

49.148 *Apotomis lineana* ([Denis & Schiffermüller])
Except for a mid-19th century record in VC62 the few Yorkshire occurrences date from 2012 and are

49.138 *Cochylis molliculana*, Kirk Smeaton 24 Aug 19 Dave Williamson new for Yorkshire.

restricted to vice-counties 61 & 63. It may well be overlooked; the last two years have seen a slight increase in records.

61. North Cliffe Wood, 29.7.2019 (ADN); Lund, 30.7.2019 (DA); North Ferriby, 3.8.2019 (IM).

63. Austerfield, 24.7.2019 (SB).

49.196 *Bactra lacteana* Caradja
This is only the fourth county occurrence but it is not easy to distinguish from *B. lancealana*; all records come from vice-counties 64 & 65.

64. Coniston Cold, 15.9.2019 gen. det. CHF (ARh).

49.201 *Ancylis unguicella* (Linnaeus)
An infrequently recorded moth but it has been found in all five vice-counties.

63. Keighley Moor, 22.5 & 23.7.2019 (IHa).

64. Collingham, 24.5.2019 (PH); Stainburn Forest, 31.5.2019 (CHF).

49.202 *A. uncella* ([Denis & Schiffermüller])
A local moth found infrequently in vice-counties 61 to 63.

61. Elvington, 12.7.2019 (JSm).

49.208 *A. subarcuan*a **(Douglas)**
A very local moth with only ten previous records. All recent occurrences have been at Strensall Common.
62. Strensall Common, 16.6.2019 det. RWo (PMa).

49.211 *A. myrtillan*a **(Treitschke)**
Often numerous in moorland localities in vice-counties 62 to 65. Records of wanderers to the lower ground are uncommon.
63. Brecks, Rotherham, 30.5.2019 (MSm).

49.237 Epinotia signatana High Batts NR 12 Jul 19 Charles Fletcher new for VC65

49.219 *Thiodia citrana* **(Hübner)**
The three previous Yorkshire occurrences were all at Spurn.
61. Hunmanby Gap, 26 & 29.7.2019 (KC).

49.220 *Rhopobota myrtillana* **(Humphreys & Westwood)**
Patchily distributed but can be locally common in vice-counties 62 to 64.
62. Lealholm, 13.5.2019 (GF); Hawnby, larvae in spun bilberry tips, moths em. 7.7.2019 (RWo); Broxa, 12.7.2019 (GF, RWo, AR).

49.228 *Epinotia sordidana* **(Hübner)**
Infrequently recorded in vice-counties 61 to 64.
64. Askham Bog, 29.9.2019 gen. det. CHF (AF, TJC).

49.237 *E. signatana* **(Douglas)**
Since the first county record in 2014 this moth has proved to be locally common in VC61. There are two recent VC62 occurrences with evidence of continuing spread in 2019 from vice-counties 63 & 65.
61. Tophill Low NR, 12, 18 & 21.7.2019 (MHo, GF); Wheldrake, 23.7.2019 (JOHS); Hunmanby Gap, 29 & 30.7.2019 (KC); Kilnwick & Lund, frequent (MCo).

49.261 Crocidosema plebejana 7 Oct 19 Tadcaster David Baker new for VC64

63. Wintersett CP. 9.7.2019 gen. det. HEB (PSm). NEW VC RECORD.
65. High Batts NR, 12.7.2019 (CHF, TMW, DMS *et al.*). NEW VC RECORD.

49.261 *Crocidosema plebejana* **(Zeller)**
We have six previous records in vice-counties 61 & 62. That in VC64 is by far the most inland occurrence in the county.
61. Muston, 20.10.2019 (PQW).
64. Tadcaster, 7.10.2019 conf. (gen. det.) HEB (DBa). NEW VC RECORD.

49.274 *Eucosma metzneriana* **(Treitschke)**
A moth that is spreading northwards in Britain, there is a single previous record at Spurn in 2017. These Yorkshire records are the most northerly in Britain.
61. Hollym Carrs, 4.8.2019 (MCo).

49.299 *Pseudococcyx postican*a **(Zetterstedt)**
With only four previous records in vice-counties 62 & 63 this pine feeding moth appears surprisingly scarce in the county.
64. Stainburn Forest, 31.5.2019 (CHF). NEW VC RECORD.

49.318 *Dichrorampha vancouverana* McDunnough
Like many *Dichrorampha* species this moth is likely to be under recorded. Most frequent in the south of the county in vice-counties 61 & 63; we have no records from VC62 and only one in VC65.
64. Alwoodley, Leeds, 24.7.2019 (PRM). NEW VC RECORD.

49.299 Pseudococcyx posticana Stainburn Forest 31 May 19 Charles Fletcher new for VC64

49.319 *D. flavidorsana* Knaggs

The same comment also applies to this moth. It is very thinly recorded in vice-counties 61 to 64.

61. Catwick, 27.8.2019 gen. det. (JM).
62. Huntington, York, 27.8.2019 gen. det. RWo (AF).

49.343 *Cydia amplana* (Hübner)

An immigrant moth that may now be resident in south-east England. There have been five occurrences in Yorkshire since the first in 1999; all have been in coastal localities in vice-counties 61 & 62.

61. Hunmanby Gap, three on 29.7.2019 (KC).
62. Skelton, 27 & 30 7.2019 (DM).

49.343 *Cydia amplana*, one of three at Hunmanby Gap on 29 July 19 Keith Clarkson

COSSOIDEA
COSSIDAE

50.001 Goat Moth *Cossus cossus* (Linnaeus)

Two larval records from a new site. All records in the last 50 years have come from the south-east corner of VC63 where it turns up infrequently. It is not impossible that there are still colonies in other parts of the county.

63. Potteric Carr NR, larvae 15 & 24.8.2019 (IAs, NCl).

50.002 Leopard Moth *Zeuzera pyrina* (Linnaeus)

Another healthy year for this spectacular moth of open scrubby areas with records spread across all five vice-counties.

61. Tophill Low NR, 22.7.2019 (MHo, DF); Lund, 23.7.2019 (DA); Stillingfleet Lodge, 3.8.2019 (DBa).
62. Haxby, 21.7.2019 (TJC).
63. Sprotbrough, 25.6, 23 & 25.7.2019 (DBo); Austerfield, 29.6, 10, 16 & 25.7.2019 (SB); Kirk Smeaton, 25.7.2019 (DWi); Swinefleet, 8.7.2019 (MJP).
64. Knaresborough, 21 & 25.7.2019 (LK); Ellington Banks (MOD), 22.7.2019 (CHF, JCW, SMP, AWh); Sharow, 23 & 25.7.2019 (JCW); Askham Bog, 25.7.2019 (AF, TJC, YB, NH); Collingham, 3.8.2019 (PH).
65. Asenby, 13.7.2019 (K&DH); Brompton-on-Swale, 23.7.2019 (TCo); Hutton Conyers, 25.7.2019 (CHF).

50.002 Leopard Moth Kirk Smeaton VC63 Dave Williamson

SESIIDAE
52.003 Lunar Hornet Moth
Sesia bembeciformis (Hübner)

Very few records this year, and unusually all of adults. This species is usually easily recorded by looking for larval tunnels in cut willow stumps and must be more common than these records suggest. Unlike other members of the family, it does not come to pheromones.

61. Tophill Low NR, 7 & 12.7.2019 (MHo, DF).
62. Thirsk, 3.7.2019 (UR).
63. Wintersett Reservoir, 7.7.2019 (PSm et al.); Potteric Carr NR, 18.8.2019 (DMG).

52.008 Red-tipped Clearwing *Synanthedon formicaeformis* (Esper)

A good year for this willow-feeding species.
Most records as usual were of moths coming to pheromones. Rodley is a new site.

61. Tophill Low NR, 22, 27 & 28.6.2019 (MHo, DF).
63. Austerfield, 15, 22 & 30.6, 14.7.2019 (SB); Thorne Moors, 22.6.2019 (MWa et al.).
64. Rodley NR, 30.6 & 21.7.2019 (JWC, JG).

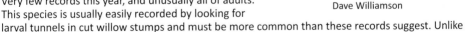

52.012 Yellow-legged Clearwing
S. vespiformis (Linnaeus)
All three records of this oak-feeding species were
from new sites.
63. Brockadale, 22.6.2019 (UR); Rivelin Dams,
30.6.2019 (PMe); Wentworth Castle, 21.8.2019 (RHa).

52.013 Currant Clearwing
S. tipuliformis (Clerck)
Records scattered across the county; a mixture
of daytime observations and moths coming to
pheromones.
61. Skidby, 29.6.2019 (ADN).
62. York, 18.6.2019 (CM).
63. Swinefleet, 30.5, 9 & 16.6.2019 (MJP); Rotherham, 21.6.2019 (MSm); Thackley, 13.7.2019 (NAA).
64. Baildon, larva on 2.3.2019 (DPa).

52.013 Currant Clearwing 29 June 19 Skidby VC 61.
Andy D Nunn

52.014 Six-belted Clearwing Bembecia ichneumoniformis ([Denis & Schiffermüller])
A good year for this moth of calcareous grassland with bird's-foot trefoil. Most records were of
moths attracted to pheromones and the biggest numbers as usual were from Brockadale. Several
records were from new sites. The St Aidan's NR records were in two separate VCs.
61. Tophill Low NR, 27, 28 & 29.6.2019 (MHo, DF); Market Weighton, 7.7.2019 (PA).
63. Forgemasters Tip Treeton Dyke, 28.6.2019 (DWh); Brockadale NR, 1, 2, 3, & 12.7.2019 (SB); St
Aidan's NR, 3 & 8.7.2019 (PRM, DN); Darton, 5.7.2019 (RBu); Potteric Carr NR, 15.7.2019 (SB); Low
Moor, 18. & 25.7.2019 (MVP); Lindrick Common (Woodsetts), 18.7.2019 (DWh); 64. St Aidan's NR,
11.7.2019 (JG).

ZYGAENOIDEA
ZYGAENIDAE
54.002 Forester Adscita statices (Linnaeus)
Scattered records as usual from the south of the county. Barrow Colliery is a new site.
63. Thorpe Marsh NR, 30.5 & 21.6.2019 (MT); Barrow Colliery site, Worsbrough, 18.6.2019 (CB).

54.003 Cistus Forester A. geryon (Hübner)
Records from the two main populations in the county. The Arncliffe site was new and held the
biggest numbers this year.
62. Moor Ings Bank, 15 & 24.5.2019 (DWa).
64. Kilnsey, 6, 14, 18 & 29.6, 3.7.2019 (PMi, ARh); Arncliffe, Cowside, 29.6.2019 (PMi); Dib Scar,
2.7.2019 (PMi).

Nemophora degeerella (conjoined) 15 june 19
Mike Smethurst

08.002 Incurvaria masculella David Baker

SECTION 2. BUTTERFLIES

HESPERIDAE
Skippers
57.001 Dingy Skipper *Erynnis tages* (Linn. 1758)

Broods: Normally **1**, but a partial 2nd possible even as far north as Yorkshire. Resident, often overlooked. Less common, moth-like species, mainly found in relation to chalk and limestone or old coal tip habitats on the N York Moors, Yorkshire Wolds, and on industrial sites like railway goods yards.

Yorkshire 2019: This year has not been as successful for Dingy Skippers as we have previously seen with lower total counts across all VCs. The county total was 60% of last years' (985 vs 1633) and the lowest county total for at least the last 10 years. This year has been the earliest the species has been seen since 2015 with first sightings coming in from late April (20th). As usual, most sightings took place during May with the peak counts in all VCs in May. However, as was the case last year, the season was over early again by the start of July with most VC's last sightings coming in during June. *Jennifer Watts*

FIRST SIGHTINGS
VC61: 20/04 **1** Enthorpe *Andrew Ashworth*
VC62: 28/04 **1** Sunny Bank West *R Parks & I Armitage*
VC63: 30/04 **12** South Kirby Stack *Chris Parkin*
VC65: 10/05 **1** Nosterfield LNR *Martin Bland*
VC64: 12/05 **2** Moor Lane *Steve Mattock*

PEAK COUNTS
VC64: 14/05 **15** Low Grantley *Mike Barnham*
VC65: 14/05 **9** Beverley Wd, Great Smeaton *John Edwards*
VC61: 15/05 **41** Enthorpe *Andrew Ashworth*
VC63: 17/05 **74** South Kirby Stack *Chris Parkin*
VC62: 21/05 **22** Pickering *Dave O'Brien*

LAST SIGHTINGS
VC65: 22/05 **2** Thornborough *Mike Barnham*
VC64: 07/06 **1** Bishop Wood *Nick Hall*
VC63: 27/06 **2** Cudworth Marsh *Cliff Gorman*
VC61: 29/06 **2** Enthorpe *Andrew Ashworth*
VC62: 04/07 **1** Red Dike, Dalby Forest *Paul Ingham*

Dingy Skipper *Erynnis tages* Sneaton forest 2019
John Money

STATISTICS 2019
Monthly: flight days (total butterflies) **countywide:** Apr **5** (53), May **24** (835), Jun **17** (96), Jul **1** (1).
Total flight days/flight season length: **47/ 76** days.
Total reports (total butterflies) **a) countywide: 189** (985) = mean **5.21** butterflies per observation.
b) by VC: VC61: **31** (236), VC62: **47** (179), VC63: **86** (501), VC64: **18** (50), VC65: **7** (19).
Tetrads recorded (i.e., 2x2km OS grid squares): **69** out of 1510 visited and 4120 in Yorkshire.

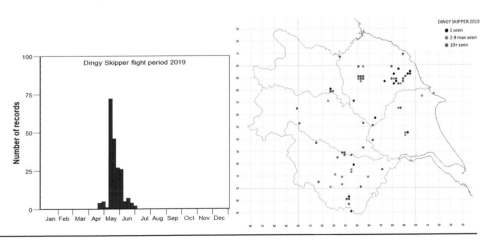

57.005 Essex Skipper *Thymelicus lineola* (Ochsenheimer 1808)

Broods: 1. Rare resident. Arrived at the southern edges of county in 1996 as part of a national expansion northward. Locally present near Doncaster (VC63), along the banks of the Ouse between Goole and RSPB Blacktoft Sands, strong numbers along the north bank of the Humber to Spurn (VC61). There has been a marked expansion since 2015 and Essex Skipper is now spreading in VC61 and VC63. The first confirmed sightings in VC62 (expansion from the south) and VC64 (presumed expansion from the north) occurred in 2018.

Yorkshire 2019: The populations in VC63 and VC61 continue to spread. The Essex Skipper was again seen, though still in a handful of locations, in VC62 and VC64. The sighting of Essex Skipper in Langdale Forest (VC62) by Ian and Pauline Popely is unexpected being in an isolated location, being about 40-km south-east and north-east of the nearest Essex Skipper colonies in VC62 (NZ41) and VC61 (SE74) respectively, and represents a new 10-km square (SE99) record of some interest. Does the species hop great distances (perhaps transported in hay for horses but that doesn't seem likely given the location), or are we simply missing the majority of the Essex Skippers that are around? The expansion of Essex Skipper still requires close monitoring and I ask recorders to make a special effort to double-check any Small Skippers seen as they might be Essex Skippers. Take a close-up photograph of the antennae and sex brand (if male) – we need to have photographs if we are to verify Essex Skipper in new areas. Please consult the Yorkshire Butterflies and Moths Report Argus 81 (2017) for Sean Clough's excellent photos on how to distinguish between Small, Essex and Large Skippers. For a recent account of how Essex Skipper have spread in Yorkshire please see Smith, DRR (2018). How have recent lepidopteral colonisers fared in Yorkshire? *The Naturalist*, **143**, 107-129. ***David Smith***

FIRST SIGHTINGS

VC63: 02/07 **1** Goole Moor Tram *Martin Warne*
VC61: 16/07 **1** Kilnsea Wetlands *Chris & H Frost*
VC61: 16/07 **1** Kilnsea, Humber Bank *C & H Frost*
VC61: 16/07 **1** Spurn Bird Obs. Church Field *C & H Frost*
VC61: 16/07 **1** North Cave Wetlands *Paul Ashton*
VC64: 30/07 **1** Bishop Wood *Mike Barnham*
VC64: 30/07 **1** Fairburn Ings RSPB *Anon*
VC62: 01/08 **1** Hipperley Beck, Langdale *I & P Popely*

PEAK COUNTS

VC62: singletons
VC63: 16/07 **15** Brockadale NR *Paul & Joyce Simmons*
VC61: 02/08 **10** Sunk Island, Humber Bank *A Gibson*
VC64: singletons

LAST SIGHTINGS

VC62: 04/08 **1** Hilton Fishing Lakes *Martin Partridge*
VC64: 05/08 **1** St Aidan's Goose Fields *A Tiffany*
VC61: 08/08 **1** Wawne *Robert Atkinson*
VC61: 08/08 **1** Spurn Bird Obs. *Chris & Howard Frost*
VC63: 18/08 **1** St Aidan's RSPB *D McMahon*

STATISTICS 2019

Monthly: flight days (total butterflies **county-wide**: Jul **19** (159), Aug **8** (68).
Total flight days/flight season length: 27/ 48 days.
Total reports (total butterflies) **a) countywide: 67** (227) = mean **3.39** butterflies per observation.
b) by VC: VC61: **29** (87), VC62: **3** (3), VC63: **32** (134), VC64: **3** (3).
Tetrads recorded (i.e., 2x2km OS grid squares): **35** out of 1510 visited and 4120 in Yorkshire

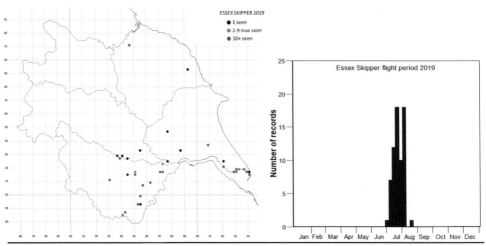

ESSEX SKIPPER 2019
● 1 seen
◉ 2-9 max seen
● 10+ seen

Essex Skipper flight period 2019

57.006 Small Skipper *Thymelicus sylvestris* (Poda 1761)

Broods: 1. Widespread resident.

Yorkshire 2019: The bulk of this year's Small Skippers have come from VC63 & VC64, and mainly during July and early August. Although it was a long flight season, there were not many records in June, and only three in September. It seems that the persistent rain that started in late May, and lasted well into June reduced the number of suitable recording days during June. The longest unbroken number of flight days countywide was 48, from the 27th of June to the 13th of August. Compared with last year (countywide) the butterfly count is up by nearly two thousand (+27%). Records countywide in 2019 were nearly double those of 2018, and the number of flight days was up by twenty five percent more than in 2018. Peak counts this year are interesting falling in vice county order; the highest count being 308 in VC65, and the lowest counts of 62 and 61 being in VC61 & VC62 respectively. *Dave Hatton*

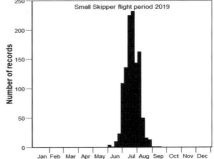

FIRST SIGHTINGS
VC61: 01/06   **1** Spurn Point NNR *Martin Stoyle*
VC64: 06/06   **1** Stainburn Forest *David & Joan Alred*
VC62: 16/06   **1** Easingwold *Kenneth Hale*
VC63: 16/06   **9** Thorpe Marsh NR *Mick Townsend*
VC65: 20/06   **2** Baldersby *Tim Helps*

PEAK COUNTS
VC61: 11/07   **62** Three Hagges Wd *Jesika Bone*
VC62: 12/07   **61** Yatts Farm, Pickering *Dave O'Brien*
VC63: 15/07 **153** Littleworth Pk, Barnsley *Chris Parkin*
VC64: 24/07 **102** Conyngham Flds, Knarsbro *M Barnham*
VC65: 25/07 **308** Willow Bridge, Catterick *D Oldham*

LAST SIGHTINGS
VC61: 22/08   **1** Kiplingcotes NR *Paul Ashton*
VC62: 23/08   **1** Crosscliff Dalby Forest *Paul Ingham*
VC63: 26/08   **1** Goole Moor Trams *Martin Warne*
VC64: 10/09   **1** Great Wd, Goldsborough *M Barnham*
VC65: 13/09   **1** Old Glebe, Leyburn *John Smith*

STATISTICS 2019
Monthly: flight days (total butterflies) **countywide:**
Jun **15** (184), Jul **31** (7,579), Aug **26** (1,192), Sept **3** (3).
Total flight days/flight season length: **75/ 105** days.
Total reports (total butterflies) **a) countywide: 1,325**
(8,958) = mean **6.76** butterflies per observation.
b) by VC: VC61: **156** (843), VC62: **103** (461) VC63:
444 (3,892) VC64: **464** (2,847) VC65: **158** (915).
Tetrads recorded (i.e., 2x2km OS grid squares):
311 out of 1510 visited and 4120 in Yorkshire.

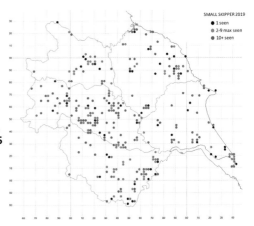

Essex Skipper *Thymelicus lineola* Whitgift P Relf

Small Skipper *Thymelicus sylvestris* Skelton Cleveland Damian Money

57.009 Large Skipper *Ochlodes sylvanus* (Esper 1779)

Broods: 1. Widespread resident, but thin on the ground.

Yorkshire 2019: Whilst both the number of flight days and length of season remained similar to the last few seasons this species declined by approximately 25% on last year. In fact, the total number of sightings is the poorest recorded for several years. The emergence of butterflies was delayed with sightings in May and June down by 50% on 2018; in contrast July boasted an increase of 50% on the previous year. VC63, which has been a strong hold for this species, and VC62 both suffered a significant decline in the number of sightings whereas the other three regions all recorded a notable increase. Chris Parkin managed to record a peak count of 51 in VC63 despite the decline in this area. Peak counts in other areas were similar or slightly higher than previous records; three peak counts were recorded in June, despite the month's poor results, including 60 by Andrew Rhodes. *Philip Brook*

FIRST SIGHTINGS

VC64: 24/05 **1** Coniston Cold *Andrew Rhodes*
VC61: 26/05 **1** North Cave Wetlands *Edgar Mail*
VC63: 31/05 **1** Oakhill Goole *Peter Hinks*
VC65: 03/06 **1** Ilton *Mike Burnham*
VC62: 06/06 **3** Hawnby Sunny Bank Wd *Dave O'Brien*

PEAK COUNTS

VC62: 23/06 **19** Harwood Dale Forest *G Featherstone*
VC65: 27/06 **21** Catterick Training Area *David Oldham*
VC64: 29/06 **60** Coniston Cold *Andrew Rhodes*
VC63: 05/07 **51** Littleworth Park, Barnsley *Chris Parkin*
VC61: 21/07 **24** Speeton *Pam Cook*

LAST SIGHTINGS

VC61: 01/08 **1** Thorngumbald *Molly & Bruce Bursell*
VC62: 01/08 **1** Langdale Forest *Ian & Pauline Popely*
VC63: 07/08 **1** Blackwater Dyke *Martin Warne*
VC65: 12/08 **2** Leyburn Old Glebe *John Smith*
VC64: 17/08 **1** Moor Lane *Steve Mattox*

Large Skipper *Ochlodes sylvanus* Three Hagges Wood-meadow Jesika Bone

STATISTICS 2019

Monthly: flight days (total butterflies) **countywide:** May **5** (10), Jun **27** (1,375), Jul **28** (1,454), Aug **11** (36).
Total flight days/flight season length: **71/** 86 days.
Total reports (total butterflies) **a) countywide: 739** (2,875) = mean **3.89** butterflies per observation.
b) by VC: VC61: **118** (284), VC62: **77** (194), VC63: **206** (1,036), VC64: **308** (1,282), VC65: **30** (79).
Tetrads recorded (i.e., 2x2km OS grid squares):
240 out of 1510 visited and 4120 in Yorkshire.

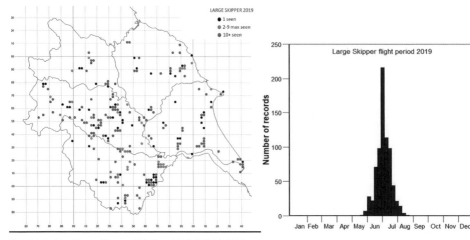

LARGE SKIPPER 2019
● 1 seen
◉ 2-9 max seen
● 10+ seen

Large Skipper flight period 2019

Number of records

Jan Feb Mar Apr May Jun Jul Aug Sep Oct Nov Dec

PIERIDAE
'Whites'
58.003 Orange-tip *Anthocharis cardamines* (Linn. 1758)

Broods: 1. Widespread common resident, flying spring/early summer.

Yorkshire 2019: The remarkable success of 2018 for the Orange-tip continued as numbers increased by almost 50% on the year in 2019. To put this into context, 2019's total number of individuals observed for just one vice-county (VC64, n = 2,970 individuals), exceeded the average annual count for the whole of Yorkshire for the last decade. The unprecedented warmth of the late winter and early spring saw the butterfly out on the wing in all five VCs by the end of March, and as is usual for this single-brooded species of spring, this also brought the flight season to an earlier end. *Andrew Suggitt*

FIRST SIGHTINGS

VC62: 17/03 **1** Easingwold *Kenneth Hale*
VC64: 24/03 **1** East Keswick *Melanie Smith*
VC63: 25/03 **1** Thorne Moor *Helen Kirk*
VC65: 29/03 **1** Brompton-on Swale *Paul Kipling*
VC61: 30/03 **1** Three Hagges Woodmeadow *T J Crawford*

PEAK COUNTS

VC61: 17/04 **20** Walmgate Stray *Edgar Mail*
VC61: 24/04 **20** Three Hagges Wd *Jesika Bone*
VC63: 19/04 **68** Hollins Wd *Chris Parkin*
VC65: 24/04 **24** West Tanfield *Pauline Percival*
VC62: 13/05 **18** Pickering Wds *Peter Hinks*
VC64: 20/05 **40** Lower Grass Wd *N & M Tuck*

LAST SIGHTINGS

VC62: 09/06 **1** Snainton *Paul Ingham*
VC63: 15/06 **1** Goole *Peter Hinks*
VC61: 20/06 **1** Hornsea Rail Trail *C & H Frost*
VC65: 21/06 **2** Tees Railway Walk *Simon Hodgson*
VC64: 08/07 **1** Green Hammerton *Alistair Taylor*

Orange-tip *Anthochoris cardamines* York Stray
Jesika Bone

STATISTICS 2019

Monthly: flight days (total butterflies) **countywide:** Mar **7** (71), Apr **26** (3,541), May **29** (2,902), Jun **20** (323), Jul **1** (1).

Total flight days/flight season length: **85/** 114 days.

Total reports (total butterflies) **a) countywide: 2,245** (6,840) = mean **3.05** butterflies per observation.
b) by VC: VC61: **348** (792), VC62: **199** (415), VC63: **328** (1,923), VC64: **1,099** (2,970), VC65: **271** (740).

Tetrads recorded (i.e., 2x2km OS grid squares): **610** out of 1510 visited and 4120 in Yorkshire.

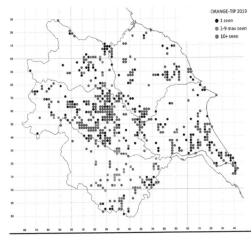

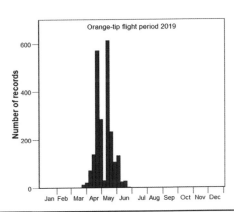

58.006 Large White *Pieris brassicae* (Linn. 1758)

Broods: 2+. Widespread resident and regular migrant both from the S and from the NE (i.e., Baltic area - in Aug).
Yorkshire 2019: The 2019 season was a poor year for the Large White with a 40% decline in individuals seen compared to 2018; a dramatic end to the five-year recovery following the very low numbers seen in 2014. The season started early for the Large White on 20th March (compared to 6th April in 2018) but the first brood closed with 68% fewer individuals spotted compared to 2018. The second brood fared only slightly better with a 35% decline compared to 2018. Reports were down 18% year-on-year at 2,634. VC61 actually showed a small annual increase in both records and butterflies whilst all other VCs showed a 20%+ decline in individuals; VC64 individuals reduced by 53%. Butterflies were spotted on 81% of days in a season which was the longest since 2015. *Mark Hasson*

FIRST SIGHTINGS
VC61: 20/03 **2** Bamforth Farm, Wawne *Robert Atkinson*
VC62: 28/03 **1** Scalby *Lee & Jax Westmoreland*
VC62: 28/03 **1** Scarborough *Lee & Jax Westmoreland*
VC64: 29/03 **1** Staveley NR *Ray Baker*
VC65: 29/03 **3** Broken Brea, Brompton-on Swale *Paul Kipling*
VC63: 17/04 **1** Hoyle Mill *Chris Parkin*

PEAK COUNTS 1st Brood
VC63: 30/04 **5** Oakhill, Goole *Peter Hinks*
VC62: 13/05 **3** Pickering Wds *Peter Hinks*
VC64: 14/05 **5** Horsforth *David & Nyree Fearnley*
VC65: 22/05 **4** West Tanfield *Pauline Percival*
VC61: 09/06 **6** Spurn Point NNR *Andy Mason*

PEAK COUNTS 2nd Brood
VC63: 17/07 **70** Woolley Grange *Geoff Carr*
VC61: 29/07 **21** Bamforth Fm, Wawne *Robert Atkinson*
VC64: 01/08 **25** Staveley West *Angela Ponsford*
VC65: 03/08 **40** Nosterfield LNR *Steve Worwood*
VC62: 17/08 **15** Snainton *Paul Ingham*

LAST SIGHTINGS
VC65: 08/10 **1** Baldersby *Tim Helps*
VC61: 12/10 **1** Langtoft *David Woodmansey*
VC61: 12/10 **1** North Cave Wetlands NR *Paul Ashton*
VC63: 16/10 **1** Potteric Carr NR *Peter Hinks*
VC62: 17/10 **1** Scarborough *Lee & Jax Westmoreland*
VC64: 18/10 **1** St Aidan's RSPB *P Morris*

STATISTICS 2019
Monthly: flight days (total butterflies) **countywide:**
Mar **3** (8), Apr **17** (90), May **24** (221), Jun **25** (197), Jul **31** (2,710), Aug **31** (3,262), Sep **30** (652), Oct **12** (26).
Total flight days/flight season length: **173/** 213 days.
Total reports (total butterflies) **a) countywide:** 2,634 (7,166) = mean **2.72** butterflies per observation.
b) by VC: VC61: **549** (1,436), VC62: **317** (770), VC63: **454** (1,807), VC64: **974** (2,140), VC65: **340** (1,013).
Tetrads recorded (i.e., 2x2km OS grid squares): **495** out of 1510 visited and 4120 in Yorkshire.

Large White *Pieris brassicae* P Relf

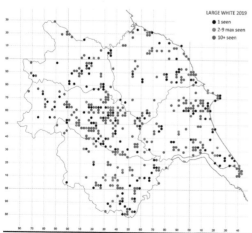
LARGE WHITE 2019
● 1 seen
◐ 2-9 max seen
● 10+ seen

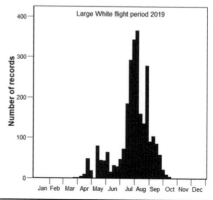
Large White flight period 2019

58.007 Small White *Pieris rapae* (Linn. 1758)

Broods: 2+. Widespread, common resident and regular migrant.

Yorkshire 2019: Whereas the previous year (2018) saw just a single March record of Small White in Yorkshire, the species got off to an exceptionally early start in 2019 with three February records. Although there was a break for the best part of a month after this, Small White was, unusually, flying in all VCs in the county by the end of March. Numbers overall were down on last year; the first brood was rather patchy. The second brood was stronger but individual reports rarely broke into three figures. There was some evidence of migration along the coast but numbers were far from exceptional. Although February records extended the usual flight season, none were seen in November and the season had come to a close rather earlier than usual, by the last week in October. Overall, Small White seems to be holding its own in the county despite annual fluctuations in numbers. *Paul Fletcher*

FIRST SIGHTINGS
VC61: 20/03 **1** Wawne *Robert Atkinson*
VC63: 21/03 **1** Low Cudworth *R Hibbert & L Corrall*
VC65: 21/03 **4** Richmond *Arnold J Robson*
VC62: 25/03 **1** York *Emma Waters*
VC64: 28/03 **1** Ferrensby *Mike Barnham*
VC64: 28/03 **1** Ilkley *Dave Howson*

PEAK COUNTS 1st Brood
VC63: 21/04 **22** Cudworth *Chris Parkin*
VC64: 09/06 **17** Coniston Cold *Andrew Rhodes*
VC61: 01/06 **11** Spurn NNR *Christine & Howard Frost*
VC62: 13/05 **7** Pickering *Peter Hinks*
VC65: 03/06 **6** Wensley *Jennie White*
VC65: 14/06 **6** Broken Brea *Paul Kipling*

PEAK COUNTS 2nd Brood
VC61: 26/08 **112** Spurn NNR *Phil Morgan*
VC64: 10/09 **110** Flaxby *Mike Barnham*
VC63: 29/07 **92** Cudworth *Chris Parkin*
VC62: 26/07 **67** Skelton Castle *Damian Money*
VC65: 08/08 **37** Broken Brea *Paul Kipling*

LAST SIGHTINGS
VC61: 12/10 **1** Skipsea *Peter Swallow*
VC61: 12/10 **2** Sledmere House *Peter Mayhew*
VC64: 17/10 **1** St Aidan's RSPB *P Morris*
VC62: 19/10 **1** Haxby *Terry Crawford*
VC63: 23/10 **3** Cudworth *Chris Parkin*
VC65: 23/10 **1** Nosterfield LNR *David Belshaw*

STATISTICS 2019
Monthly: flight days (total butterflies) **countywide:** Mar **11** (46), Apr **21** (418), May **26** (582), Jun **26** (448), Jul **31** (5,986), Aug **31** (6,438), Sep **30** (3,205), Oct **14** (141).

Total flight days/flight season length: **189/218 days.**

Total reports (total butterflies) **a) countywide: 4,257** (17,264) = mean **4.06** butterflies per observation.

b) by VC: VC61: **849** (4,344), VC62: **337** (1,338), VC63: **1,090** (5,796), VC64: **1,552** (4,497), VC65 **429** (1,289).

Tetrads recorded (i.e., 2x2km OS grid squares): **674** out of 1510 visited and 4120 in Yorkshire.

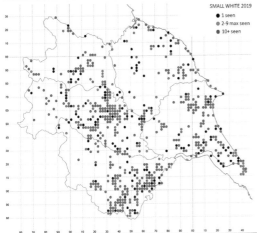

SMALL WHITE 2019
● 1 seen
● 2-9 max seen
● 10+ seen

Photo - Small White *Pieris rapae* Martin Partridge

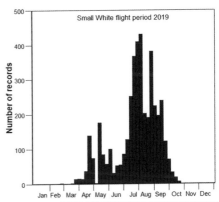

Small White flight period 2019

58.008 Green-veined White *Pieris napi* (Linn. 1758)

Broods: 2+. Common and widespread resident favouring damp areas and upland habitats.

Yorkshire 2019: Despite an earlier start and later finish to the season for the Green-veined White than in 2018, along with a 10% increase in the number of reports submitted, the number of butterflies recorded in the county declined by around 15% when compared to the previous year. Given the butterfly's preference for damp areas, the dry weather of 2018 may well have contributed to this reduction. Once again, VC64 holds the record for the most reports submitted and butterflies recorded. In addition to the counts noted below, Stephen Root recorded 65 butterflies at Knaresborough, Paul and Joyce Simmons recorded 57 at Brockadale, Chris Parkin submitted three counts in excess of 50 for Cudworth, and Robert Atkinson contributed the seven highest counts for VC61 from Wawne. *Jax Westmoreland*

FIRST SIGHTINGS

VC63: 28/03	**1** Cudworth	*Chris Parkin*
VC63: 28/03	**1** Thorne & Crowle Moors	*Martin Warne*
VC61: 29/03	**1** Wawne	*Robert Atkinson*
VC64: 29/03	**1** Harlow Carr	*John Edwards*
VC65: 11/04	**1** Broken Brea	*Paul Kipling*
VC62: 17/04	**1** Walmgate Stray, York	*Peter Mayhew*

PEAK COUNTS 1st Brood

VC61: 13/05	**14** Hull	*Sean Clough*
VC65: 15/05	**57** Catterick	*David Oldham*
VC64: 22/05	**45** Scar Close NR	*John Hamnett*
VC62: 26/05	**10** Wykeham Forest	*Paul Ingham*
VC63: 02/06	**32** Sheffield	*Ange Garrod*

PEAK COUNTS 2nd Brood

VC64: 28/07	**115** Goldsborough	*Mike Bramham*
VC63: 01/08	**58** Woolley Stack	*Chris Parkin*
VC65: 01/08	**25** Broken Brea	*Paul Kipling*
VC62: 03/08	**20** Snainton	*Paul Ingham*
VC61: 07/08	**45** Wawne	*Robert Atkinson*

LAST SIGHTINGS

VC65: 23/09	**1** High Force	*Valerie Standen*
VC64: 28/09	**1** Pateley Bridge	*John Shillcock*
VC61: 02/10	**1** Wawne	*Robert Atkinson*
VC62: 17/10	**1** Scarborough	*Lee & Jax Westmoreland*
VC63: 17/10	**1** South Kirby	*Chris Parkin*

STATISTICS 2019

Monthly: flight days (total butterflies) **countywide:** Mar **2** (12), Apr **21** (655), May **29** (1,734), Jun **27** (1,260), Jul **31** (2,376), Aug **31** (2,949), Sep **27** (571), Oct **7** (17).

Total flight days/flight season length: 175/ 204 days.

Total reports (total butterflies) **a) countywide: 2,900** (9,574) = mean **3.30** butterflies per observation.

b) by VC: VC61: **349** (939), VC62: **245** (595), VC63: **437** (2,186), VC64: **1,352** (4,282), VC65: **517** (1,572).

Tetrads recorded (i.e., 2x2km OS grid squares): **608** out of 1510 visited and 4120 in Yorkshire.

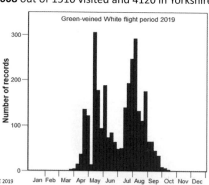

Green-veined White flight period 2019

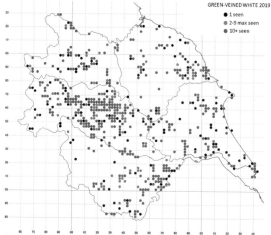

GREEN-VEINED WHITE 2019
- ● 1 seen
- ● 2-9 max seen
- ● 10+ seen

Green-veined White *Pieris napi*
Martin Partridge

58.010 Clouded Yellow *Colias croceus* (Geoffroy 1785)

Broods: Multiple. Highly mobile migrant, occasionally reaching Yorkshire from the continent, mainly southern Europe, or as offspring from butterflies which came earlier in year to southern England. Numbers are usually low but can vary considerably from year to year, with big invasions tens of years apart.

Yorkshire 2019: There was a small east-coast immigration of butterflies to Spurn and Wawne near Hull with a peak of 10 being sighted on August 20th. There were 18 records (totalling 32 butterflies), 11 records of which came from Spurn and 5 from Wawne. There were no records in VC62 or VC65. There were just 2 reports from VC63; singletons on 23rd and 25th August in the Goole area. VC64 had by far the most records (24 records amounting to 89 butterflies) of Clouded Yellow, though undoubtedly, the same butterflies were being reported by different recorders. VC64 had 5 records of individual butterflies between 22nd April (Brotherton) and the 23rd August at St Aidan's RSPB reserve. On Saturday 24th August, at Ripon City Wetlands, 10 Clouded Yellows were seen. The isolated appearance of a large number of Clouded Yellow so far inland raises some doubts as to whether there was a deliberate release at this location. Altogether there were 17 records (totalling 82 butterflies) from the Ripon City Wetlands until the last sighting on September 10th. ***Paul & Joyce Simmons***

Tetrads recorded (i.e., 2x2km OS grid squares): **14** out of 1510 visited and 4120 in Yorkshire.

Clouded Yellow *Colias croceus* Wakefield 2019 Tim Melling

58.013 Brimstone *Gonepteryx rhamni* (Linn. 1758)

Broods: 1. Long-lived, very mobile, hibernating resident.

Yorkshire 2019: I have records back to 2010 and this year had the highest number of butterflies with almost 400 more than 2014, the next highest count, but also the highest number of reports. The number of butterflies per report has remained pretty constant. Brimstone were seen on most days from the first sightings apart from a large gap from 28th February until 14th March when none were seen anywhere in the county. April and May had the largest numbers. Mike Barnham found 2 eggs and 1 larvae at Thornborough on 22nd May (VC65), and Sean Clough found 3 larvae in a Hull garden on 15th June (VC61). Most of the records were of just 1 or 2 butterflies, with quite a few of 3, but not many reports of double figures. VC63 had the most multiple counts. Reports were well spread out in all the VCs. *Nyree Fearnley*

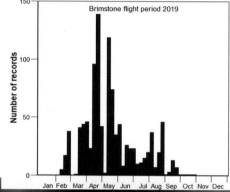

FIRST SIGHTINGS
VC63: 12/02 **2** Carlton Marsh *Chris Parkin*
VC64: 14/02 **1** East Keswick *Avis Meades*
VC65: 14/02 **1** Nosterfield LNR *Anon*
VC61: 16/02 **1** North Cave Wetlands *R Goodison*
VC62: 21/02 **2** Haxby, York *Terry Crawford*

PEAK COUNTS
VC64: 28/03 **53** Bishop Wd *L Corrall & R Hibbert*
VC64: 30/04 **22** Brockadale NR *P & J Simmons*
VC62: 12/05 **17** Pickering Wds *I Armitage & R Parks*
VC65: 12/05 **20** Nosterfield Qu *David Belshaw*
VC61: 15/05 **11** Enthorpe *Andrew Ashworth*

LAST SIGHTINGS
VC62: 20/09 **1** Goathland Moor *Norman Wilf*
VC61: 21/09 **1** Filey Dam *Lynda Cox*
VC64: 21/09 **1** Harrogate *Michael P Laycock*
VC65: 23/10 **1** Nosterfield LNR *D Belshaw*
VC63: 29/10 **1** Thorp Marsh *B Evans B Foster & M Townsend*

Brimstone *Gonepteryx rhamni* John Money.

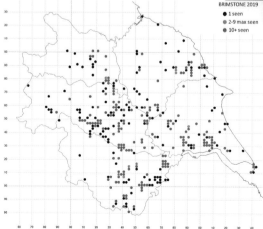

STATISTICS 2019
Monthly: flight days (total butterflies) **countywide:** Feb **13** (78), Mar **12** (286), Apr **23** (547), May **23** (463), Jun **20** (160), Jul **20** (92), Aug **20** (196), Sep **9** (33), Oct **4** (4).
Total flight days/flight season length: **144/ 260 days.**
Total reports (total butterflies) **a) countywide: 1,022** (1,859) = mean **1.82** butterflies per observation.
b) by VC: VC61: **225** (363), VC62: **97** (166), VC63: **263** (612), VC64: **357** (566), VC65: **80** (152).
Tetrads recorded (i.e., 2x2km OS grid squares): **333** out of 1510 visited and 4120 in Yorkshire.

NYMPHALIDAE
Nymphalids - the multicoloured species plus the 'Browns'.
59.002 Wall *Lasiommata megera* (Linn. 1767)
Broods: 2. Very localised yet widespread resident which has declined dramatically in S England. The situation appears more hopeful in Yorkshire. Populations seem to suffer from very wet weather. Nationally, a 'species of concern'.

Yorkshire 2019: There was a reduction of ~15% in total number of individual Wall recorded in 2019 compared to 2018. The number of days Wall was seen on the wing was similar to 2018; the start of the season was about three weeks earlier than the delayed emergence of 2018 but finished a month earlier than the extended season in the exceptional hot year of 2018. Numbers of sightings increased marginally compared to 2018 in VCs 61 and 62, with a slightly larger increase in VC65. Sightings in VC64 were relatively stable. Sightings halved in the stronghold of VC63 in 2019 compared to 2018 – this may be attributable to reduced observer effort rather than real drops in numbers. *Steve Mattock*

FIRST SIGHTINGS
VC61: 21/04 **2** Flamborough *Dennis Baker*
VC62: 29/04 **1** Skelton Castle *Damian Money*
VC64: 12/05 **1** Moor Ln Upper Poppleton *Steve Mattock*
VC65: 12/05 **1** Whitcliff *Catherine Jones*
VC63: 13/05 **1** S Kirkby Stack *Les Corrall & Ralph Hibbert*
VC63: 13/05 **6** Thurlstone Edge *Chris Parkin*

PEAK COUNTS 1st Brood
VC61: 21/05 **8** Spurn NNR *Howard & Christine Frost*
VC63: 24/05 **10** Dunford Bridge *Dave Holmes*
VC62: 29/05 **14** Lingrow Cliffs, Port Mulgrave *John Edwards*
VC65: 01/06 **7** Nosterfield LNR *Martin Bland*
VC64: 06/06 **10** Dacre Banks *Mike Barnham*

PEAK COUNTS 2nd Brood
VC61: 08/08 **13** Spurn NNR *Howard & Christine Frost*
VC65: 23/08 **11** Crofton-on-Tees *David Phillips*
VC64: 24/08 **12** Dacre Banks *Mike Barnham*
VC62: 25/08 **7** Chafer Wd, Ebberston *Paul Ingham*
VC63: 25/08 **27** Thurlstone High Bank *Dave Holmes*

LAST SIGHTINGS
VC62: 01/09 **1** Snainton *Paul Ingham*
VC63: 05/09 **5** S Kirkby Stack *Les Corrall & Ralph Hibbert*
VC65: 14/09 **1** Whitcliffe *Catherine Jones*
VC61: 19/09 **1** Spurn NNR *Robert Goddison*
VC64: 20/09 **3** Coniston Cold *Andrew Rhodes*

STATISTICS 2019
Monthly: flight days (total butterflies)
countywide: Apr **3** (4), May **19** (212), Jun **19** (142), Jul **6** (22), Aug **27** (542), Sep **10** (27).
Total flight days/flight season length: **84/** 153 days.
Total reports (total butterflies) **a) countywide: 391** (949) = mean **2.43** butterflies per observation.
b) by VC: VC61 **66** (156), VC62: **40** (89), VC63: **56** (246), VC64: **146** (312), VC65: **83** (146).
Tetrads recorded (i.e., 2x2km OS grid squares): **159** out of 1510 visited and 4120 in Yorkshire.

Wall *Lasiommata megera* Dave O'Brien

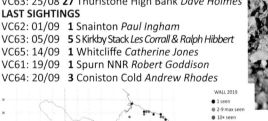

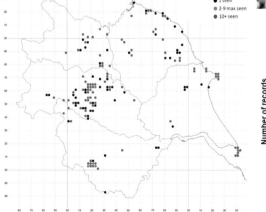
WALL 2019
● 1 seen
● 2-9 max seen
● 10+ seen

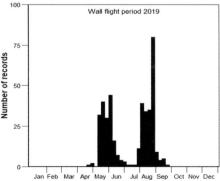
Wall flight period 2019

59.003 Speckled Wood *Pararge aegeria* (Linn. 1758)

Broods: 3+. Mobile resident which is present throughout the county having expanded from the south starting in the 1990s. See Smith, DRR (2018). How have recent lepidopteral colonisers fared in Yorkshire? *The Naturalist*, 143, 107-129.

Yorkshire 2019: More reports came in and more flight days were recorded for Speckled Wood in 2019 versus 2018, so a drop of roughly 1,000 in number of individuals observed across Yorkshire is probably a genuine one. The apparent fall in numbers was reflected in all the VCs except for a rejuvenated VC65. That said, we probably shouldn't describe 2019 as a bad year for Speckled Wood in Yorkshire either; as I mentioned in last year's report, a total of around 10,000 seems to be the post-recolonization norm and we weren't far off that. *Andrew Suggitt*

FIRST SIGHTINGS
VC63: 01/03 **1** Cudworth Marsh *Richard Laverack*
VC62: 25/03 **1** St Nicholas Fields York *Emma Walters*
VC64: 28/03 **1** Little Preston *J. Martin*
VC65: 30/03 **1** Nosterfield LNR *Ken Limb*
VC61: 31/03 **1** Thwaite Grdns Cottingham *A Ashworth*

PEAK COUNTS 1st Brood
VC62: 20/04 **31** Strensall Common *Terry Crawford*
VC63: 21/04 **42** Cudworth Railway North *Chris Parkin*
VC65: 23/04 **12** Scorton Qu *Mark Hewitt*
VC61: 24/04 **15** Kiplingcotes Chalk Pit NR *Peter Hinks*
VC64: 24/04 **33** Grass Wds Transect *Andrew Rhodes*

PEAK COUNTS 2nd and 3rd Brood
VC61: 22/08 **15** Thorngumbald *M Bruce & P Bursell*
VC62: 23/08 **24** Deepdale *Graham Featherstone*
VC65: 01/09 **30** Nosterfield LNR *Christine Weaver*
VC64: 10/09 **41** Otley Wetlands *Paul Purvis*
VC63: 14/09 **62** Hollins Wd *Chris Parkin*

LAST SIGHTINGS
VC61: 08/10 **1** Flamborough S Landing *D Woodmansey*
VC64: 23/10 **1** St Aidan's RSPB *G.Y. Leach*
VC65: 23/10 **1** Tees Railway Walk *Simon Hodgson*
VC63: 31/10 **1** Brierley *Chris Parkin*
VC62: 02/11 **1** Hilton *Martin Partridge*
Photo, Rolf Farrell.

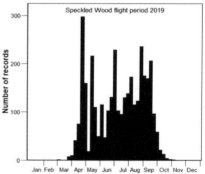

Speckled Wood flight period 2019

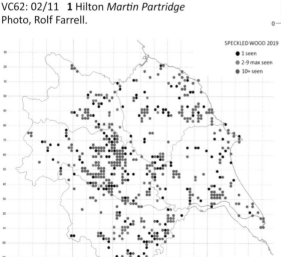

SPECKLED WOOD 2019

● 1 seen
● 2-9 max seen
● 10+ seen

STATISTICS 2019
Monthly: flight days (total butterflies) **countywide:** Mar **6** (21), Apr **24** (1,464), May **29** (839), Jun **28** (954), Jul **31** (1,353), Aug **31** (2,154), Sep **28** (2,235), Oct **16** (120), Nov **1** (1).
Total flight days/flight season length: **194**/ 247 days.
Total reports (total butterflies) **a) countywide: 3,433** (9,141) = mean **2.66** butterflies per observation.
b) by VC: VC61: **431** (850), VC62: **373** (915), VC63: **775** (2,950), VC64: **1,413** (3,382), VC65: **441** (1,044).
Tetrads recorded (i.e., 2x2km OS grid squares): **587** out of 1510 visited and 4120 in Yorkshire.

59.004 Large Heath *Coenonympha tullia* (Müller 1764)

Broods: 1. Sedentary resident of mires and mosses - N York Moors (VC62), Humberhead Peatlands (VC63 – Thorne, Crowle & Hatfield Moors) and Bowland Fells, western Pennines (VC64).

Yorkshire 2019: Flight days were up on 2018 by eighteen. This said, numbers of Large Heath recorded was down 25% on 2018. The probable reason was a period of wet weather coinciding with the peak flight period in June leading to butterflies failing to emerge or staying under cover. The damp weather made access to the transects difficult underfoot and several visits were curtailed, or part completed, due to rain. There were Large Heath records from all suitable habitats on Thorne Moor but they were in lower numbers than 2018. Fen Bog also showed a drop in the number of visits made and consequently the numbers recorded. Hatfield Moor had two records of four individuals on two consecutive days. Another reason for the lower counts on Large Heath this year is Les Corrall and Ralph Hibbert, who over the past years have managed to predict the peak flight days for Large Heath on Thorne Moor with amazing accuracy, were unable to visit the moor. *Ron Moat*

FIRST SIGHTINGS
VC63: 25/05   **1** Thorne Moor *Martin Warne*
VC62: 18/06   **2** Fen Bog *Peter Liddle*
PEAK COUNTS
VC63: 21/06 **247** Thorne Moor *M Warne & H Kirk*
VC62: 26/06   **6** Fen Bog *Dave O'Brien*
LAST SIGHTINGS
VC62:12/07   **1** Fen Bog *Peter Mayhew*
VC63:21/07   **3** Thorne Moor *Martin Warne*

STATISTICS 2019
Monthly: flight days (total butterflies)
countywide: May **2** (17), Jun **16** (1,020), Jul **10** (119).
Total flight days/flight season length: **28/** 58 days.
Total reports (total butterflies) **a) countywide:**
139 (1,156) = mean **8.30** butterflies per observation.
b) by VC: VC62: **3** (9), **VC63**:**136** (1147).
Tetrads recorded (i.e., 2x2km OS grid squares): **11** out of 1510 visited and 4120 in Yorkshire.

Large Heath *Coenonympha tullia* ab. *lanceolata*
North York Moors
3 7 2019 Tim Melling

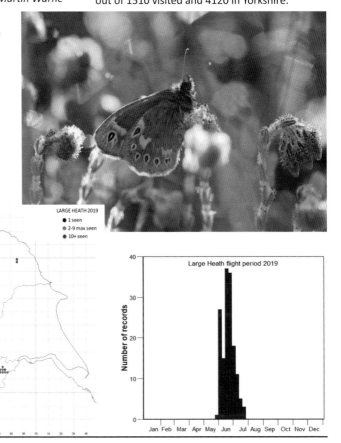

LARGE HEATH 2019
● 1 seen
◉ 2-9 max seen
● 10+ seen

Large Heath flight period 2019

59.005 Small Heath *Coenonympha pamphilus* (Linn. 1758)

Broods: 1 to 3. Widespread resident, often more common in upland areas.

Yorkshire 2019: Over the last 15 years of reporting on Small Heath the county total has shown little change. The overall statistics are similar to last year (2018) but this masks regional differences. Numbers in VC61 and 62 show a long-term decline. In VC61 numbers fell from 4,296 in 2006 to 387 in 2019 (the lowest record in this VC). VC62 numbers have declined from 2,867 in 2006 to 516 in 2019 (third lowest record in this VC). However, VC63, 64 and 65 show an upward trend. VC64 numbers were 739 butterflies in 2007 but 3,712 in 2019 (their highest total for which I have records), whilst VC63 totals have risen from 646 in 2007 to 2,259 in 2019 (their second highest total for which I have records). VC65 numbers have increased slowly from 56 in 2008 to their highest total of 452 this year. It is difficult to speculate on the causes of an increase in western regions and decline in the east but the differences for this species are quite marked. *Paul and Joyce Simmons*

FIRST SIGHTINGS

VC63: 30/04   **1** Orgreave *Steve Branch*
VC64: 12/05   **1** Moor Lane Upper Popltn *Steve Mattock*
VC61: 14/05   **1** Spurn Point *Phil Morgan*
VC62: 16/05   **1** Hawnby Hill *Steven Kirtley Dave O'Brien*
VC65: 03/06   **1** Druids Plantation, Ilton *Mike Barnham*

PEAK COUNTS

VC63: 27/06 **142** Orgreave *Steve Branch*
VC64: 27/06 **171** Blue Crag, Arncliffe *Ian Court*
VC61: 02/07   **23** North Wolds Site *David Smith*
VC65: 13/07   **84** Cross Gill Top, Catterick *Tim Helps*
VC62: 14/07   **40** South Gare *Damian Money*

LAST SIGHTINGS

VC62: 08/09   **1** Steeple Cross, Clvlnd Way *John Edwards*
VC64: 23/09   **2** Staveley East *Anna Wallin*
VC65: 23/09   **1** Ellerton Moor, Catterick *David Oldham*
VC63: 02/10   **2** Littleworth Park, Barnsley *Chris Parkin*
VC61: 08/10   **1** Spurn Bird Observatory *Howard Frost*

STATISTICS 2019

Monthly: flight days (total butterflies) **countywide:**
Apr **1** (2), May **19** (625), Jun **27** (2,544), Jul **29** (3,044), Aug **26** (944), Sep **12** (164), Oct **2** (3).
Total flight days/flight season length: 116/ 162 days.
Total reports (total butterflies) **a) countywide: 1,194** (7,326) = mean **6.14** butterflies per observation.
b) by VC: VC61: **105** (387), VC62: **126** (516), VC63: **154** (2,259), VC64: **683** (3,712), VC65: **126** (452).
Tetrads recorded (i.e., 2x2km OS grid squares): **225** out of 1510 visited and 4120 in Yorkshire.

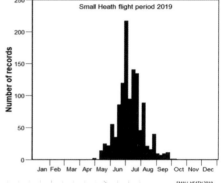

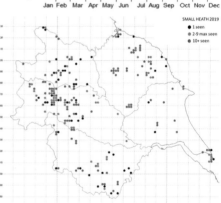

[59.008 Scotch Argus *Erebia aethiops* (Esper 1777)]

Broods: 1. Formerly a Yorkshire resident in Upper Wharfedale. Appears to have become extinct in 1955 probably due to habitat change and the depredations of collectors. Has recently been subject to several unreported and apparently unofficial introductions to places for which there are no previous records. Currently, there are only two remaining natural sites for this species in England both in Cumbria.

Yorkshire 2019: There has been the continued presence of Scotch Argus for eight years now in known locations in VC64, radiating out from the site of probable introduction at Park Rash (near Kettlewell) in or prior to 2012. The butterfly has been seen flying in the usual locations: Bastow Wood, Park Rash, Caseker Gill, Sleets Gill and a withheld location. The earliest sighting was on 02/08 (James Dickinson, location withheld) of 21 Scotch Argus, all but one being male. The last sighting was on 23/08 of 3 Scotch Argus (Janet Turnbull, location withheld). Altogether, there were 441 butterflies recorded in 2019, with a peak of 114 in Bastow Wood (Ernie Scarfe on 12/08). The numbers of butterflies reported is twice that of 2018 and is by some ways the best year we have had since the butterfly was introduced. *David Smith*
Tetrads recorded (i.e., 2x2km OS grid squares): **6** out of 1510 visited and 4120 in Yorkshire.

59.009 Ringlet *Aphantopus hyperantus* (Linn. 1758)

Broods: 1. Widespread and expanding resident, unusual in that it can fly in dull conditions and even light rain.

Yorkshire 2019: Ringlet populations remain stable in Yorkshire. After threatening a slight decline over the last couple of years, a phenologically unremarkable 2019 saw Ringlet numbers return almost to their 2016 level, representing an increase of 11% compared to 2018. Particularly encouraging was a doubling of abundance in VCs 61 and 65; the former has shown signs of decline in recent years, whilst the latter reached its highest abundance since the boom years of 2013-14. VC64 reinforced its reputation as the stronghold for this species, with over 44% of individuals and 48% of records coming from here. Nevertheless, a decline in abundance of 23% in VC63 compared to 2018 (despite an 11% increase in records submitted) will need to be watched carefully; declines have now been recorded for four consecutive years in this vice-county with little change in the number of records, indicating that recorders here are seeing fewer Ringlets at a time. *Callum Macgregor*

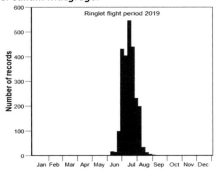

FIRST SIGHTINGS
VC63: 23/05 **1** Barnsley *Alwyn Timms*
VC64: 06/06 **1** Burley *Susan Barton*
VC61: 09/06 **1** Spurn Point *Andy Mason*
VC62: 15/06 **2** Ruswarp *Wendy Holliday*
VC65: 23/06 **1** Nosterfield LNR *David Belshaw*

PEAK COUNTS
VC61: 04/07 **124** Thorngumbald *M Bruce P Bursell*
VC63: 08/07 **378** Rawcliffe Bridge *John Hitchcock*
VC65: 10/07 **198** Catterick Garrison *David Oldham*
VC62: 12/07 **157** Yatts Farm, Pickering *Dave O'Brien*
VC64: 16/07 **370** Duck St Qu Greenhow *M Barnham*

LAST SIGHTINGS
VC61: 17/08 **1** Wharram Qu *David Smith*
VC62: 21/08 **1** Snainton *Paul Ingham*
VC65: 26/08 **1** High Force *Valerie Standen*
VC64: 30/08 **2** Barlow Common *David Firth*
VC63: 19/09 **1** Orgreave *Steve Branch*

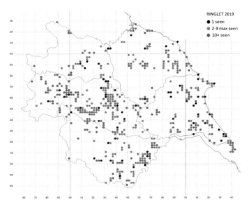

STATISTICS 2019
Monthly: flight days (total butterflies) **countywide:** May **1** (1), Jun **18** (1,531), Jul **31** (23,803), Aug **22** (1,005), Sep **1** (1).
Total flight days/flight season length: **73/** 120 days.
Total reports (total butterflies) **a) countywide: 2,427** (26,341) = mean **10.85** butterflies per observation.
b) by VC: VC61: **319** (2,750), VC62: **233** (1,989), VC63: **381** (6,724), VC64: **1,185** (11,669), VC65: **309** (3,209).
Tetrads recorded (i.e., 2x2km OS grid squares): **504** out of 1510 visited and 4120 in Yorkshire.

59.010 Meadow Brown *Maniola jurtina* (Linn. 1758)

Broods: 1. Common and widespread resident on grassland sites often in large numbers.

Yorkshire 2019: The steady decline in this species was dramatically reversed this year with sightings matching numbers last seen in 2014. Each VC reported an increase in sightings compared to last year (2018), with greater than 50% increases in every VC except VC62 (where it increased by 'only' ~20%). The season started in June where numbers were down on 2018. However, July witnessed an amazing doubling of sightings compared to 2018. There were a number of very large sighting counts: PM Haigh's peak count of 574 at St Aidan's, then Chris Parkin's phenomenal count of 700+ at Littleworth Park in Barnsley. Both these counts were significantly higher than last year's peak counts. Three-figure sightings are relatively unusual but Chris Parkin managed to record over 4500+ in 15 three-figure counts representing ~40% of VC63's sightings. *Philip R Brook*

FIRST SIGHTINGS
VC64: 01/06 **1** Barlow Common *Jill Carter*
VC62: 03/06 **1** Oakley Garth, Ruswarp *Wendy Holliday*
VC61: 06/06 **2** Spurn Point *Phil Morgan*
VC63: 09/06 **10** St Aidan's RSPB *J Pickering*
VC63: 09/06 **1** St Aidan's RSPB *P M Haigh*
VC65: 17/06 **1** Nosterfield LNR *Martin Bland*
PEAK COUNTS
VC62: 03/07 **165** Walmgate Stray, York *Peter Mayhew*
VC61: 11/07 **306** Three Hagges Wd *Jesika Bone*
VC63: 15/07 **706** Littleworth Pk, Barnsley *Chris Parkin*
VC64: 17/07 **574** St Aidan's Hillside *P M Haigh*
VC65: 23/07 **176** Catterick Training Area *David Oldham*
LAST SIGHTINGS
VC65: 29/08 **1** Tees Railway Walk *Martin Bland*
VC62: 01/09 **2** Walmgate Stray, York *Peter Mayhew*
VC61: 10/09 **1** North Cave Wetlands *Paul Ashton*
VC63: 21/09 **1** Totley, Sheffield *Bill Smyllie*
VC63: 21/09 **2** Edlington Pit Wd *Tony Butler*
VC64: 23/09 **3** Staveley East *Anna Wallin*
STATISTICS 2019
Monthly: flight days (total butterflies) **countywide:** Jun **25** (3,970), Jul **31** (22,861), Aug **30** (4,897), Sep **12** (117).
Total flight days/flight season length: **98/ 115** days.
Total reports (total butterflies) **a) countywide: 2,700** (31,845) = mean **11.79** butterflies per observation.
b) by VC: VC61: **349** (3,411), VC62: **223** (1,240) VC63: **428** (12,190) VC64: **1,336** (12,573) VC65: **364** (2,431).
Tetrads recorded (i.e., 2x2km OS grid squares): **527** out of 1510 visited and 4120 in Yorkshire.

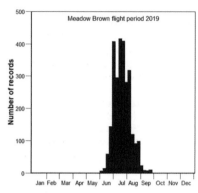

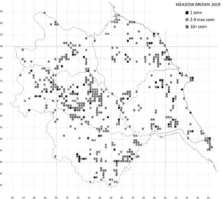

59.011 Gatekeeper *Pyronia tithonus* (Linn. 1771)

Broods: 1. Expanding resident with northern limit of national distribution in lowland areas on a line between Flamborough and Ripon approx. Expansion currently appears stalled.

Yorkshire 2019: The improved summer conditions in 2019 led to the first upturn in the fortunes of Gatekeeper since 2015, giving the best county totals since 2009. VC63 continues to be the Yorkshire stronghold, with a wide range of habitats covered by a good number of observers. The restored colliery sites and limestone areas held the highest counts. VC64 had one third of the VC63 total with many records coming from transects, particularly from Fairburn and St. Aidan's RSPB reserves. VC61 has recovered some ground since its very poor year in 2018, with records from a good selection of sites in the vice-county. VC62 has not followed this year's upward trend, with only 38 butterflies recorded compared with 47 last year, chiefly from the York area which seems to be the northern limit in the east of Yorkshire. VC65 continues to have a very small and scattered population. *Paul & Joyce Simmons*

FIRST SIGHTINGS
VC61: 17/06 **1** Sutton-on-Hull *David Howson*
VC63: 28/06 **1** Canklow *Steve Branch*
VC64: 28/06 **2** Weston *Sue Griffiths*
VC62: 21/07 **3** Warthill, York *Peter Izzard*
VC65: 24/07 **1** River Ure, Redmire *Clive Wood*
PEAK COUNTS
VC64: 25/07 **151** Farnham Gravel Pits *Mike Barnham*
VC63: 26/07 **468** Littleworth Pk, Barnsley *Chris Parkin*
VC62: 30/07 **8** Warthill, York *Peter Izzard*
VC61: 01/08 **95** Thorngumbald *M Bruce & P Bursell*
VC65: 02/08 **2** Hutton Conyers *Charles Fletcher*

Gatekeeper *Pyronia tithonus* Brockadale John Money

LAST SIGHTINGS

VC62: 13/08 **1** Water Lane, York *Mike Walton*
VC65: 24/08 **1** West Tanfield *Pauline Percival*
VC64: 30/08 **3** Barlow Common *David Firth*
VC63: 03/09 **1** Canklow *Steve Branch*
VC61: 19/09 **1** Wawne *Robert Atkinson*

STATISTICS 2019

Monthly: flight days (total butterflies) **countywide:** Jun **4** (33), Jul **30** (6,339), Aug **30** (4,613), Sep **2** (2).
Total flight days/flight season length: **66**/ 95 days.
Total reports (total butterflies) **a) countywide: 981** (10,989) = mean 11.20 butterflies per observation.
b) by VC: VC61: **158** (857), VC62: **25** (38), VC63: **342** (7,289), VC64: **448** (2,794), VC65: **9** (11).
Tetrads recorded (i.e., 2x2km OS grid squares): **253** out of 1510 visited and 4120 in Yorkshire.

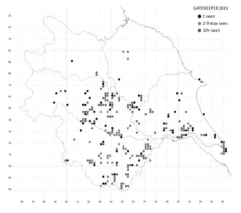

[A report of 2 Gatekeeper flying next to polytunnels at Nosterfield (VC65) on 21st May by Simon Warwick was received. This was almost a month before the next sighting of Gatekeeper in Yorkshire (17/06, VC61) and some two months before the next sighting in VC65 (24/07). The earliest of the record, coupled with the nearness of the polytunnels, would imply that pupation occurred in artificial surroundings. To avoid skewing our flight season we have not calculated the Gatekeeper season using this record. **David Smith**]

[**ERRATA 2018:** The species return for Gatekeeper had some erroneous entries. The **First Sightings** given for VC63 and VC64 were both incorrect; 'VC63: 11/06 **35** St. Aidan's RSPB *P M Haigh*' and 'VC64: 11/06 **139** St. Aidan's RSPB *P M Haigh*' should read 'VC64: 22/06 **2** High Birstwith, Harrogate *Richard Walton*' and 'VC63: 22/06 **11** Wentside Hill *Les Driffield*' respectively. The **PEAK COUNT** for VC64 was also incorrect; 'VC64: 11/06 **139** St. Aidan's RSPB *P M Haigh*' should read 'VC64: 11/07 **84** St Aidan's RSPB *P M Haigh*'. **David Smith**]

59.012 Marbled White *Melanargia galathea* (Linn. 1758)

Broods: 1. Resident, fairly sedentary species. 'Wild' populations found on the Yorkshire Wolds. Populations elsewhere often result from both officially reported and unofficial introductions or re-introductions. However, this species could well be in a period of natural expansion subject to periodic fall-backs. The species was found on Magnesian Limestone Belt areas in the 19th century but became extinct there by the **1880s**.

Yorkshire 2019: Another poor year for Marbled White; this is the third year of decline. The number of individual butterflies (2,733) in 2019 is lower than the pre-boom average of around 4,000 and some ways short of the last boom years average of around 6,000 recorded in 2013-2016. The season started in mid-June and was finished by the middle of August – the season was marginally longer than 2018's rather short season. Again there were no sightings from VC65. *Jennifer Smith*

Marbled White *Melanargia galathea* 28 6 2019
Brockadale John A Wilkinson

FIRST SIGHTINGS
VC63: 18/06 **13** Brockadale NR *L Corrall & R Hibbert*
VC63: 18/06 **1** Wenthillside *Les Driffield*
VC61: 21/06 **1** Wharram Qu *Ian Marshall*
VC64: 21/06 **2** Aberford *Dave Ramsden*
VC62: 01/07 **1** Heckdale, Dalby Forest *Ian & P Popely*
PEAK COUNTS
VC64: 02/07 **35** Ledsham YWT *Philip Brook*
VC63: 11/07 **530** Brockadale NR *L Corrall & R Hibbert*
VC62: 12/07 **60** Ellerburn Bank, Dalby *Dave O'Brien*
VC61: 14/07 **100** Enthorpe *Andrew Ashworth*
LAST SIGHTINGS
VC63: 06/08 **2** Brockadale NR *L Corrall, R Hibbert*
VC61: 08/08 **17** Thixendale *David Smith*
VC64: 13/08 **1** St Aidan's RSPB *A Tiffany*
VC62: 15/08 **3** Yatts Farm, Pickering *Dave O'Brien*
STATISTICS 2019
Monthly: flight days (total butterflies) **countywide:**
Jun **8** (211), Jul **27** (2,490), Aug **7** (32).
Total flight days/flight season length: 42/ 59 days.
Total reports (total butterflies) **a) countywide:**
155 (2,733) = mean **17.63** butterflies per
observation.
b) by VC: VC61: **28** (326), VC62: **38** (308), VC63: **51**
(1,802), VC64: **38** (297).
Tetrads recorded (i.e., 2x2km OS grid squares): **53**
out of 1510 visited and 4120 in Yorkshire.

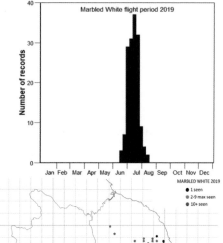

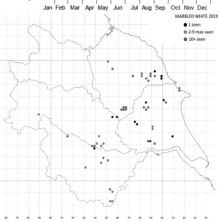

59.013 Grayling *Hipparchia semele* (Linn. 1758)
Broods: 1. Rare and very localised resident, found on disused or little used industrial areas and railway infrastructure.
Yorkshire 2019: For the third year running no Grayling were seen at the VC61 Wolds site. It is possible that the butterfly is still present in low numbers and may benefit from the altered grazing regime that has been put in place. There were also concerns about unauthorised access to this privately-owned site. To be clear, there is no public access to this site. Grayling fared better in VC62, with records coming from nine 1-km squares, including South Gare and the industrial areas to the south and west. Most of the sightings were from the Teesdale Way between South Bank and Redcar, and numbers seen will represent a small percentage of the butterflies found on the inaccessible brownfield land either side. However, it is possible that the proposed compulsory purchase and subsequent redevelopment of former British Steel land may have an adverse effect on this species. Only one Grayling was seen in VC63 which was from the Parkgate area of Rotherham where it has been seen in previous years. A look on Google Earth suggests there is quite a bit of suitable habitat in this area, but not necessarily publicly accessible, so Grayling numbers here may be higher than records suggest. *Dave O'Brien*

FIRST SIGHTINGS
VC62: 14/07 **73** South Gare, Redcar *Damian Money*
VC63: 21/07 **1** Parkgate, Rotherham *Paul Leonard*
PEAK COUNTS
VC63: 21/07 **1** Parkgate, Rotherham *Paul Leonard*
VC62: 06/08 **82** Corus, Teesside *Dave Wainwright*
LAST SIGHTINGS
VC63: 21/07 **1** Parkgate, Rotherham *Paul Leonard*
VC62: 06/08 **82** Corus, Teesside *Dave Wainwright*

STATISTICS 2019
Monthly: flight days (total butterflies)
countywide: Jul **3** (166), Aug **1** (82).
Total flight days/flight season length: 4/ 24 days.
Total reports (total butterflies) **a) countywide: 10**
(248) = mean **24.8** butterflies per observation.
b) by VC: VC62: **9** (247), VC63: **1** (1).
Tetrads recorded (i.e., 2x2km OS grid squares):
6 out of 1510 visited and 4120 in Yorkshire.

This beautiful photograph shows the typical resting position of the butterfly with the diagnostic twin eye spots on the upper forewing hidden from sight. On the broken background favoured by the butterfly the camouflage afforded by the lower under wings is striking. When looking for Grayling at a known site you quickly learn how fatal it is to not to keep exact track of where they have landed. Though their flight is quite distinctive, having a pronounced looping and gliding flight pattern, the moment they suddenly dive down to land they effectively vanish from sight on the open bare ground. A failure to note exactly where they have landed has often led to a bewildered, painstaking and often fruitless search for the resting butterfly. The only hope then is to walk in the general direction you last saw them and hope to disturb them so they fly up again. **David Smith**

Grayling *Hipparchia semele* 21 7 2019
Parkgate Rotherham VC63 Paul Leonard

59.014 Pearl-bordered Fritillary *Boloria euphrosyne* (Linn. 1758)

Broods: 1. (A partial 2nd sometimes occurs in S England.) Yorkshire's rarest butterfly confined to 2 or 3 private sites in the N York Moors National Park. See pp 178-182 of *The Butterflies of Yorkshire* (Frost ed., 2005) for a full account of this species.

Yorkshire 2019: The flight period lasted from 18th April (Common site by Jim Hall) to 6th June (Common site by Jim Hall and Ian Armitage) which was much longer than the heat wave summer of 2018. Encouraging counts were recorded from each of the three sites from which the species is usually recorded. Numbers from the valley site, recorded by Jon Hogg who walks a transect there, were at their highest since the butterfly reappeared there in 2011 following extensive scrub clearance. Jon also recorded a count of 60 from the quarry site in mid-May while Dave O'Brien's peak count of 68 came from the third site, The Common, was the county's best of 2019. Altogether there were 420 Pearl-bordered Fritillaries recorded across the three sites. Data supplied by Jim Hall, who took over The Common transect in 2017, confirms that 2020 was one of the best years of the decade for this colony. *Dave Wainwright*

Tetrads recorded (i.e., 2x2km OS grid squares): **3** out of 1510 visited and 4120 in Yorkshire.

59.015 Small Pearl-bordered Fritillary *Boloria selene* (Denis & Schiffermüller 1775)

Broods: 1. Very local resident restricted to mire habitats in VCs 62, 64 & 65.

Yorkshire 2019: On both the eastern and western sites emergence was at the expected time. The flight period was over in the second week of July in the west but, unusually on the North York Moors, there was a longer season which extended until the end of July. Numbers reported were good but not large. VC64 records were from just three sites (two being UKBMS transect sites) but it was good to have a report by Brian & Elizabeth Shorrock of a singleton from the Gisburn Forest (Stephen Park); a colony thought extinct since 1996. Another reasonable year for the Swarth Moor population (37 recorded in the season) and also on the Scar Close NNR Transect where (40) were recorded, once again more recorded during the season than ever before. There were no visits to any of the VC65 sites. *Terry Whitaker*

FIRST SIGHTINGS
VC62: 03/06 **1** Goathland, Wheeldale Gill *Dave O'Brien*
VC64: 18/06 **4** Scar Close Transect (Sect. 10) *Kay Andrews*
VC65: **No Records**

PEAK COUNTS
VC62: 23/06 **83** Harwood Dale Forest, *Graham Featherstone*
VC64: 18/06 **4** Scar Close NNR Transect (Sect. 10) *Kay Andrews*
VC64: 22/06 **4** Swarth Moor Helwith Bridge *B & E Shorrock*
VC64: 22/06 **4** Swarth Moor SSSI Transect (Sect. 2) *Ian Court*
VC64: 27/06 **4** Scar Close NNR Transect (Sect. 10) *Kay Andrews*
VC65: **No Records**

LAST SIGHTINGS
VC64: 15/07 **2** Scar Close NNR Transect *Kay Andrews*
VC64: 15/07 **Singletons** Scar Close Transect *Kay Andrews*
VC62: 29/07 **1** Langdale Frst, Hipperley Beck *I & P Popely*
VC65: **No Records**

STATISTICS 2019
Monthly: flight days (total butterflies)
countywide: Jun **13** (203), Jul **10** (68).
Total flight days/flight season length: **23/56 days.**
Total reports (total butterflies) **a) countywide: 68**
(271) = mean **3.99** butterflies per observation.
b) by VC: VC62: **21** (190), VC64: **47** (81).
Tetrads recorded (i.e., 2x2km OS grid squares): **19** out of 1510 visited and 4120 in Yorkshire.

[59.017 Silver-washed Fritillary *Argynnis paphia* (Linn. 1758)]

Broods: 1. Not uncommon in Yorkshire in the 19th century, but appeared to become extinct by the 1940s. Odd records between 1950s to 2016 could, just possibly, have been long-distance wanderers, but were more likely to have been unofficial, casual introductions. In 2017 a number of sightings of 10+ individual butterflies were reported in VC64. These were highly likely to have been unofficial introductions but they have established local populations and spread in VC64. Simultaneously, natural expansion has apparently occurred in southern Yorkshire (VC63) which, in conjunction with further dispersal in the hot summer of 2018, now means that Silver-washed Fritillary can turn up (albeit uncommonly) in any of the five Yorkshire VCs (VC61-VC65).

Yorkshire 2019: There were two separate reports from VC61 of an individual butterfly on 29/07 (Phil Morgan) and on 08/08 (David Smith) both at Tophill Low reservoir. Given the sighting of SWF at Tophill Low in 2018 this suggests that egg-laying was successful. There were seven reports (totalling 14 butterflies) from VC62: the earliest sighting was on 24/07 at Broxa Forest where Carol Dickinson, and Ian and Pauline Popely, saw five and four SWF respectively (presumably the same individuals); Dave O'Brien reported one SWF from the same location on 04/08; Ed Snell reported one SWF at Langdale (04/08); Damien Money reported one SWF in a Skelton garden on two days (23/08 and 25/08); and the last sighting was by Graham Featherstone who reported one SWF at Gundale, Pickering on 08/09. There were 19 reports (totalling 32 butterflies) from VC63; the earliest from Thorpe Salvin (an area well-known as a site of unofficial introductions) by Derek Whiteley on 20/07, and the last sighting from Brockadale NR by Paul and Joyce Simmons on 24/08. The sighting at Potteric Carr NR on 24/07 (Darren Wozencroft) was of the aberration *ocellata*. The stronghold for SWF in Yorkshire is VC64 which had 53 reports (totalling 287 butterflies) in 2019: the earliest sighting was on 04/07 at Skipton Quarry by Andrew Rhodes of one SWF; the peak count was of 35 SWF on 29/07 by Nick Hall at Bishop Wood; and

the last sighting was by Dave Ramsden at Stubbing Moor Plantation on 19/08. Around half of all SWF butterflies were reported from Bishop Wood which has been extensively colonised. Finally, VC65 which had its first SWF sighting in 2016 (at High Batts), provided two reports totalling four butterflies in 2019: the first sighting was by Mike Eccles on 04/07 at Thorpe Perrow Arboretum of three SWF; and the second sighting was by Paul Kipling on 01/08 at Broken Brea of one SWF. *David Smith*

Tetrads recorded (i.e., 2x2km OS grid squares): **34** out of 1510 visited and 4120 in Yorkshire.

Silver-washed Fritillary *ab. ocellata* VC63
Potteric Carr 14 8 2019 Darren Wozencroft

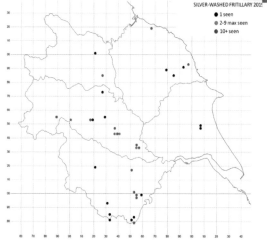

SILVER-WASHED FRITILLARY 2019
● 1 seen
● 2-9 max seen
● 10+ seen

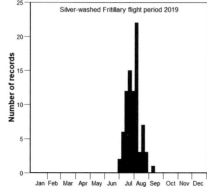

Silver-washed Fritillary flight period 2019

59.019 Dark Green Fritillary *Argynnis aglaja* (Linn. 1758)

Broods: 1. Uncommon, local resident & wanderer which has increased its range in recent years. Mainly an upland species.

Yorkshire 2019: Another year with good numbers of Dark Green Fritillary seen. It is notable that the majority of the VC64 & 65 records originated from Butterfly Transects but it is good to see the species is back in force at many old sites including Gisburn Forest & Greenhow (Duck Street Quarry) in VC64, and from the High Force NNR which produced the majority of the VC65 sightings. In VC63 records came from more widely scattered locations rather than from the honey pot of Brockadale NR. This may have had the effect of reducing the number of butterflies counted in VC63 to something more representative of the other VC's situation. It is nice to see the species has appeared on Les Driffield's new private nature reserve at Wenthillside. Compared with 2018 numbers were down in the east & south of the County. The emergence in VC62 was quite early. The VC63 emergence was slightly later than expected but as the first reports were of good numbers the start of the season was certainly missed. Numbers were slightly up in VC65. In the upland areas of VC64 it was an exceptional year which produced a doubling of butterflies from new and known locations all over the Dales. The season in VC64 also started earlier and was also longer than normal. There were two reports of singletons in VC61. *Terry Whitaker*

FIRST SIGHTINGS
VC64: 12/06   singletons Long Ashes Trnsct *P Burns*
VC63: 18/06   **19** Brockadale NR *L Corrall & R Hibbert*
VC65: 26/06   **1** Catterick Training Area, *D Oldham*
VC62: 27/06   **1** Dalby Forest, Crosscliff Brow *P Ingham*
VC61: 08/08   **1** Thixendale *David Smith*

PEAK COUNTS
VC61: singletons
VC63: 06/07   **64** Brockadale NR *Chris Parkin*
VC62: 12/07   **71** Yatts Farm, Pickering *Dave O'Brien*
VC64: 22/07   **166** Blue Scar, Arncliffe *Ian Armitage*
VC65: 29/06   **4** Catterick Training Area *David Oldham*

LAST SIGHTINGS
VC63: 06/08   **2** Brockadale *L Corrall & R Hibbert*
VC62: 15/08   **4** Yatts Farm, Pickering *Dave O'Brien*
VC61: 18/08   **1** Cycle track, Naburn *Mike Hayes*
VC65: 26/08   **1** High Force Transect *Valerie Standen*
VC64: 28/08   **1** Timble Ings *David & Joan Alred*

Dark Green Fritillary Brockadale VC63 Paul Simmons.

STATISTICS 2019
Monthly: flight days (total butterflies)
countywide: Jun **15** (115), Jul **24** (1,451), Aug **20** (222).
Total flight days/flight season length: **59/ 78 days.**
Total reports (total butterflies) **a) countywide:**
332 (1,788) = mean **5.39** butterflies per observation.
b) by VC: VC61: **2** (2), VC62: **40** (253), VC63: **28**
(390), VC64: **238** (1,106), VC65: **24** (37).
Tetrads recorded (i.e., 2x2km OS grid squares):
85 out of 1510 visited and 4120 in Yorkshire

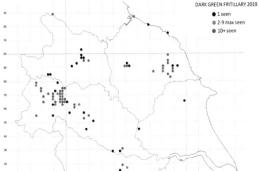

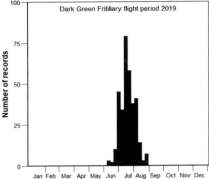

59.023 Red Admiral *Vanessa atalanta* (Linn. 1758)

Broods: Unclear. Common annual immigrant from S Europe/N Africa, increasingly wintering in UK as partial hibernator.

Yorkshire 2019: A good year for the Red Admiral, with the number of butterflies recorded being the third highest total from the last fifteen years. As usual, the main months were June to September with records tailing off from October and very few sightings after that. It does seem to have been one of the better years for the arrival of migrant butterflies. *Lee Westmoreland*

FIRST SIGHTINGS
VC61: 12/01	**4** Langtoft	*David Woodmansey*
VC64: 18/02	**1** Meanwood	*Judith Scott*
VC63: 22/02	**1** Rotherham	*Steve Branch*
VC62: 13/03	**2** Scarborough	*L & J Westmoreland*
VC65: 21/03	**1** Nosterfield LNR	*Steve Worwood*

PEAK COUNTS
VC65: 11/08	**138** Catterick Training Area	*Michael Spensley*
VC61: 18/08	**30** North Cave Wetlands	*Carole Robinson*
VC63: 26/08	**106** Cudworth Railway	*Chris Parkin*
VC62: 03/09	**71** York	*Peter Izzard*
VC64: 07/09	**33** Knaresborough	*Mike Barnham*
VC64: 20/09	**33** Coniston Cold	*Andrew Rhodes*

LAST SIGHTINGS
VC61: 18/10	**1** Brantingham	*Richard Shillaker*
VC65: 23/10	**1** Nosterfield LNR	*Martin Bland*
VC65: 23/10	**1** Tees Railway	*Simon Hodgson*
VC64: 29/10	**1** Westhouse	*Roger Neale*
VC64: 29/10	**1** Ben Rhydding	*Jenny Dixon*
VC64: 29/10	**1** Otley	*Ernie Scarfe*
VC62: 05/11	**1** Scarborough	*L & J Westmoreland*
VC63: 04/12	**1** Cudworth	*C Gorman & C Stonier*

Photo, Martin Partridge.

STATISTICS 2019
Monthly: flight days (total butterflies) **countywide:** Jan **1** (4), Feb **5** (6), Mar **7** (13), Apr **12** (33), May **14** (45), Jun **28** (906), Jul **31** (1,859), Aug **31** (3,404), Sep **30** (3,676), Oct **27** (571), Nov **3** (6), Dec **1** (1).

Total flight days/flight season length: **190/** 327 days.

Total reports (total butterflies) **a) countywide: 3,631** (10,524) = mean **2.90** butterflies per observation. **b) by VC:** VC61: **749** (2,238), VC62: **364** (1,311), VC63: **662** (2,111), VC64: **1,393** (3,612), VC65: **463** (1,252).

Tetrads recorded (i.e., 2x2km OS grid squares): **679** out of 1510 visited and 4120 in Yorkshire.

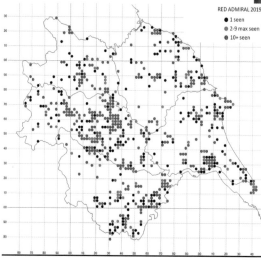

RED ADMIRAL 2019
- ● 1 seen
- ● 2-9 max seen
- ● 10+ seen

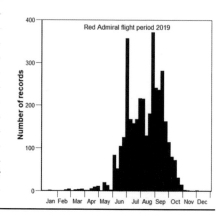

Red Admiral flight period 2019

59.024 Painted Lady *Vanessa cardui* (Linn. 1758)

Broods: Unclear. Annual immigrant from N Africa and continental Europe in varying numbers from year to year.

Yorkshire 2019: A long flight season with increased numbers of reports and butterflies observed made this 'a once in a decade' year for the migratory Painted Lady; the phenomenon last being observed in 2009. Occasional sightings of butterflies flying as early as February were received. Large numbers began to arrive in June increasing steadily to a peak in August. Counts were lower overall than those observed in 2009 (~26,000 compared to ~39,000) and the recorded flight days were also fewer (137 vs 175) but a dramatic improvement compared to the past 9 years was still observed. With more data still to come (e.g., from the Big Butterfly Count) these numbers will increase. As well as the sightings listed below other reports worthy of mention are 300 from Pauline Popely at Langdale Forest, 250 from Steve Worwood at Nosterfield, 188 from Chris Parkin at Woolley Stack, and 142 from Howard and Christine Frost in Kilnsea. An amazing year for the butterfly. *Jax Westmoreland*

FIRST SIGHTINGS

VC64: 24/02   **2** Baildon *Peter Hughes*
VC64: 24/02   **1** Selside *Helen Sergeant*
VC63: 27/02   **1** Sheffield *Pete Bibby*
VC61: 21/04   **2** Spurn *Howard & Christine Frost*
VC65: 25/05   **1** Muker *Stephen Kirtley*
VC62: 31/05   **3** Ruswarp *Wendy Holliday*

PEAK COUNTS

VC62: 30/07 **342** Skelton Castle *Damian Money*
VC64: 03/08 **120** Baildon *Peter Hughes*
VC65: 13/08 **453** Catterick *Michael Spensley*
VC61: 26/08 **158** Spurn *Phil Morgan*
VC63: 26/08 **215** Cudworth *Chris Parkin*

LAST SIGHTINGS

VC62: 10/10   **1** York *Mike Walton*
VC64: 12/10   **1** Lindley Rsvr *David & Nyree Fearnley*
VC61: 15/10   **1** Wawne *Robert Atkinson*
VC63: 23/10   **1** Cudworth *Chris Parkin*
VC65: 23/10   **1** Nosterfield LNR *David Belshaw*

Photo, Steve Relf.

STATISTICS 2019

Monthly: flight days (total butterflies) **countywide:**
Feb **2** (4), Mar **0** (0), Apr **1** (2), May **3** (8), Jun **27** (4,868), Jul **31** (5,288), Aug **31**(13,555), Sep **28** (1,769), Oct **14** (69).
Total flight days/flight season length: **137/ 242 days.**
Total reports (total butterflies) **a) countywide:**
4,401 (25,563) = mean **5.81** butterflies per observation.**b) by VC: VC61: 721** (4,368), VC62: **427** (4,637), VC63: **721** (4,140), VC64: **1,875** (8,175), VC65: **657** (4,243).
Tetrads recorded (i.e., 2x2km OS grid squares): **807** out of 1510 visited and 4120 in Yorkshire.

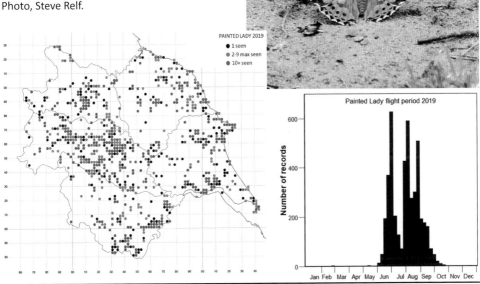

PAINTED LADY 2019
● 1 seen
● 2-9 max seen
● 10+ seen

Painted Lady flight period 2019

59.026 Peacock *Aglais io* (Linn. 1758)

Broods: 1 with small partial 2nd noted in some recent years. Common, mobile, long-lived, hibernating resident and partial migrant.

Yorkshire 2019: A great improvement on recent years with the second highest total of the millennium and an increase of 340% on last year. Most of the butterflies were seen in July (19%) and August (61%) with a further 10% in April. The recent swing to VC64 from VC63 continued with 36% of all Peacocks in VC64 and 24% in VC63. It was a good year in VC65. It was a poor year in VC61 which now only provides about 10% of sightings where it used to provide over 30%. Both VC64 and VC65 recorded their highest ever numbers. The cold spell in March may have led to an almost simultaneous spring peak across all VCs in April. Average counts rose by between ~125% (VC62) to ~225% (VC65). In total 29 counts of over 100 were made, with three from Langdale Forest (VC62) and four from the Cudworth area (VC63). *David Woodmansey*

FIRST WINTER SIGHTINGS
VC65: 01/01 **1** Nosterfield LNR *Royanne Wilding*
VC63: 04/01 **3** Thorpe Marsh NR *Mick Townsend*
VC61: 28/01 **1** Beverley Rail Stn *David Woodmansey*
VC64: 14/02 **1** Coniston Cold *Andrew Rhodes*
VC64: 14/02 **1** Thorlby *Caroline Moorhouse*
VC62: 27/02 **1** Rievaulx Abbey *John Edwards*
VC62: 27/02 **1** Goathland *Wilf Norman*

FIRST SIGHTINGS Spring
VC63: 18/03 Several sightings (5) of 1 to 8 Peacocks
VC61: 19/03 **1** Wawne *Robert Atkinson*
VC62: 20/03 Several sightings (6) of 1 to 4 Peacocks
VC64: 20/03 Several sightings (4) of 1 Peacock
VC65: 21/03 Several sightings (7) of 1 to 3 Peacocks

STATISTICS 2019
Monthly: flight days (total butterflies)
countywide: Jan **5** (14), Feb **14** (59), Mar **13** (879), Apr **27** (2,464), May **23** (949), Jun **26** (330), Jul **28** (4,914), Aug **31** (15,582), Sep **28** (478), Oct **18** (49), Nov **3** (4), Dec **1** (1).
Total flight days/flight season length: 217/ 337 days. **Total reports** (total butterflies) **a) countywide: 4,106** (25,723) = mean **6.26** butterflies per observation. **b) by VC:** VC61: **640** (2,805), VC62: **432** (3,250), VC63: **710** (6,168), VC64: **1,769** (9,434), VC65: **555** (4,066). **Tetrads recorded** (i.e., 2x2km OS grid squares): **751** out of 1510 visited and 4120 in Yorkshire.

FIRST MULTIPLE SIGHTINGS
VC63: 04/01 **3** Thorpe Marsh *Mick Townsend*
VC64: 17/02 **2** Farnham Grvl Pits *Harrogate Nats*
VC61: 20/03 **3** Beverley *David Turner*
VC61: 20/03 **4** Everthorpe Grange *R Leach*
VC61: 20/03 **5** Three Hagges Wd *Jesika Bone*
VC62: 20/03 **2** Saltburn-by-the-Sea *M Barnham*
VC62: 20/03 **2** Wydale *Paul Ingham*
VC62: 20/03 **2** Snainton *Paul Ingham*
VC62: 20/03 **3** Haxby *Terry Crawford*
VC62: 20/03 **4** Walmgate Stray, York *Peter Mayhew*
VC65: 21/03 **2** Baldersby *Tim Helps*
VC65: 21/03 **2** Nosterfield LNR *Steve Worwood*

PEAK COUNTS Spring
VC61: 20/04 **57** Spurn Point *Andy Mason*
VC63: 20/04 **43** Barrow Tip *Chris Parkin*
VC64: 20/04 **50** Grimwith Reservoir *Roy Baker*
VC65: 21/04 **21** Ainderby Steeple *Nick Morgan*
VC62: 22/04 **20** Langdale Forest *Ian & Pauline Popely*

PEAK COUNTS Summer
VC64: 29/07 **183** Walshford *Mike Barnham*
VC63: 01/08 **375** Barnsdale Qu *L Corrall & R Hibbert*
VC65: 03/08 **580** Catterick Training Area *M Spensley*
VC61: 04/08 **120** Enthorpe *Andrew Ashworth*
VC62: 18/08 **260** Langdale Forest *Ian & Pauline Popely*

LAST SIGHTINGS
VC64: 17/10 **1** Burley *Janet Kyriakides*
VC64: 17/10 **2** Timble Ings *Karen Bullimore*
VC62: 23/10 **1** Skelton Castle *Damian Money*
VC65: 23/10 **1** Baldersby *Tim Helps*
VC65: 23/10 **1** Nosterfield LNR *David Belshaw*
VC65: 23/10 **1** Tees Railway Walk (S3) *S Hodgson*
VC63: 29/11 **1** Ickles, Rotherham *Steve Branch*
VC61: 03/12 **1** Spurn Point *Phil Morgan*

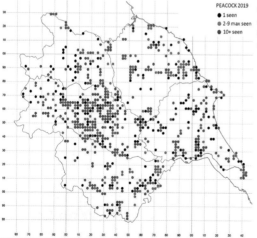

PEACOCK 2019
● 1 seen
● 2-9 max seen
● 10+ seen

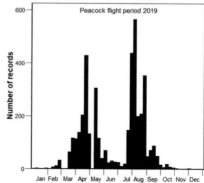

Peacock flight period 2019

59.027 Small Tortoiseshell *Aglais urticae* (Linn. 1758)

Broods: 1 to 3 partial. Mobile, hibernating resident and partial migrant with populations currently in marked decline.

Yorkshire 2019: This season has shown huge increases in numbers of Small Tortoiseshells recorded compared to 2018, with the total number of butterflies recorded increasing by 47% from 7,470 recorded butterflies in 2018 to 13,179 recorded in 2019. The month that yielded the largest record of butterflies was July 2019, where a total of 4,524 individuals were spotted. This is a dramatic increase on July 2018 where 2,545 individual butterflies were recorded. The number of flight days also increased by 13% from 202 days to 228 over the year, indicating the prevalence of the species during the year. There was also an increase shown in early emergent butterflies from 1 individual recorded in February 2018 to 15 being recorded in February 2019. The flight season was longer in 2019 than 2018 due to the earlier emergence of the butterfly in 2019. *Emily Summer*

FIRST SIGHTINGS
VC63: 01/01 **1** Cudworth Marsh *Les Corrall*
VC62: 23/01 **1** Abbey Steps, Whitby *Mike Barnham*
VC65: 08/02 **2** Scotton *Patricia Illingworth*
VC61: 11/02 **1** Aldbrough Cliff *Adrian Johnson*
VC64: 15/02 **1** Brotherton *David Wadding*

PEAK COUNTS Overwintered
VC65: 22/03 **21** Scotton *Andrew Murray*
VC63: 25/03 **47** Hoyle Mill *Chris Parkin*
VC62: 29/03 **15** Walmgate Stray, York *Peter Mayhew*
VC61: 17/04 **20** Walmgate Stray, York *Edgar Mail*
VC64: 24/04 **12** Gallows Hill NR, Otley *Simon Bryant*

PEAK COUNTS Summer
VC63: 21/06 **57** Canklow *Steve Branch*
VC64: 23/07 **117** Wormald Green *Mike Barnham*
VC62: 26/07 **22** Skelton Castle *Damian Money*
VC65: 12/08 **206** Catterick Training Area *M Spensley*
VC61: 13/08 **30** Bird Obs. Church Fld, Spurn *H Frost*

PEAK COUNTS Late summer
VC61: 18/08 **19** Thorngumbald *M Bruce & P Bursell*
VC61: 23/08 **19** Withernsea *Christine & Howard Frost*
VC65: 29/08 **42** Baldersby *Tim Helps*
VC64: 11/09 **58** Coniston Cold *Andrew Rhodes*
VC62: 13/09 **41** Breezy Knees Gdn, York *Peter Izzard*
VC63: 16/09 **60** Thurlstone *Alwyn Timms*

LAST SIGHTINGS
VC63: 23/10 **1** Wibsey, Bradford *L Johnson*
VC62: 05/11 **1** Scarborough *Lee & Jax Westmoreland*
VC65: 07/11 **2** Scotton *Patricia Illingworth*
VC61: 10/11 **1** Brantingham *Richard Shillaker*
VC64: 29/11 **1** Leeds Bradford Airport *Alex Whitaker*

STATISTICS 2019
Monthly: flight days (total butterflies) **countywide:** Jan **2** (3), Feb **15** (198), Mar **18** (693), Apr **26** (1,090), May **26** (334), Jun **27** (1,088), Jul **31** (4,524), Aug **30** (2,878), Sep **26** (2,230), Oct **23** (136), Nov **4** (5), Dec **0** (0).
Total flight days/flight season length: 228/ 333 days.
Total reports (total butterflies) **a) countywide: 4,113** (13,179) = mean **3.20** butterflies per observation..**b) by VC:** VC61: **674** (1,953), VC62: **415** (1,348), VC63: **743** (2,923), VC64: **1,731** (4,924), VC65: **550** (2,031).
Tetrads recorded (i.e., 2x2km OS grid squares): **737** out of 1510 visited and 4120 in Yorkshire.

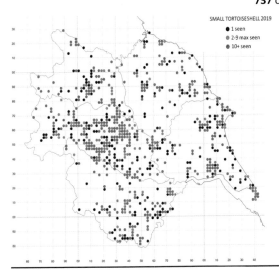

SMALL TORTOISESHELL 2019
● 1 seen
● 2-9 max seen
● 10+ seen

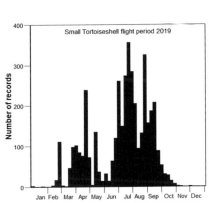

59.031 Comma *Polygonia c-album* (Linn. 1758)

Broods: 1 to 2. Long-lived, hibernating resident which has expanded northward across the county over the last 20 years or so.

Yorkshire 2019: The mild autumn/winter going into 2019, coupled with mild and sunny spells throughout late February and March, seems to have resulted in greatly improved numbers of butterflies for the spring emergence in 2019 compared with 2018. A notable peak occurred on March 28th, with 40 individuals seen in Bishop Wood by Les Corrall and Ralph Hibbert. This was at a contrast with an unsettled May/June which led to comparatively poor numbers of butterflies seen in these months this year. Overall, however, there were a greater number of flight days noted for every vice county, and a marked increase in the total number of individuals sighted, with a mean number of individuals per observation of 2.19 compared with 1.9 in 2018. Lots of warm and sunny days from July through September saw good numbers through the later part of the year with an exceptional highlight of 84 individuals seen in Hollins Wood by Chris Parkin on September 14th. *Elizabeth Ingram*

FIRST SIGHTINGS
VC61: 12/01 **1** Langtoft E Lea *David H Woodmansey*
VC63: 12/02 **7** Cudworth Marsh *Chris Parkin*
VC64: 23/02 **3** Ilkley *David & Nyree Fearnley*
VC64: 23/02 **3** Otley *Carmen Horner & F Horner*
VC64: 23/02 **1** Middleton Wds, Ilkley *David Howson*
VC64: 23/02 **1** East Wd, Otley *Paul Purvis*
VC62: 24/02 **1** Wydale *Paul Ingham*
VC62: 24/02 **1** Snainton *Paul Ingham*
VC65: 25/02 **2** Richmond *Arnold J Robson*

PEAK COUNTS Overwintered
VC61: Several sightings (8) of 2 Comma
VC63: 25/03 **27** Hoyle Mill *Chris Parkin*
VC64: 28/03 **40** Bishop Wd *Les Corrall & Ralph Hibbert*
VC65: 28/03 **3** Broken Brea, Brompton-on-Swale *P Kipling*
VC65: 29/03 **3** Broken Brea, Brompton-on-Swale *P Kipling*
VC65: 06/04 **3** Nosterfield LNR *Martin Bland*
VC62: 22/04 **4** Clifton Backies, York *Mike Walton*

PEAK COUNTS Mid-summer Brood
VC63: 17/07 **23** Hoyle Mill *Chris Parkin*
VC62: 26/07 **12** Skelton Castle *Damian Money*
VC64: 30/07 **25** Bishop Wd, Selby *Mike Barnham*
VC61: 01/08 **13** Thorngumbald *M Bruce & P Bursell*
VC65: 06/08 **10** Broken Brea, Brompton-on-Swale *P Kipling*
VC65: 12/08 **10** Broken Brea, Brompton-on-Swale *P Kipling*

PEAK COUNTS Late-summer Brood
VC63: 14/09 **84** Hollins Wd *Chris Parkin*
VC61: 16/09 **8** Spurn Point *Peter Hinks*
VC62: 16/09 **8** Haxby, York *Terry Crawford*
VC64: 26/09 **12** Knaresborough *Mike Barnham*
VC65: 28/09 **20** Nosterfield LNR *David Belshaw*

LAST SIGHTINGS
VC65: 23/10 **1** Nosterfield LNR *David Belshaw*
VC62: 26/10 **1** Scarborough *Lee & Jax Westmoreland*
VC63: 31/10 **2** Brierley *Chris Parkin*
VC61: 02/11 **1** High Esk *Phil Morgan*
VC64: 16/11 **1** Norwd Edg Hopkinson Gill *D & N Fearnley*

STATISTICS 2019
Monthly: flight days (total butterflies) countywide: Jan **1** (1), Feb **10** (133), Mar **13** (403), Apr **24** (287), May **17** (65), Jun **13** (50), Jul **30** (1,127), Aug **31** (851), Sep **29** (1,041), Oct **22** (366), Nov **2** (2), Dec **0** (0).
Total flight days/flight season length: **192/** 309 days.
Total reports (total butterflies) **a) countywide: 1,967** (4,326) = mean **2.20** butterflies per observation.
b) by VC: VC61: **263** (428), VC62: **194** (355), VC63: **550** (1,791), VC64: **779** (1,374), VC65: **181** (378).
Tetrads recorded (i.e., 2x2km OS grid squares): **434** out of 1510 visited and 4120 in Yorkshire.

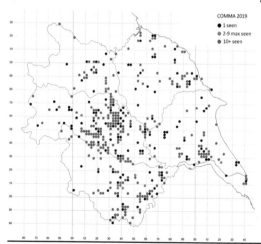

COMMA 2019
● 1 seen
● 2-9 max seen
● 10+ seen

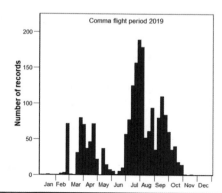

Comma flight period 2019

Number of records

Jan Feb Mar Apr May Jun Jul Aug Sep Oct Nov Dec

Comma Rockley Old Hall by Geoff Carr

RIODINIDAE
Metalmarks

60.001 Duke of Burgundy *Hamearis lucina* (Linn. 1758)

Broods: 1 (spring). One of our rarest residents confined to a small number of sites mainly on private land on the southern edge of the North York Moors in the Helmsley and Pickering areas. These are subject to an annual programme of recording and site management with the support of key landowners and the National Park.

Yorkshire 2019: Despite concerns that the drought conditions in the summer of 2018 might have affected breeding success Duke of Burgundy had a second excellent year. We obtained records for 12 known sites in the Helmsley area, found one new site which may be occupied, and obtained peak counts of 53, 59,43 and 103 on our largest sites (the highest ever records for two of these sites). The decline in the numbers of sites where we have recorded Duke of Burgundy in the Helmsley area from 2000 onwards appears to have been reversed. The results for the Pickering sites were also re-markably good with records for four of the five locations where it has been recorded in recent years near Pickering, the discovery of a single butterfly in Gundale 2.5 km away where it has not been recorded for over 30 years, and 2 adults seen on the extinct Pexton site in Thornton Dale 3 km from any known colony. These records confirm that female butterflies are travelling surprising distances to colonize or re-colonise new sites. The Branch maintains a programme of management of monitoring and management of all known sites in North Yorkshire – if you want to help please do contact me (see contact details back of the Report). *Robert Parks*

FIRST SIGHTINGS
VC62: 20/04   **6** Hawnby *Stephen Kirtley*
PEAK COUNTS
VC62: 15/05 **103** Helmsley area *Dave Wainwright*
LAST SIGHTINGS
VC62: 06/06   **4** Hawnby *Ian Armitage*

STATISTICS 2019
Monthly: flight days (total butterflies) **countywide:**
Apr **6** (39), May **12** (539), Jun **2** (9).
Total flight days/flight season length: **20/** 48 days.
Total reports (total butterflies) **a) countywide: 57**
(587) = mean **10.30** butterflies per observation.**b)**
by VC: VC62: **57** (587).**Tetrads recorded** (i.e., 2x2km
OS grid squares): **12** out of 1510 visited and 4120 in
Yorkshire.

Duke of Burgundy 22 May 2019 Hawnby Hill
John Money.

LYCAENIDAE
Blues & Hairstreaks
61.001 Small Copper *Lycaena phlaeas* (Linn. 1761)

Broods: 2 occasionally partial 3. Fairly mobile resident.

Yorkshire 2019: Inevitably this year saw a decline compared to the record-breaking 2018 season (when there were 1,070 reports of 3,414 individual butterflies). Nevertheless, 2019 was still a good year for Small Copper (based on number of reports and individual butterflies counted) compared to the relatively subdued seasons of the last five years or so (excepting 2018). The first brood started properly in the second week of May and was thereafter uncharacteristically strong. The strength of the first brood presumably arose from greater numbers of overwintering larvae from the exceptional 2018 season. The second brood in July to September was though uncharacteristically poor compared to most years; we would expect the second brood numbers to be at least three times stronger than the first brood, though as mentioned, the first brood in 2019 was bolstered from 2018 larvae. There was a lingering presence in October restricted largely to VC63 indicating a possible third brood. The flight season was long entirely due to an isolated exceptionally early sighting in mid-March (VC62) which was followed by a gap of five weeks when no Small Copper were reported anywhere in Yorkshire. The majority of sightings were in VC63 and VC64 as is usual, but the peak count came from Catterick (VC65), indicating a strengthening in the numbers of this beautiful butterfly in north-west Yorkshire. It is usual to encounter this widely-distributed butterfly species in small discrete colonies in varied habitats where it favours warm and dry surroundings (open sunny areas with low vegetation such as is found in rough grassland and disused quarries for instance), as well as wandering in our gardens and parks. The female will only lay her eggs on sunny days and the summer was warmer than average in July and August so this might mean we will have a good year in 2020. *David Smith*

FIRST SIGHTINGS
VC62: 13/03 **1** Scarborough *Lee & Jax Westmoreland*
VC64: 20/04 **1** Burley Moor *Anne & Peter Riley*
VC61: 21/04 **1** Fordon Chalk Bnk *David Woodmansey*
VC63: 26/04 **1** Thorne Moor *Martin Warne*
VC63: 26/04 **1** Goole Moor Tram *Martin Warne*
VC65: 12/05 **1** Nosterfield LNR *David Belshaw*

PEAK COUNTS
VC63: 20/05 **10** St Aidan's RSPB *A Tiffany*
VC62: 23/05 **14** Pickering *I Armitage, D O'Brien & R Parks*
VC64: 24/08 **18** Coniston Cold *Andrew Rhodes*
VC61: 27/08 **15** Calley Heath YWT NR *David Miller*
VC65: 13/09 **44** Catterick Training Area *Catherine Jones*

LAST SIGHTINGS
VC62: 20/09 **1** Newton Mulgrave Moor *Wendy English*
VC61: 26/09 **1** Wawne *Robert Atkinson*
VC64: 02/10 **1** Pateley Bridge *John Shillcock*
VC65: 10/10 **1** Tees railway walk *Simon Hodgson*
VC63: 28/10 **2** Hatfield, Doncaster *Ian & Kath Weeks*

STATISTICS 2019
Monthly: flight days (total butterflies)
countywide: Mar **2** (2), Apr **4** (8), May **22** (282), Jun **22** (169), Jul **23** (146), Aug **29** (571), Sep **24** (160), Oct **8** (17).

Total flight days/flight season length: **134/** 230 days.

Total reports (total butterflies) **a) countywide: 762** (1,355) = mean **1.78** butterflies per observation.**b) by VC:** VC61: **97** (159), VC62: **86** (165), VC63: **193** (288), VC64: **294** (567), VC65: **92** (176).

Tetrads recorded (i.e., 2x2km OS grid squares): **250** out of 1510 visited and 4120 in Yorkshire.

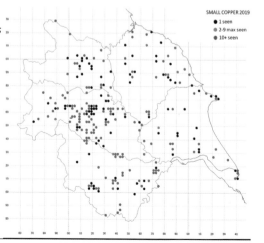

SMALL COPPER 2019
● 1 seen
◉ 2-9 max seen
● 10+ seen

Small Copper flight period 2019

Number of records

Jan Feb Mar Apr May Jun Jul Aug Sep Oct Nov Dec

61.004 Purple Hairstreak *Favonius quercus* (Linn. 1758)

Broods: 1. Localised resident, mainly found in association with oaks.

Yorkshire 2019: Numbers overall were lower than in 2018 and records came from fewer sites. Half of the VC61 sightings were from the reliable Everthorpe Grange locality, but a number of records came from the eastern half of this VC where this species has been under-recorded in recent years. In VC62, records came from only 4 sites, although numbers were higher than in 2018. Typically, most records came from VCs 63 & 64, although from fewer sites than previously. Both VCs returned 3-figure highest counts, with VC64 also producing the last record of the year. Records from VC65 came from more sites than in 2018, and in far higher numbers, although most of the records were from a single site. *Dave O'Brien*

FIRST SIGHTINGS

VC62: 03/07 **1** Skelton Castle *Damian Money*
VC65: 04/07 **2** Bedale Bypass *Martin Bland*
VC63: 06/07 **3** Cudworth Marsh *Cliff Gorman*
VC61: 10/07 **2** Everthorpe Grange *Rosemary Roach*
VC64: 12/07 **1** Burley in Wharfdale *Corrie Hardaker*

PEAK COUNTS

VC61: 13/07 **6** Everthorpe Grange *Rosemary Roach*
VC61: 16/07 **6** Burton Constable *H & C Frost*
VC63: 16/07 **231** Thorpe Marsh *B Evans, B Foster, M Townsend*
VC65: 23/07 **22** Ainderby Steeple *Nick Morgan*
VC62: 24/07 **9** Ruswarp *Wendy Holliday*
VC64: 25/07 **238** Cardale, Harrogate *Mike Barnham*

LAST SIGHTINGS

VC61: 03/08 **1** Everthorpe Grange *R Roach*
VC65: 08/08 **1** Broken Brea *Paul Kipling*
VC62: 09/08 **1** Ruswarp *Wendy Holliday*
VC63: 13/08 **1** St Aidan's RSPB *D McMahon*
VC64: 24/08 **1** Brimham Moor *Mike Barnham*

STATISTICS 2019

Monthly: flight days (total butterflies) **countywide:** Jul **24** (1,148), Aug **11** (34).
Total flight days/flight season length: **35/** 53 days.
Total reports (total butterflies) **a) countywide: 145** (1,182) = mean **8.15** butterflies per observation.
b) by VC: VC61: **28** (83), VC62: **11** (38), VC63: **34** (568), VC64: **59** (445), VC65: **13** (48).
Tetrads recorded (i.e., 2x2km OS grid squares): **75** out of 1510 visited and 4120 in Yorkshire.

Purple Hairstreak *neozephyrus quercus*
Martin Partridge

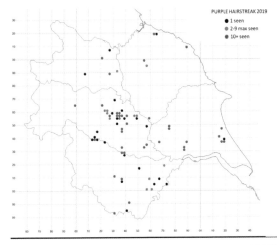

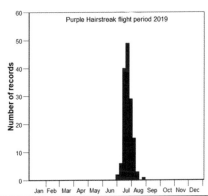

61.005 Green Hairstreak *Callophrys rubi* (Linn. 1758)

Broods: 1. Localised resident, mainly associated with upland areas.

Yorkshire 2019: This was by far the best year of the past 10 years for which I have records. There were almost 500 more individual butterflies than the next best year of 2014 (1648). However, there were also considerably more reports this year than previously (2018 reports = 135) ; the mean of butterflies seen per observation this year (8.67) thus being not much greater than in 2018 (7.60). The resurrection of consistent recording from Spurn is welcome and there were six 1-km squares where Green Hairstreak was seen in the Spurn NNR. Can anyone find any other sites in VC61? VC64 remains the hot spot. On 22 April, David Leather saw 115 on Ilkley Moor across several locations. The moors above Addingham also provided multiple locations of double figures from mid-April to mid-May. The number of flight days was above average with a long flight period too. The count of 287 at Catterick was the highest ever for that site. *Nyree Fearnley*

FIRST SIGHTINGS

VC61: 17/04 **1** Kilnsea Wetlands *Tim Collins, Howard & Christine Frost, David & Jenny Smith*
VC64: 17/04 **16** Otley Chevin *David & Nyree Fearnley*
VC64: 17/04 **3** Bingley Moor *Ian Grange*
VC65: 20/04 **2** Ellingstring *David Coltman*
VC62: 21/04 **1** Boltby *Peter Mayhew*
VC63: 21/04 **7** Flaight Hill *David Dodsworth*

PEAK COUNTS

VC64: 28/04 **50** Upper Barden Rsv *Ernie Scarfe*
VC62: 13/05 **11** Hawnby *Dave O'Brien & Robert Parks*
VC61: 14/05 **42** Spurn NNR *Howard & Christine Frost*
VC63: 14/05 **75** Snailsdone Reservoir *Alwyn Timms*
VC65: 14/05 **287** Catterick Training Area *David Oldham*

LAST SIGHTINGS

VC63: 25/05 **4** Flaight Hill *David Dodsworth*
VC65: 03/06 **30** Catterick Training Area *David Oldham*
VC64: 10/06 **2** Malham Tarn *Denis Lord*
VC61: 18/06 **3** Spurn NNR *Howard & Christine Frost*
VC62: 05/07 **1** Worlds End *Peter Mayhew*

Photo, P Relf

STATISTICS 2019

Monthly: flight days (total butterflies) **countywide:** Apr **13** (847), May **21** (1,263), Jun **8** (66), Jul **1** (1).

Total flight days/flight season length: **43/** 80 days.

Total reports (total butterflies) **a) countywide: 251** (2,177) = mean **8.67** butterflies per observation.

b) by VC: VC61: **31** (297), VC62: **32** (95), VC63: **18** (273), VC64: **160** (1,110), VC65: **10** (402).

Tetrads recorded (i.e., 2x2km OS grid squares): **94** out of 1510 visited and 4120 in Yorkshire.

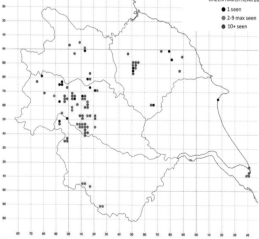

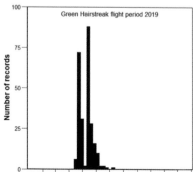

GREEN HAIRSTREAK 2019
● 1 seen
● 2-9 max seen
● 10+ seen

Green Hairstreak flight period 2019

61.006 White-letter Hairstreak *Satyrium w-album* (Knoch 1782)

Broods: 1. In Yorkshire, a resident usually associated with Wych Elms.

Yorkshire 2019: Although White-letter Hairstreak enjoyed a longer flight period in 2019, this was otherwise a very disappointing year, with fewer reports and lower numbers of butterflies seen than in 2018. Worryingly, there were signs of Dutch elm disease at several locations in VC62, with two mature trees at one site completely killed. If this is the same in other VCs, potentially we could see quite a decline of this species. In VC61, all records were of singles, mostly from the Cottingham area (Thwaite Gardens as seen by Andrew Ashworth), as well as in Hornsea (Lynda Cox) and Low Catton (Rob Andrews). All of the VC62 sightings came from the same site in Ruswarp where the recorder has reported an outbreak of Dutch elm disease. Most of the records came from VCs 63 & 64, where the butterfly was quite widely spread throughout both VCs, although numbers were lower than in previous years, with no double-figure counts made. Records came from more sites in VC65 than in previous years, with the only double-figure count coming from a site near Northallerton. No records of eggs or larvae were received in 2019. *Dave O'Brien*

FIRST SIGHTINGS
VC63: 16/06 **1** Burkinshaw, Bradford *Martyn Priestley*
VC64: 27/06 **1** Middle Hookstone, Harrogate *M P Laycock*
VC65: 29/06 **2** Nosterfield *Martin Bland*
VC62: 01/07 **3** Ruswarp *Wendy Holliday*
VC61: 11/07 **1** Thwaite Gardens *Andrew Ashworth*

PEAK COUNTS
VC62: 01/07 **3** Ruswarp *Wendy Holliday*
VC63: 05/07 **5** Hugset Wood *Geoff M Carr*
VC65: 07/07 **30** Myers Lane, Thrintoft *Nick Morgan*
VC61: singletons (between 11/07 and 21/07)
VC64: 23/07 **7** Quarry Moor, Ripon *Mike Barnham*

LAST SIGHTINGS
VC61: 21/07 **1** Hornsea *Lynda Cox*
VC62: 14/08 **1** Ruswarp *Wendy Holliday*
VC65: 08/08 **2** Clints, Marske *Naomi Meredith*
VC63: 15/08 **1** Sheffield *Ange Garrod*
VC64: 15/08 **1** East Keswick *Melanie Smith*

STATISTICS 2019
Monthly: flight days (total butterflies)
countywide: Jun **5** (14), Jul **25** (176), Aug **7** (11).
Total flight days/flight season length: 37/ 61 days.
Total reports (total butterflies) **a) countywide: 100** (201) = mean **2.01** butterflies per observation.
b) by VC: VC61: **6** (6), VC62: **4** (7), VC63: **24** (40), VC64: **56** (101), VC65: **10** (47).
Tetrads recorded (i.e., 2x2km OS grid squares): **62** out of 1510 visited and 4120 in Yorkshire.

White-letter Hairstreak *Satyrium w-album*
Martin Partridge

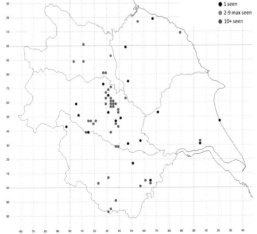

WHITE-LETTER HAIRSTREAK 201
● 1 seen
● 2-9 max seen
● 10+ seen

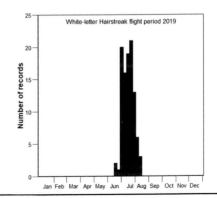

[61.010 Small Blue *Cupido minimus* (Fuessly 1775)]

Broods: 2. (i.e., in S England - situation in Yorkshire variable but usually only 1 brood). Thought to have been extinct in Yorkshire since the **1950s** if not earlier. Colonies discovered in 2010 and 2015 probably the result of unreported introductions. Details of the locations are withheld to protect this species on sensitive sites.

Yorkshire 2019: The colony discovered in 2010 was visited nine times on eight different days. A total of 73 adults were seen. The earliest sighting at this location was 12th May (Dave Ramsden) of five males, the peak number was 17 on the 20th May (Mike Barnham), and the last sighting was of one male on the 5th August (Dave McMahon). The August sighting indicates that there were two broods at this location. The numbers were considerably less than in 2018 (when 223 adults were recorded in the season at this location). The colony discovered in 2015 was visited 24 times on 15 different days. A total of 388 adults were seen – similar to the total of 412 adults seen in the 2018 season. The earliest sighting at this location was 23rd May (Alwyn Timms) of 13 adults, the peak number was 35 on the 21st June (Chris Parkin), and the last sighting was of 10 adults on the 23rd August (Alwyn Timms). This means that there was also a second brood at this meta-colony location. Though one of the main locations was stripped of vegetation last year by contractors the kidney vetch has re-grown and the Small Blue colony has re-established itself. It is amazing sometimes how resilient nature is. ***David Smith***
Tetrads recorded (i.e., 2x2km OS grid squares): **3** out of 1510 visited and 4120 in Yorkshire.

Small Blue *Cupido minimus* mating Alwyn Timms

61.012 Holly Blue *Celastrina argiolus* (Linn. 1758)

Broods: 1 to 3 partial. Fairly recent coloniser spreading N. Some populations may be cyclical (peaking every 4 and 6yrs) due to the predations of the parasitic ichneumon wasp *Listrodomus nycthemerus*. Please see Smith, DRR. (2018). Time series analysis of Holly Blue records in Yorkshire - uncovering a parasitoid. *The Naturalist*, *143*, 166-173.

Yorkshire 2019: Whilst for me it never felt like a particularly good year for this species when the records came in it turned out to be the second best year on record for the county – the best year since 2002 for VC62 – and all other VC's also having a good year. The first sighting on 16th March was one of the earliest on record being a fortnight earlier than the mean. There were not many other records though during the month and it was April before Holly Blue emerged in any numbers and then it had its best ever spring brood beating the previous record from last year. The spring brood was the strongest by a ratio of 1.4:1. The Holly Blue is a widespread species tending to do better in our more southern VCs. The flight period was typical with the last being observed on the wing on 26th September. ***Dave Ramsden***

FIRST SIGHTINGS	PEAK COUNTS 1st Brood
VC62: 16/03 **1** Easingwold *Kenneth Hale*	VC65: 19/04 **3** West Tanfield *Pauline Percival*
VC63: 26/03 **1** Balby *Diane Wardley*	VC62: 13/05 **15** Snainton *Paul Ingham*
VC61: 28/03 **1** Beverley *David Turner*	VC63: 13/05 **9** Brockadale NR *Paul & Joyce Simmons*
VC64: 29/03 **1** Otley *Simon Bryant*	VC64: 24/05 **8** Knaresborough *Mike Barnham*
VC65: 17/04 **1** Bedale *Martin Bland*	VC61: 06/06 **22** Kilnsea *Howard & Christine Frost*

PEAK COUNTS 2nd Brood
VC61: 01/08   **5** Hunmanby *Phyl Abbott*
VC65: 01/08   **5** Baldersby *Tim Helps*
VC62: 05/08 **24** Scarborough *Lee & Jax Westmoreland*
VC63: 18/08   **8** Goole *Peter Hinks*
VC64: 23/08   **5** Knaresborough *Mike Barnham*
LAST SIGHTINGS
VC61: 12/09   **1** Walkington *Richard Shillaker*
VC63: 13/09   **1** Goole *Peter Hinks*
VC64: 19/09   **1** Knaresborough *Mike Barnham*
VC65: 19/09   **1** Baldersby *Tim Helps*
VC62: 26/09   **1** Scarborough *Lee & Jax Westmoreland*

STATISTICS 2019
Monthly: flight days (total butterflies)
countywide: Mar **5** (9), Apr **18** (480), May **26** (731), Jun **22** (141), Jul **22** (243), Aug **30** (686), Sep **19** (59).
Total flight days/flight season length: **142/** 195 days.
Total reports (total butterflies) **a) countywide:**
1,482 (2,349) = mean **1.59** butterflies per observation.
b) by VC: VC61: **419** (645), VC62: **169** (377), VC63: **274** (445), VC64: **504** (718), VC65: **116** (164).
Tetrads recorded (i.e., 2x2km OS grid squares): **318** out of 1510 visited and 4120 in Yorkshire.

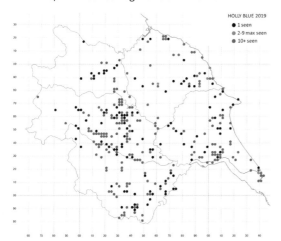

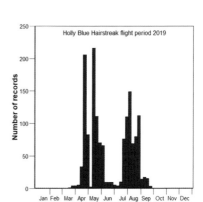

Holly Blue Hairstreak flight period 2019

[61.014 Silver-studded Blue *Plebejus argus* (Linn. 1758)]

Broods: 1 to 2. Brood situation in Yorkshire not known, probably only one. This resident species is thought to have become extinct in Yorkshire in the late **1800s**. An unreported introduction has taken place at Lindrick Common, hence the bracketed status of this species.
Yorkshire 2019: A report was provided (via twitter by Vin Browne) of Silver-studded Blue being seen on the 6th August. *David Smith*

Silver-studded Blue *Plebejus argus* Martin Partridge

61.015 Brown Argus (BA) *Aricia agestis* (Denis & Schiffermüller 1775)
61.016 Northern Brown Argus (NBA) *Aricia artaxerxes* (Fabricius 1793)

Broods: BA 1 to 3. NBA 1 (although a partial 2nd is not impossible in ideal weather conditions.) These 2 species are dealt with together as they are difficult to tell apart. ID is best made by site, with NBA now thought to be found only in rock rose habitats in the Pennine Dales, whilst BA is mainly associated with wild geranium species which are more widespread and may even occur round the edges of large fields farmed intensively, although on the Yorkshire Wolds and N York Moors there are sedentary BA colonies found on rock rose. Geranium-based BA has been expanding northward in recent years.

Yorkshire 2019: BA. The first sighting was on 28th April at Fordon Chalk Banks with ten Brown Argus seen. This first sighting was seventeen days earlier than in 2018. The total county wide flight period was three days shorter than in 2018 with the last observations being on 30th September. The flight period appears to have moved to earlier in the year with no sign of a possible third brood as was possibly witnessed in 2018 at Nosterfield LNR. The total number of sightings at 831 and reports (295) shows increased levels of recording. The number of Brown Argus seen in VC64 has increased significantly with only a small increase in the number of reports. The number of reports and total number of sightings in VC62 remain low when compared to the other vice counties. Most sightings come from no further north than the middle of the North York Moors.

NBA. The first sightings were made at several locations in VC64 on 6th June which was five days later than in 2018. The first sighting in VC65 was not made until two weeks later. Large numbers were again seen in June in 2019 in VC64 with reduced reporting; however much greater numbers were seen in July (June to July ratio of 1.57:1 in 2019 compared to 10.47:1 in 2018) with sightings extending a week into August. The flight period appears to have moved to later in the year when compared to 2018, and was extended to 63 days compared to 49 days in 2018, five days above the average. The number of Northern Brown Argus recorded in VC64 (750) was 10% lower than the highest ever counts of 2018 (837). Again the vast majority of Northern Brown Argus records come from VC64. *Martin Partridge*

Brown Argus

FIRST SIGHTINGS
VC61: 28/04 **10** Fordon Chalk Banks *Edgar Mail*
VC63: 12/05 **1** South Kirby Stack *Chris Parkin*
VC64: 15/05 **1** St Aidan's Hillside *D McMahon*
VC64: 15/05 **2** Barlow Common *Claire Burton*
VC65: 15/05 **1** Nosterfield LNR *David Belshaw*
VC62: 21/05 **23** Yatts Farm, Pickering *Dave O'Brien*

PEAK COUNTS 1st Brood
VC61: 28/04 **10** Fordon Chalk Banks *Edgar Mail*
VC62: 21/05 **23** Yatts Farm, Pickering *Dave O'Brien*
VC65: 22/05 **17** Centre Henge, Thornbrgh *M Barnham*
VC64: 06/06 **10** St Aidan's Hillside *A Tiffany*
VC63: 09/06 **12** St Aidan's RSPB *J Pickering*

PEAK COUNTS 2nd Brood
VC64: 18/08 **38** Knaresborough *Mike Barnham*
VC65: 23/08 **7** Nosterfield LNR *Martin Bland*
VC63: 24/08 **15** South Kirby *Chris Parkin*
VC62: 26/08 **8** Ellerburn Bank *Dave O'Brien*
VC61: 27/08 **7** Calley Heath YWT NR *David Miller*

LAST SIGHTINGS
VC62: 26/08 **8** Ellerburn Bank *Dave O'Brien*
VC65: 19/09 **1** Nosterfield LNR *David Belshaw*
VC61: 20/09 **1** Wawne, Bamforth Farm *Robert Atkinson*
VC64: 20/09 **1** St Aidan's RSPB *P Morris*
VC63: 30/09 **1** South Kirby Stack *L Corrall & R Hibbert*

Northern Brown Argus

FIRST SIGHTINGS
VC64: 06/06 **3** Bastow Wd, *I & B Blomfield*
VC64: 06/06 **7** Dib Scar, Conistone *I & B Blomfield*
VC64: 06/06 **1** Lea Grn & Bastow Wd *Ian Court*
VC64: 06/06 **2** Low Ox Pasture Kilnsey *P Millard*
VC64: 06/06 **4** Long Ashes transect *Ian Court*
VC65: 20/06 **7** Haw Bank, Carperby *Ian Court*

PEAK COUNTS
VC65: 20/06 **7** Haw Bank, Carperby *Ian Court*
VC64: 27/06 **82** Blue Cragg, Arncliffe *Ian Court*

LAST SIGHTINGS
VC65: 24/07 **1** Swinithwaite *D Fearnley, P Millard & A Rhodes*
VC65: 24/07 **1** Morpeth Scar, W Burton *D Fearnley et al.*
VC64: 08/08 **1** near Kilnsey *Paul Millard*

Brown Argus Aricia agestis Tim Melling

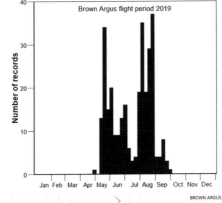

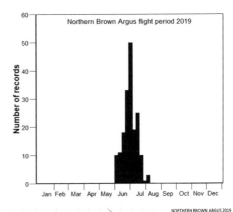

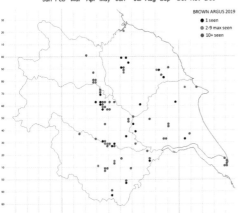

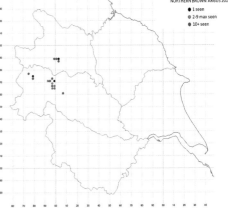

STATISTICS 2019

Brown Argus
Monthly: flight days (total butterflies)
countywide: Apr **1** (10), May **16** (175), Jun **19** (153), Jul **14** (77), Aug **27** (384), Sep **12** (32).
Total flight days/flight season length: **89/** 155 days.
Total reports (total butterflies) **a) countywide: 295** (831) = mean **2.82** butterflies per observation.
b) by VC: VC61: **63** (126), VC62: **19** (67), VC63: **102** (294), VC64: **71** (246), VC65: **40** (98).
Tetrads recorded (i.e., 2x2km OS grid squares): **85** out of 1510 visited and 4120 in Yorkshire.

Northern Brown Argus
Monthly: flight days (total butterflies)
countywide: Jun **13** (462), Jul **14** (294), Aug **3** (5).
Total flight days/flight season length: **30/** 64 days.
Total reports (total butterflies) **a) countywide: 180** (761) = mean **4.23** butterflies per observation.
b) by VC: VC64: **176** (750), VC65: 4 (11).
Tetrads recorded (i.e., 2x2km OS grid squares): **17** out of 1510 visited and 4120 in Yorkshire.

Morpeth Scar Swinithwaite VC65 Paul Millard

61.018 Common Blue *Polyommatus icarus* (Rottemburg 1775)

Broods: 1 to 3. (2nd & 3rd are often partial and usually only on lower land. Spring and summer broods may overlap. Complicated variability according to weather, height and latitude.) Fairly widespread resident on suitable grasslands with Bird's-foot-trefoil.

Yorkshire 2019: Although records of this delightful butterfly remained healthy in 2019, the second highest of the last decade (and a new high in VC65), numbers did not follow suit. These dropped 25% on 2018, being the sixth best of the last decade. The mean count per record was the lowest for which I have data (since 2005). Since the 2012 crash, mean counts per record have only once (in 2015) attained the minimum of the previous seven years, and are suggestive of a decline in the abundance of this species in Yorkshire over the last 15 years. There were again few large counts, although two of 500+ at Duck Street Quarry, Greenhow, must have been very beautiful experiences. Phenologically it was an unremarkable year with no April records and just a single October record, and second generations strongest in VC61 and VC63 as usual, though present in all VCs. *Peter Mayhew*

FIRST SIGHTINGS

VC62: 02/05 **1** Goathland *Wilf Norman*
VC61: 11/05 **1** Thorngumbald *M Bruce & P Bursell*
VC63: 12/05 **1** Hob Hill, Stanbury *David Dodsworth*
VC64: 13/05 **1** Ripon *Jeremy Dunford*
VC64: 13/05 **1** Lin Dyke Link *Rachael Tulloch*
VC64: 13/05 **3** Lin Dyke Link *Rachael Tulloch*
VC64: 13/05 **1** Staveley West *Angela Ponsford*
VC65: 15/05 **1** Scotton *Patricia Illingworth*

PEAK COUNTS 1st Brood

VC65: 22/05 **19** Thornborough *Mike Barnham*
VC61: 01/06 **28** Spurn NNR *Christine & Howard Frost*
VC63: 18/06 **59** Littleworth Park, Barnsley *Chris Parkin*
VC62: 03/07 **27** Spaunton Qu *Dave O'Brien*
VC64: 16/07 **691** Duck Street Qu *Mike Barnham*

PEAK COUNTS 2nd Brood

VC62: 01/08 **3** Langdale Forest *Ian & Pauline Popely*
VC62: 03/08 **3** Strensall Common *Terry Crawford*
VC65: 03/08 **7** Nosterfield LNR *Steve Worwood*
VC63: 08/08 **77** Littleworth Park, Barnsley *Chris Parkin*
VC61: 13/08 **38** Kilnsey Wetlands *Howard Frost*
VC64: 24/08 **25** Harewood Whin, Rufforth *Martin Roberts*

Common Blue Raindale 2 July 2019 Peter Mayhew

LAST SIGHTINGS

VC62: 05/09 **2** Dalby Heckdale *Ian & Pauline Popely*
VC65: 17/09 **1** Leyburn Old Glebe *Jennie White*
VC64: 20/09 **2** St Aidan's RSPB *P Morris*
VC61: 21/09 **1** North Cave Wetlands *Paul Ashton*
VC63: 02/10 **1** Littleworth Pk, Barnsley *Chris Parkin*

STATISTICS 2019

Monthly: flight days (total butterflies) **countywide:** May **22** (347), Jun **28** (1,375), Jul **27** (2,523), Aug **31** (1,548), Sep **20** (287), Oct **1** (1).
Total flight days/flight season length: **129/ 154** days.
Total reports (total butterflies) **a) countywide: 1,146** (6,081) = mean **5.31** butterflies per observation. **b) by VC: VC61: 211** (886), **VC62: 67** (184), **VC63: 342** (2,037), **VC64: 419** (2,749), **VC65: 107** (225).
Tetrads recorded (i.e., 2x2km OS grid squares): **262** out of 1510 visited and 4120 in Yorkshire.

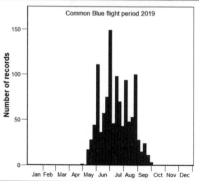

Common Blue flight period 2019

Exotic and Rare Species 2019 (not listed elsewhere)

Every few years or so Camberwell Beauty *Nymphalis antiopa* are seen in Yorkshire. This is a very mobile hibernating species not known to breed in the wild in the UK. This remains a rare but regular immigrant from central or southern Europe (usually June/July sightings) and Scandinavia (usually Aug/Sept sightings), though particular weather patterns can trump these assumptions. In the last decade (2019-2009) there have been a number of reports: one in 2016 (plausible but not confirmed) and one in 2014, two in 2013, two in 2011, and one in 2010. This year we had two sightings. A Camberwell Beauty (invariably sightings are of single butterflies) was seen in Victoria Dock, east Hull (VC61) on July 11th by Dominic Henri. The prevailing wind direction in the preceding days

Camberwell Beauty Victoria Dock Dominic Henri.

was from the south-east (9th July) and south-west (10/11th July). The butterfly was in a Damson tree near unmanaged green space. The Hull dock area is associated with this butterfly with some arguing that imported wood from Finland could be the source. This is increasingly unlikely these days with the pre-processing (sawing, chemical treatment, plastic shrink wrapping) of wood happening abroad before it comes to the UK having become much more common practice. Another sighting was from Beverley (VC61) via twitter with photo provided (identifier details withheld). The exact date is unclear (22nd Aug or few days before). There was a report of a Swallowtail on the 'Sunday Gardening on BBC Radio Leeds' Facebook page with a clear photograph (identifier details withheld). The butterfly was seen in Harrogate (VC64) on 13th August and appeared to be the Continental Swallowtail *Papilio machaon* subsp. *gorganus* because of the thinner veiling and generally less intense markings. The British subspecies *Papilio machaon* subsp. *britannicus* is much more sedentary and restricted to the Norfolk Broads, has broader veining and more intense colouring, and the adults fly late May into early July with only a partial second emergence in August in warm years. There was a sighting by Graham Lowe at Hornsea (VC61) on the 9th September of a female *Dryas iulia* (the Julia butterfly), a species of brush-footed butterfly resident

Long-tailed Blue Bentley Doncaster 9th Sept 2019 via MickTownsend

in Brazil, central America and the southern USA. This is a species popular with Butterfly Houses being both long-lived and very active. This will have likely been an escapee from the Bugtopia Butterfly House at Hornsea freeport. (Photo page 131)

Finally, there was a report and hardcopy photo of a Long-tailed Blue *Lampides boeticus* found in a conservatory in Bentley near Doncaster (VC63). The sighting was passed on by Mick Townsend. The sighting date was sometime between 2nd-9th September. There was a significant influx of Long-tailed Blue in the south of England in the last weeks of August 2019 (with some 50 or so records of adults seen flying in the southern counties bordering the English Channel from Cornwall to Kent), with one sighting from Glamorgan, south Wales. The Doncaster record could be the most northerly sighting of the influx seen in 2019 in the UK, as well as being a first for Yorkshire. **David Smith**

Exotic species cover escapees from butterfly houses, accidental imports with fruit and vegetables, or other deliveries from outside the area of the British Isles. Rare species are any which are not currently listed each year in our Report. If you see or hear of any exotic specimens being seen, or if you come across a rare species (like Essex Skipper on a new site, or a rarity such as Swallowtail, Camberwell Beauty, or anything else not recorded in our Report annually), we would very much appreciate it if you could fill up a Rare Species Record Form to enable us to archive a full record of your sighting. Forms are available from your regional VC Co-ordinator, County Recorder or from the Yorkshire Branch website and can be transmitted electronically. Please see back of the Report for addresses. If at all possible exotic and rarity reports should be accompanied by any photos taken or by a scan of any field notes and diagrams made at the time.

Section 3. Macro Moths (the larger moths plus Pyralids)

PYRALOIDEA
PYRALIDAE

62.002 *Lamoria zelleri* (Joannis)
This moth first appeared in 2012 at Spurn, from
which area all subsequent records have come.
These are the first occurrences away from there.
61. Muston, 23.7.2019 (PQW); Hollym Carrs, 4.8.2019 (MCo).

62.021 *Oncocera semirubella* (Scopoli)
This distinctive moth seems to be spreading
northwards; it was also recorded for the first time in
Nottinghamshire during the year. It is also said to be
an occasional immigrant and the fact that both these
moths occurred on the same date might point to
immigration as their origin, we may never know!
62. Haxby, 26.7.2019 (TJC). NEW VC RECORD.
65. Semerwater, 26.7.2019 (CHF, JCW, DMS, TMW). NEW COUNTY RECORD.

62.021 *Oncocera semirubella* Semerwater 26 Jul 19
Charles Fletcher new for Yorkshire.

62.025 *Dioryctria sylvestrella* (Ratzeburg)
Since 2005 this moth has occurred in small numbers in vice-counties 61 to 64. The VC62 record is
from the same locality which provided the first in VC62 in 2018.
61. Easington, 10.7.2019 (MFS).
62. Sunbeck Wood, Brafferton Spring, 25.8.2019 (TAB).

62.032 *Nephopterix angustella* (Hübner)
We have two previous records, both in VC61, in 2010 & 2017. It is uncertain whether these are
immigrants or come from resident populations in the south of England.
61. North Ferriby, 29.7.2019 (IM); Kilnsea, 13.9.2019 (MA).

62.050 *Euzophera cinerosella* (Zeller)
Locally common in the extreme south of VC63 although seen rather less frequently during the past few
years. Otherwise there are three records in VC61 and one in VC65; it remains unrecorded in VC62.
64. Alwoodley, Leeds, 18 & 22.7.2019 (PRM). NEW VC RECORD.

62.053 *Ancylosis oblitella* (Zeller)
A mainly immigrant moth, there is a single previous record at Spurn in 1996.
61. Easington, three on 25.8.2019, moths seen on 26 & 27.8.2019 may be re-trapped individuals
from the 25th (MFS).

62.060 *Vitula serratilineella* (Ragonot) = *edmandsii* sensu auct.
The second county record, the first at Spurn in 1997 was the first in the British Isles. It was
subsequently found to be resident in Northumberland.
61. Easington, indoors 31.8.2019 gen. det. HEB (BRS).

62.062 *Plodia interpunctella* (Hübner)
This cosmopolitan pest of stored foodstuffs is probably under recorded as it is seldom encountered
outdoors. Widely recorded in small numbers it has been seen more frequently in 2019. There is
presently no record from VC65.
62. Pickering, indoors 23.7.2019 (LW); North Ferriby, indoors 6.8.2019 (IM); Tollerton, 23.8.2019
(MB); York, in bag of sunflower seeds 22.8, 22 & 30.9.2019 (BB).
63. Sheffield, 23.2.2019 (RFu); Potteric Carr NR, in stored bird seed 2 & 6.4.2019 (per RI&JCH).
64. Menston, 17.6.2019 (P&KL); Rodley NR, 2019 (PM).

62.077 *Endotricha flammealis* ([Denis & Schiffermüller])
First seen in Yorkshire in 1991; over the past twenty years it has become a common moth over most
of the county and has now reached the far north-west.
65. Hutton Conyers, 25 & 29.7.2019 (CHF). NEW VC RECORD.

CRAMBIDAE

63.002 *Loxostege sticticalis* (Linnaeus)
An immigrant moth, irregular in appearance; it has occurred most often in the Spurn area of VC61 although there are records from all five Yorkshire vice-counties. In some years it has been quite numerous but this is the first in Yorkshire since 2012.
61. Stillingfleet Lodge, 3.8.2019 (DBa).

63.005 *Pyrausta despicata* (Scopoli)
This is a quite widespread, although local, moth within the county. However, surprisingly, the only previous VC62 record is provided by an undated manuscript entry for Buttercrambe by Arthur Smith (d. 1957) of York in his copy of *Porritt* (1904).
62. Scarborough, 25.7 & 4.8.2019 (L&JW).

63.005 *Pyrausta despicata*, Scarborough
Jax Westmoreland 25 Jul 19 second for VC62

63.008 *P. ostrinalis* (Hübner)
Frequent in the Yorkshire Dales but with an increased number of records in 2019. Otherwise there are only one or two records each in the four remaining vice-counties and all date from the 19th century.
64. Kilnsey, 6.6 to 8.7.2019 (ARh, PM); Arncliffe, 29.6.2019 (PMi); Dib Scar, 11.7.2019 (DM, LWi); Bastow Wood, Grassington, 4.8.2019; Kettlewell, 8.8.2019 (PMi); Strans Wood, Yockenthwaite, 15.8.2019 (PMi, ARh, DF).

63.014 *Sitochroa palealis* ([Denis & Schiffermüller])
There have been several occurrences in vice-counties 61 to 63 in recent years but this is the only one in 2019 and from a new locality.
63. Old Moor RSPB reserve, 14.7.2019 (UR).

63.015 *S. verticalis* (Linnaeus)
The single previous county record was in VC61 in 1939.
63. West Melton, 25.6.2019 (HEB). NEW VC RECORD.

63.028 *Ostrinia nubilalis* (Hübner)
This moth is an immigrant or wanderer from populations further south in Britain. In recent years it has occurred quite regularly most years in VC61, additionally there are single records from vice-counties 64 & 65. This is the only one in 2019.
61. Lund, 27.7.2019 (MCo).

63.048 *Palpita vitrealis* (Rossi)
This formerly scarce immigrant moth has become much more frequent since 2012 and now occurs almost annually.
61. Hollym Carrs, 4.8.2019 (MCo).
64. Sharow, 21.9.2019 (JCW).

63.048 *Palpita vitrealis* Sharow 21 Sept 19
Jill Warwick one of only two in the county this year

63.054 Box Moth *Cydalima perspectalis* (Walker)
This moth is a major pest of Box plants and is spreading rapidly northwards. It first appeared in York-shire in 2014 with three further records in 2017. Although the defoliating larvae have yet to be found in Yorkshire the increase in records during 2019 suggests that it will not be long before they occur.
61. Leconfield, 11.7.2019 (R&HC); North Ferriby, 25.7.2019 (IM); Kilnsea, 23.9.2019 (JHF) & 25.9.2019 (JCr).
62. Huntington, York, 29.6.2019 (AF); Romanby, 4.8.2019 (AM); Scarborough, 12.9.2019 (AR).
63. Cudworth, 5.7.2019 det. HEB (from photo) (CG); Sprotbrough, 15.7.2019 (DBo); Sheffield, 3.8.2019 (UR); Fishlake, 25.9.2019 (RP).
64. Harrogate, 27.7.2019 (RB); Wetherby, 3.9.2019 (UR).

63.058 *Evergestis extimalis* (Scopoli)
As an immigrant or wanderer from further south this moth occurs most years in coastal areas of vice-

counties 61 & 62.

61. Kilnsea, 16 & 17.7.2019 (JCr).

62. South Gare, 15.7.2019 (IE); Skelton, 26.7.2019 (DM).

63.065 *Scoparia ancipitella* (La Harpe)

There are several 19th century records, after
which no more were recorded until 1990. It
has since been found very infrequently in vice-
counties 62 to 64.

64. Guisecliffe Woods, 19.7.2019 gen. det. (CHF, JCW).

63.076 *Euchromius ocellea* (Haworth)

A scarce and irregular immigrant with four previous
county records; three in VC61 and an inland occurrence in VC63 in 1985. These two records from adjacent localities in 2019 may refer to the same individual.

63.087 *Crambus hamella* York 27 Aug 19
Alastair Fitter. Third for VC62

61. Kilnsea, 10.7.2019 (JHF); Easington, 11.7.2019 det. BRS (MFS).

63.087 *Crambus hamella* (Thunberg)

Most frequently seen in VC63 with a few records in VC61. There are only two previous VC62
occurrences, the most recent in 1956. Unrecorded in the more northerly vice-counties of 64 & 65.

62. Huntington, York, 27.8.2019 gen. det. RWo (AF).

63.100 *Catoptria margaritella* ([Denis & Schiffermüller])

This inhabitant of boggy moorland is frequent in vice-counties 62 to 65 and occurs less often on the
lower ground in vice-counties 61 & 63. The numbers seen at Semerwater in 2019 were exceptional.

65. Semerwater, in excess of 3000 on 26.7.2019 (CHF, JCW, DMS, TMW).

63.112 *Platytes alpinella* (Hübner)

In recent years this moth has occurred regularly inland in the south of VC63 as well as in coastal
areas of VC61. The York record is an indication of a wider distribution.

61. Kilnsea, 18 & 19.7 & 27.8.2019 (JHF); Wheldrake, 25.7.2019 (JOHS).

62. Huntington, York, 24.7.2019 (AF). NEW VC RECORD.

63. Thorne Moors, 29.7.2019 (MWa *et al.*)

63.120 *Schoenobius gigantella* ([Denis & Schiffermüller])

Since 2013 this moth has occurred annually and in increasing numbers in the south of Yorkshire but
is presently restricted to localities in vice-counties 61 & 63.

61. Tophill Low NR, 28.6 & 12.7.2019 (MHo, GF); North Ferriby, 4,5 & 10.7 & 28.8.2019 (IM); Lower
Derwent Valley, 20.7.2019 (CSR); Lund, 25.7.2019 (MCo); Spurn NNR., 27.6 & 6.7.2019 (MFS).

63. Barnsley, 15.7.2018 (JW); Austerfield, 1.6.2019 (SB); Potteric Carr NR, 1 & 29.6, 5 & 24.7.2019
(RI&JCH, HEB); Blacktoft Sands, 26.7.2019 (MJP).

DREPANOIDEA
DREPANIDAE

65.002 Oak Hook-tip *Watsonalla binaria* (Hufnagel)

This species seems to be in long-term decline. After healthier numbers in 2018, 2019 brought a
return to the normal low numbers.

61. North Cliffe Wood, 31.5.2019 (IM, ADN); Kilnwick, 25.7.2019 (MCo); Tophill Low NR, 23.8.2019
(MHo, DF); Hunmanby Gap, 4.9.2019 (KC).

62. Strensall Village, 30.5, 12.7 & 5.8.2019 (YB); Great Smeaton, 25.7.2019 (JE); Strensall Common,
29.7 & 1.8.2019 (YB); Wykeham Causeway, 29.7.2019 (AR, JHo); Romanby, 4.8.2019 (AM).

63. Austerfield, several dates (SB); West Melton, 24.7, 10 & 21.8.2019 (HEB); Pledwick, Wakefield,
25.7.2019 (MHe); Fishlake, 17.8.2019 (RP); Carlton, 23.8.2019 (DSm).

64. Tadcaster, 3.8.2019 (AAl); Askham Bryan, 5.8.2019 (DLa).

65.003 Barred Hook-tip *W. cultraria* (Fabricius)

An average year for this moth of beech woodland.

61. Lund, 1.6.2019 (DA).

62. Broxa Forest, 18.7.2019 (AR, JHo); Adderstone Wood (Dalby), 31.7.2019 (SF).
64. Coniston Cold, 6, 21, 23 & 24.8.2019 (ARh); Skyreholme, 27.8.2019 (PMi); Alwoodley, 30.8.2019 (PRM); Pateley Bridge, 23.8.2019 (T&PB).

65.011 Poplar Lutestring *Tethea or* ([Denis & Schiffermüller])
This species has a very localised population in parts of VC62 and we receive on average one record per year. This record is encouragingly from a new site. The nearest populations are in Lincolnshire and Cumbria.
62. Wykeham Causeway, 28.7.2019 (AR, JHo).

65.013 Common Lutestring *Ochropacha duplaris* (Linnaeus)
A big drop in numbers this year means that we should list all 29 records. These are the lowest numbers for many years.
61. North Cliffe Wood., 29.6 & 28.7.2019 (DA, JMo); Rudston, 19.7.2019 (HEB).
62. Skelton, 18.6.2019 (DM); Moorsholm, 2.7.2019 (SF); Clay Bank Plantation, 10.7.2019 (SF); Wykeham Causeway, 14 & 30.7, 2.8.2019 (AR, JHo, SF, RWo, JH, AWr); Low Dalby, 24.7.2019 (JW); Scarborough, 21.8.2019 (L&JW).
63. Carlton Marsh NR, 28.6.2019 (HEB, CG et al.); Hatfield Moors, 16.7 & 15.8.2019 (HEB, DWi); Lindholme, 16.7.2019 (P&JS); West Melton, 1.8.2019 (HEB).
64. Brimham Rocks, 21.6.2019 (CHF); Baildon, 14 & 28.7, 2.8.2019 (JG); Little Preston, 22.7.2019 (JMa); Dob Park, 22.7.2019 (CGH); Askham Bog, 25.7.2019 (AF, TJC, YB, NH); Alwoodley, 27.7.2019 (PRM).

65.014 Oak Lutestring *Cymatophorina diluta* ([Denis & Schiffermüller])
An exciting record of this rare species from the Bowland area in the extreme west of VC64; the first in the county since 1996. The main population in the north of England is in north Lancashire and south Cumbria, so this indicates a slight expansion to the south-east. It has declined over much of the country.
64. New Laithe Farm, 24.8.2019 (MB).

LASIOCAMPOIDEA
LASIOCAMPIDAE

66.002 Pale Eggar *Trichiura crataegi* (Linnaeus)
This continues to be an uncommon moth in the county although numbers were up a little this year and encouragingly there were records from three new sites.
61. Muston, 25.8.2019 (PQW); Newton Upon Derwent, 26.8.2019 (IRH).
62. Great Smeaton, 9, 22, 26, 27 & 30.8.2019 (JE); Tollerton, 25.8.2019 (MBe); Great Barugh, 26.8.2019 (PC).
63. Austerfield, 17 & 21.8.2019 (SB).
64. Tadcaster, 3.8.2019 (AAl); Bellflask, 18.8.2019 (BM); Mickley, 25.8.2019 (CHF, JCW. JH, FC).
65. Healey, 17.8.2019 (DMS, IW).

66.003 Lackey *Malacosoma neustria* (Linnaeus)
84 records of 126 moths represents a further increase in numbers but still significantly fewer than 10 to 20 years ago. Records came from 23 sites, all in the south-eastern quarter of the county.

66.005 Small Eggar *Eriogaster lanestris* (Linnaeus)
A major survey for larval webs in June produced records from an amazing 80 sites in the usual Malton/Pickering area with some spread into two new 10K squares. From a national perspective, our population is very important and this study may throw some light on its habitat requirements and be able to suggest better hedgerow management.
62. Pickering/Malton area, 80 records of larval webs 4.5 to 26.6.2019 (SN); south of Kirkbymoorside, larval webs 14.6.2019 (TWr).

66.008 Fox Moth *Macrothylacia rubi* (Linnaeus)
42 records of 49 moths or larvae represents another good year and there are too many records to list individually. The 17 records of adults were nearly all from light traps and were mostly (but not all) females, as the males are less common at light. Records came from all the usual upland areas of the county and several of our lowland heaths. There were unusually no records from VC65.

BOMBYCOIDEA
SATURNIIDAE

68.001 Emperor Moth *Saturnia pavonia* (Linnaeus)
We used to receive few records of this species and list them all, but the outstandingly successful

pheromone lure which is now currently available has revolutionised recording of this spectacular moth. Over half of the 90 records we received this year were of adult males coming to pheromones, and there were probably more as not everyone logged the method. There were seven records of females at light and five of larvae in July and August. Records came from all the usual upland areas and lowland heaths across all five vice-counties. Summer sightings of adults put on iRecord were invariably of Emperor Dragonfly!

SPHINGIDAE

69.004 Convolvulus Hawk-moth *Agrius convolvuli* (Linnaeus)
Another poor year for this spectacular migrant moth. All records except for one were from coastal areas.
61. Driffield, 2.9.2019 (J&JL); Spurn, 12 & 25.9.2019 (MA, JHF); Easington (Spurn), 21 & 22.9.2019 (MFS).
62. Scarborough, 15.8.2019 (KCo); Beck Hole (Whitby), 25.9.2019 (AJ).
65. Masham, 2.10.2019 (UR).

69.005 Death's-head Hawk-moth *Acherontia atropos* (Linnaeus)
Of the Spurn records, one came to light and one was found the following day along the narrow neck. The larva at Guisborough was found on a path close to a large patch of bittersweet.
61. Spurn, 1 & 2.6.2019 (MFS, UR).
62. Guisborough, larva on 3.9.2019 (BMc).

69.006 Privet Hawk-moth *Sphinx ligustri* (Linnaeus)
It is nice to be able to say that we have too many records of Privet Hawk-moth to list individually. We received 40 records of 50 moths from 15 sites, all in VC61, the eastern part of VC63 and the south of VC62. Seven of these were new sites so it appears to be well established in the south-east of the county.

69.007 Pine Hawk-moth *S. pinastri* (Linnaeus)
This is another species where we normally list all records but we received record numbers in 2019 with 42 records of 49 moths from 26 sites. Six were from new sites. It has been a year of consolidation rather than spread, though the situation is looking particularly healthy in the south of VC62.

69.010 Humming-bird Hawk-moth *Macroglossum stellatarum* (Linnaeus)
At the time of writing we were aware of 148 records of 154 moths from 86 sites all across the county though these numbers are always swollen considerably when we eventually receive records from all the on-line schemes. The first record on 27th February was unusual but was likely to be a migrant rather than an over-wintering moth as it arrived during a very warm spell with southerly winds. The last one was in Ripon on 20th October but the main wave arrived in June and July. Nectaring was most common on buddleia but was also noted on red valerian, lavender, viper's bugloss, verbena and honeysuckle.

69.014 Bedstraw Hawk-moth *Hyles gallii* (Rottemburg)
After a blank year in 2018, a total of eight records of this spectacular migrant made 2019 a much better year, with records dotted all over the county.
61. Stillingfleet Lodge, 3.8.2019 (DBa); Catwick, 7.8.2019 (JM); Easington (Spurn), 2.9.2019 (GFr).
62. Cayton (Scarborough), 3.8.2019 (PJD).
63. Oxenhope, 29.7.2019 (DBu).
65. Hutton Conyers, 29.7 & 4.8.2019 (CHF); Scorton, larva 14.10.2019 (CNi).

69.014 Bedstraw Hawk-moth VC 61 David Baker   69.006 Privet Hawk-moth VC 61 Mike Smethurst

GEOMETROIDEA
GEOMETRIDAE

70.002 Purple-bordered Gold *Idaea muricata* (Hufnagel)
Healthy numbers were noted by day from various sites on Thorne Moors with a record total of 25 moths reported. This marsh cinquefoil-feeding species is very local in the country with widely scattered populations.
63. Thorne Moors, 12.6 to 8.7.2019 (MWa et al.).

70.004 Least Carpet *I. rusticata* ([Denis & Schiffermüller])
A large increase in numbers accompanied by considerable spread in its range to northern VC62, the west of VC63 and into VC64. Other species which have undergone rapid spread sometimes contract back for a period of consolidation before further expansion and it will be interesting to see whether this happens with Least Carpet.

70.004 Least Carpet 1 Aug 19 Peter Riley first for VC64

61. Easington (Spurn), 21 moths from 24.7 to 4.8.2019 (MFS); Spurn, 7 moths from 25 to 29.7.2019 (JHF, JCr, MA); Hunmanby Gap, 26 & 27.7.2019 (NC, KC); Flamborough, 27.7.2019 (MiP).
62. Skelton, 31.7.2019 (DM). NEW VC RECORD.
63. Kirk Smeaton, 25.7.2019 (DWi); Pledwick, Wakefield, 25.7.2019 (MHe); Luddenden, 27.7.2019 (MHy).
64. Burley-in-Wharfedale, 1.8.2019 (P&AR). NEW VC RECORD.

70.006 Dwarf Cream Wave *I. fuscovenosa* (Goeze)
65 records of 123 moths from 15 sites is a healthy total. As usual nearly all the records were from the Spurn area and from the south-east of VC63 though there was one further up the coast at Muston where it is fairly regular.

70.015 Small Scallop *I. emarginata* (Linnaeus)
This is typically a moth of damp heathy areas where the larvae feed on bedstraws. It is perhaps surprising that it had never been seen before in VC64. Our populations are the most northerly in the country.
62. Strensall Common, 7.7.2019 (YB).
63. Austerfield, 8 & 16.7.2019 (SB); Crowle Moor, 11.7.2019 (DWi); Hatfield Moors, 16.7.2019 (DWi).
64. Askham Bog, 8.7.2019 (AF, TJC, PMa et al.). NEW VC RECORD.

70.018 Plain Wave *I. straminata* (Borkhausen)
This species continues to be confused with the unbanded form of Riband Wave and we cannot be certain that all the records in our database are correct. It is a little unkind of us to demand a photo for every record so we tend to query those from new areas or from inexperienced observers. When identifying this species, try not just to rely solely on the degree of "kinking" of the outer cross line which can be tricky on worn specimens but also look for the smooth silky appearance of Plain Wave and the pattern of dashes at the end of the wings rather than the dots and dashes of Riband Wave. Plain Wave is locally common for example on some of our lowland heaths, and quite rare in gardens.
62. Strensall Common, 7, 8 & 16.7.2019 (YB, PMa); Haxby, 9, 22 & 24.7.2019 (TJC); Broxa, 12.7.2019 (GF); Low Dalby, 24.7.2019 (JW); Brompton, 26.7.2019 (AR, JHo); Wykeham Causeway, 2.8.2019 (SF).
63. Balby, 23 & 24.6.2019 (PG); Sprotbrough, 17.7.2019 (DBo); Austerfield, 25.7.2019 (SB); Potteric Carr NR, 7.8.2019 (RI&JCH).
64. Little Preston, 25, 26, 27 & 29.7.2019 (JMa); Bellflask, 25.8.2019 (BM).

70.023 Mullein Wave *Scopula marginepunctata* (Goeze)
A scarce moth with all 13 county records coming from VC61, usually from the Spurn area.
61. Spurn, 12.7.2019 (JHF).

70.025 Lesser Cream Wave *S. immutata* (Linnaeus)
Records from some of its regular sites. A rather local moth which is often misidentified.
61. Spurn, 30.6.2019 (JHF).
63. Austerfield, 10, 20, 24 & 25.7.2019 (SB); Hatfield Moors, 16.7.2019 (DWi).

70.026 Smoky Wave *S. ternata* (Schrank)

A good year with records from typical upland areas, mostly of adults seen by day. The Ilkley record of 31st May was the earliest ever and was confirmed with a good photograph.

62. Fen Bog, 28.6, 12 & 15.7.2019 (GF, PMa); Hole of Horcum, 12.7.2019 (PMa); Tranmire Bog, 23.7.2019 (DA); Cropton Forest, 23.7.2019 (PA).
63. Keighley Moor, 9 & 10.6.2019 (IHa).
64. Ilkley, 31.5 & 8.7.2019 (P&JB); Brimham Rocks, 21.6.2019 (CHF et al); Dib Scar, 2.7.2019 (PMi); Bastow Wood, 7.7.2019 (PMi, LWi).

70.027 Cream Wave 18 May 19 Haxby T J Crawford

70.027 Cream Wave *S. floslactata* (Haworth)

We receive a lot of records of this species and find a lot are misidentifications for other "Waves", particularly those records from July onwards. It is a woodland moth, often seen by day and not likely to be seen in gardens. For new sites, inexperienced recorders and moths flying late in the season we need a photo to confirm this species.

61. Spurn, 12, 15 and 25.7.2019 (JHF); Skipwith Common, 17.7.2019 (NC, SC).
62. Haxby, 18.5.2019 (TJC); Glaisdale, 27.5.2019 (GF); Turkey Carpet, 21.6.2019 (SF).
63. Haw Park, 1.6.2019 (PSm et al.); Austerfield, 1.6 & 20.7.2019 (SB).
64. Bishop Wood, 21 & 22.5.2019 (CM, SB).

70.028 Rosy Wave *S. emutaria* (Hübner)

The new Atlas tells us that there is a thriving population at Spurn. Unfortunately, it can no longer be described as thriving, as for the second year in a row numbers were very low.

61. Spurn, 22.6, 9, 11, 12 & 27.7.2019 (MFS, JHF).

70.032 Birch Mocha *Cyclophora albipunctata* (Hufnagel)

A typical year for this moth of heathy areas with lots of birch. Market Weighton is a new site.

61. Market Weighton, 3.6.2019 (PA).
62. Strensall Common, 25.5, 19 & 29.6 & 27.8.2019 (YB); Broxa, 12.7.2019 (GF).
63. Thorne Moors, 18 & 29.5.2019 (RM); Hatfield Moors, 16.7.2019 (HEB).

70.036 Maiden's Blush *C. punctaria* (Linnaeus)

The dramatic rise in numbers of records seems to have stalled and as expected there was a slight reduction this year to 69 records of 84 moths from 33 sites. There were several new sites at the periphery of the range such as Sheffield, Pontefract and Brafferton, but no real expansion this year. It is likely that it is biding its time before another expansion in the next few years.

70.037 Clay Triple-lines *C. linearia* (Hübner)

A poor year with only 14 records of 17 moths, so the lowest totals since 2012. Four sites however were new so it is likely that it is more widespread than these records suggest. Nationally it certainly seems to be doing well.

62. Wykeham Causeway, 23.6 & 30.7.2019 (AR, JHo); Strensall Common, 24.6.2019 (YB); Strensall Village, 24.6.2019 (YB); Bickley Gate, 30.6.2019 (AR, JHo); Scarborough, 10.7.2019 (L&JW); Low Dalby, 16.7.2019 (JW); Brafferton Spring Wood, 25.8.2019 (TAB).
63. Kirk Smeaton, 24.6.2019 (P&JS); Sprotbrough, 11.7.2019 (DBo); Brockadale NR, 18.7.2019 (P&JS).
64. Nether Poppleton, 16.7.2019 (D&HT); Alwoodley, 25.7.2019 (RWi).
65. Healey, 24.7.2019 (DMS, IW).

70.038 Vestal *Rhodometra sacraria* (Linnaeus)

A good year for this attractive migrant species after a blank year in 2018.

61. Hunmanby Gap, 10.7.2019 (KC); Easington (Spurn), 14, 17 & 23.8.2019 (MFS); Spurn, 14.10.2019 (JHF).
62. Haxby, 23 & 24.8.2019 (TJC).
63. Fishlake, 27.8.2019 (RP).
64. Menston, 2.7.2019 (CGH); Sharow, 22.9.2019 (JCW).
65. Scotton, Catterick, 5.6.2019 (MSa); Worton, 7.7.2019 (WS); Healey, 21.9.2019 (DMS, IW).

70.041 July Belle *Scotopteryx luridata* (Hufnagel)
A very local moth of heathy areas. It is surprising that it has never been recorded at Strensall before.
62. Strensall, 5.8.2019 (YB).
65. Foxglove Covert, 18.6.2019 (FCMT).

70.043 Chalk Carpet *S. bipunctaria* ([Denis & Schiffermüller])
A very encouraging set of records from its usual site which include the earliest records ever in the county. The usual flight time is July and August but our Flamborough moths (confirmed by photographs) emerged remarkably early this year.
61. Flamborough, eight records of nine moths from 23.5 to 22.7.2019 (AAI).

70.046 Oblique Carpet *Orthonama vittata* (Borkhausen)
The stronghold of this moth of wet areas is in the Lower Derwent Valley, but it is being found increasingly in more upland western parts of the county.
61. Wheldrake, 33 records of 52 moths from 29.5 to 9.9.2019 (JOHS); Lower Derwent Valley, 13 records of 26 moths from 29.5 to 29.9.2019 (CSR, NC, SC); Elvington, 25.8.2019 (JSm).
62. Newtondale, 17.6.2019 (SF).
64. Coniston Cold, 4.6, 5 & 22.8.2019 (ARh); Askham Bog, 23.8.2019 (AF); West Bradford, 1.6.2019 (BH); New Laithe Farm, 26.6.2019 (MBr).
65. Semerwater, 26.6.2019 (CHF, JCW, DSm, TMW).

70.048 Red Carpet *Xanthorhoe decoloraria* (Esper)
Records from typical areas in the west of VC64 and 65.
64. Malham Tarn, 25.7.2019 (DCGB); Near Thruscross, 1.8.2019 (CGH); Grass Wood, 3.8.2019 (PMi).
65. Lartington, 24.7.2019 (PWe).

70.060 Small Argent and Sable *Epirrhoe tristata* (Linnaeus)
Scattered records from typical upland areas with plenty of heath bedstraw.
62. Fen Bog, 28.6 & 12.7.2019 (GF, PMa); Stony Moor, 2.7.2019 (PMa).
65. Redmire - Apedale, 2.6.2019 (UR).

70.062 Wood Carpet *E. rivata* (Hübner)
This moth is easily confused with the smaller Common Carpet. If you record it from a new site, we need to see a picture and importantly we need to know the forewing length as it is significantly larger than Common Carpet. There are no consistent differences between the genitalia of either sex so dissection is no help. Very local in VC61 and 63.
61. North Frodingham, 27.6.2019 (AAI).

70.063 Galium Carpet *E. galiata* ([Denis & Schiffermüller])
Records from the usual upland western fringes of the county and from Flamborough. The Flamborough moths are cut off from the larger population in the Pennines by 60-70 miles.
61. Flamborough, 21 & 26.6, 11.7.2019 (AAI).
63. Golcar, 24.8.2019 (CSR).
64. Ingleborough NR,18.6.2019 (TMW, JP); Moughton, 23.7.2019 (TMW).

70.068 Beautiful Carpet *Mesoleuca albicillata* (Linnaeus)
A poor year for this attractive woodland moth. It only every appears in small numbers but the population may be larger than we think as it is not strongly attracted to light.
61. North Cliffe Wood, 5.7.2019 (IM, ADN).
62. Wykeham Causeway, 23.6.2019 (AR, JHo); Broxa, 12.7.2019 (GF).
63. Austerfield, 10.7.2019 (SB); Haw Park, 25.7.2019 (PSm et al.).
65. Foxglove Covert, 16.7.2019 (FCMT).

70.069 Dark Spinach *Pelurga comitata* (Linnaeus)
The smallest number of records since 1997 and the third very poor year in a row. It has declined over much of the country, particularly in the Midlands, and this could be linked to changes in land use resulting in a loss of weedy areas with goosefoots and oraches.
61. Market Weighton, 11.7 & 17.8.2019 (PA); North Frodingham, 31.7.2019 (AAI); North Cliffe Wood, 8.8.2019 (IM, ADN).
62. Wykeham Causeway, 11.7.2019 (AR, JHo); Saltburn, 24.7.2019 (IE); Skelton, 3.8.2019 (DM).

63. West Melton, 27.7.2019 (HEB).
64. Moughton, 23.7.2019 (TMW).
65. Hutton Conyers, 25.7.2019 (CHF).

70.070 Mallow *Larentia clavaria* (Haworth)

A good year with records across three vice counties. The VC62 records were the first since 2010. All three VC63 larval records were on *Malva sylvestris* and these were the first larval records on our database for over a century.
61. Catwick, 21.9.2019 (JM); Easington (Spurn), 22, 25 & 27.9, 4 & 5.10.2019 (MFS); Spurn, 25.9.2019 (JHF).
62. Haxby, 22.9.2019 (TJC); Wykeham Causeway, 25.9.2019 (AR, JHo).
63. Boston park, larvae, 19.5.2019 (UR); Armthorpe, larva, 19.5.2019 (UR); Cantley Low Common, larva, 21.5.2019 (UR); Kirk Smeaton, 30.9 & 1.10.2019 (DWi).

70.072 Grey Mountain Carpet *Entephria caesiata* ([Denis & Schiffermüller])

Just one record so a very poor year. It is likely that climatic change has contributed to a loss of records from lower ground in the south and east of its range.
64. Malham Tarn, 30.8.2019 (UR).

70.075 May Highflyer *Hydriomena impluviata* ([Denis & Schiffermüller])

After three good years, a major drop in numbers means that we must list all records. Many woodland moths of late spring/early summer did badly this year.
61. North Ferriby, 21.4, 20.5, 1 & 16.6.2019 (IM); Tophill Low NR, 30.5.2019 (MHo, DF); North Cliffe Wood, 29.6.2019 (JM).
62. Lealholm, 25.5.2019 (GF).
63. West Melton, 18 & 25.5.2019 (HEB); Austerfield, 18 & 24.5.2019 (SB); Thorne Moors, 22.5.2019 (RM); Cudworth, 27.5.2019 (CG).
64. West Bradford, 30.4, 25.5 & 1.6.2019 (BH); High Farnhill, 23.5.2019 (NS); Little Preston, 30 & 31.5, 1, 16 & 19.6.2019 (JMa); Hackfall Woods, 1.6.2019 (CHF); Giggleswick, 2.6.2019 (RW).
65. High Batts NR, 26.5.2019 (CHF, LR, PT).

70.076 Ruddy Highflyer *H. ruberata* (Freyer)

Local and infrequently recorded. This is from one of its more regular sites.
63. Thorne Moors, 18.5.2019 (RM).

70.078 Chestnut-coloured Carpet *Thera cognata* (Thunberg)

Just a single moth at one of its usual sites amongst junipers in the Ingleborough area.
64. Moughton, 23.7.2019 (TMW).

70.082 Juniper Carpet *T. juniperata* (Linnaeus)

Very few records of this late-flying species in 2019.
61. Skidby, 23.10 & 1.11.2019 (ADN).
62. Scarborough, 18.10.2019 (L&JW); Strensall Village, 24.10.2019 (YB).
63. Rotherham, 25 & 27.10.2019 (MSm).
64. Tadcaster, several dates 15.10 to 5.11.2019 (DBa); West Bradford, 17, 20 & 23.10 & 24.11.2019 (BH); Silsden, 3.11.2019 (UR).

70.083 Cypress Carpet *T. cupressata* (Geyer)

After our first record in 2018 we now have two further records from the same area where it is obviously getting established. We are likely to see records from other parts of the county. Unlike last year's record, these are from the first generation.
64. Little Preston, 1 & 4.7.2019 (JMa).

70.084 Blue-bordered Carpet *Plemyria rubiginata* ([Denis & Schiffermüller])

Low numbers again this year and none from VC61, though it was recorded from several new sites.
62. Tollerton, 24.7.2019 (MBe); Scarborough, 25.7.2019 (L&JW); Great Smeaton, 25.7.2019 (JE); Low North Camp, 23.8.2019 (RWo, GF, AR, JHo).
63. Sprotbrough, 6.7.2019 (DBo).
64. Tadcaster, 10, 16, 17 & 23.7.2019 (DBa); Askham Bryan, 11.7.2019 (DLa); Thruscross, 1.8.2019 (CGH); West Bradford, 2.8.2019 (BH); Burley-in-Wharfedale, 6.8.2019 (P&AR); Bellflask, 14.8.2019 (BM); Skyreholme, 25.8.2019 (PMi).
65. Ainderby Steeple, 20.7.2019 (JE); Semerwater SSSI, 26.7.2019 (CHF, JCW, DMS, TMW);

Cotherstone, 22.8.2019 (PWe).

70.086 Broken-barred Carpet *Electrophaes corylata* (Thunberg)
Another woodland moth of late spring/early summer having a bad year. Taking into account the increased recording effort of recent years, this is probably the lowest total of records ever received.
62. Brompton, 24.5.2019 (M&ZH); York, 1.6.2019 (AF); Haxby, 1, 8 17 & 18.6.2019 (TJC); Wykeham Causeway, 27.6.2019 (AR, JHo); Low Dalby, 27 & 28.6.2019 (JW).
63. Fishlake, 22 & 30.5 & 22.6.2019 (RP); Potteric Carr NR, 25.5.2019 (RI&JCH, HEB); Sheffield, 1.6.2019 (UR); Hatfield Moors, 16.7.2019 (HEB).
64. Cookridge, 11.7.2005 (PL); Little Preston, 22, 24 & 31.5 & 7.6.2019 (JMa); West Bradford, 25.5.2019 (BH); Giggleswick, 1.6.2019 (RW); High Farnhill, 2.6.2019 (NS).

70.092 Spinach *Eulithis mellinata* (Fabricius)
A slightly more encouraging year though numbers are still low. Several additional claims turned out to be Barred Straw or typos for Northern Spinach. This is now a rare moth and we need a photo if it is from a new site.
62. Saltburn, 30.6.2019 (IE).
63. West Melton, 25, 26, 29 & 30.6.2019 (HEB); Rodley, 22.7.2019 (JWC).
64. Burley-in-Wharfedale, 24.6.2019 (P&AR).
65. Healey, 6.7.2019 (DMS, IW).

70.096 Autumn Green Carpet *Chloroclysta miata* (Linnaeus)
Numbers of this species have tailed off in recent years unlike the rather similar Red-green Carpet which has done much better. The VC61 records were unusual as this is more commonly a moth of the higher ground.
61. Lund, 29.9.2019 (PA, DA); Lower Derwent Valley, 3.10.2019 (NC, SC).
62. Brafferton Spring Wood, 19.4.2019 (TAB); Goathland, 25.9, 24.10.2019 (WN); Sneaton, 3.11.2019 (N&MT).
63. Keighley Moor, 19.4.2019 (IHa); Keighley, 11 & 12.9, 3.11.2019 (IHa); Halifax, 25.9.2019 (DSu); Linthwaite, 4.10.2019 (AB).
64. Coniston Cold, 22.4, 24 & 30.9.2019 (ARh); Giggleswick, 23.4 & 29.9.2019 (RW); Hawkswick, 30.4.2019 (PMi, ARh, N&DF, C&FH); Yockenthwaite, 30.4.2019 (PMi, ARh, N&DF, C&FH); Ingleborough NR, 1.6.2019 (TMW); Baildon, 24.9.2019 (JG); Bellflask, 27.9.2019 (BM).

70.099 Beech-green Carpet *Colostygia olivata* ([Denis & Schiffermüller])
A rather local moth of upland areas. A single record from one of its usual haunts.
64. Malham Tarn, 25.7.2019 (DCGB).

70.102 Striped Twin-spot Carpet *Coenotephria salicata* (Hübner)
A healthy spread of records in two broods from the usual areas. Not seen in VC62 since 1998.
64. Yockenthwaite, 30.4 & 14.8.2019 (PMi, ARh, N&DF, C&FH); Hawkswick, 30.4.2019 (PMi, ARh, N&DF, C&FH); Ingleborough NR, 1 & 18.6.2019 (TMW, JP); Colt Park, 5.6.2019 (TMW, KA); Dib Scar, 2.7.2019 (PMi); Grass Wood, 3.8.2019 (PMi); Skyreholme, 25.8.2019 (PMi).
65. Foxglove Covert, 23.8.2019 (CHF, JCW, DMS et al.).

70.104 Devon Carpet *Lampropteryx otregiata* (Metcalfe)
A remarkable year with spread to many new parts of the county including eight new sites. There are still no records in VC65 or the east of VC63 though it is surely only a matter of time. Unusually there was only one moth from the first brood. Take care not to mistake moths in May for the similar but larger Water Carpet.
61. Lower Derwent Valley, 23.8.2019 (CSR).
62. Grosmont, 22.5.2019 (DWa); Forge Valley, 30.7.2019 (AR, JHo); Brafferton Spring Wood, 4 & 25.8.2019 (TAB); Errington Copse, New Marske, 8.8.2019 (DM); Low North Camp, 23.8.2019 (RWo, GF, AR, JHo).
64. Dob Park, 12, 23 & 29.8.2019 (CGH); Sawley, 20.8.2019 (CHF); New Laithe Farm, 24.8.2019 (MB); Coniston Cold, 27.8.2019 (ARh).

70.105 Northern Winter Moth *Operophtera fagata* (Scharfenberg)
A lot of claimed Northern Winter Moths turn out to be Winter Moth which is far more likely to turn up in gardens. If you are unsure, measure the wing length and send in a photo. You are most likely to come across this moth in birch woodland. The flight time is usually November so any turning up in

January are almost certainly Winter Moths.

63. Rishworth, 3.11.2019 (EE).

64. Bellflask, 16 & 23.11.2019 (BM); Grass Wood, 20.11.2019 (PMi).

Epirrita species

We still receive confident records of these four species with no indication that the abdominal underside has been examined. Small Autumnal Moth is fairly easy, as it is small, flies earlier than the others, and is usually found in upland areas, though occasionally later and lowland examples turn up. For the other three, they really should be recorded as "November Moth agg." unless you have looked at their abdomens and compared them to the pictures on page 101 of Waring and Townsend's field guide (3rd edition). November Moth is by far the commonest, especially in gardens. Pale November and Autumnal will occasionally come to gardens but are far more likely to be found in woodland, particularly birch woodland where they are sometimes disturbed by day. This year there were over 40 confirmed records of November Moth and there were none of Autumnal Moth. Records of the other two species are listed below.

70.108 Pale November Moth *Epirrita christyi* (Allen)

65. Hutton Conyers, 1.11.2019 (CHF).

70.110 Small Autumnal Moth *E. filigrammaria* (Herrich-Schäffer)

63. Keighley Moor, 7 & 15.9.2019 (IHa).

64. Ilkley, 29.8.2019 (P&JB).

65. Healey, 6.9.2019 (DMS, IW).

70.112 Dingy Shell *Euchoeca nebulata* (Scopoli)

A fairly poor year with records from only 11 sites spread across lowland parts of the county. An easy moth to identify as it rests with its wings closed.

61. Allerthorpe Lakeland Park, 7.7.2019 (CHF); Tophill Low NR, 23.8.2019 (MHo, DF).

62. Littlebeck, 24.8.2019 (MN).

63. Potteric Carr NR, 26.5.2019 (RI&JCH); Hatfield Moors, 16.7.2019 (DWi); Thorpe Marsh NR, 22.7.2019 (DWi).

64. Little Preston, 22.6, 17.7, 2 & 23.8.2019 (JMa); Askham Bog, 8.7, 3 & 23.8.2019 (AF, TJC, PMa et al.); Bellflask, 13.7.2019 (BM); Alwoodley, 15.7.2019 (PRM).

65. Beverley Wood, Great Smeaton, 30.5.2019 (JE).

70.114 Small Yellow Wave *Hydrelia flammeolaria* (Hufnagel)

Another decrease in numbers means that we should list all records this year.

61. Lund, 24.6.2019 (MCo); North Cliffe Wood, 29.6 & 5.7.2019 (JMo, DA, IM, ADN); North Ferriby, 16.7 & 23.8.2019 (IM).

62. Husthwaite, 14.6.2019 (KG); Broxa, 28.6, 12 & 18.7.2019 (GF, AR, JHo); Strensall Common, 29.6 & 5.7.2019 (YB); Bickley Gate, 30.6.2019 (AR, JHo); Stokesley, 6.7.2019 (SF); Scarborough, 10.7.2019 (L&JW); Clay Bank Plantation, 10.7.2019 (SF); Wykeham Causeway, 14.7 & 2.8.2019 (AR, JHo, SF); Moorsholm, 17.7.2019 (SF).

63. Potteric Carr NR, 29.6.2019 (RI&JCH, HEB); Fishlake, 29.6.2019 (RP); Darnall, 16.7.2019 (PMe); Hatfield Moors, 16.7.2019 (HEB); Brockadale NR, 18.7.2019 (DWi).

64. Askham Bog, 8.7.2019 (AF, TJC, PMa et al.); Alwoodley, 2.8.2019 (PRM).

70.115 Welsh Wave *Venusia cambrica* (Curtis)

A return to normal levels after two record years. A moth of upland areas with rowan.

62. Dalby Forest, 31.5 & 24.6.2019 (AR, JHo, SF); Low Dalby, 16.6, 20, 24, 29.7 & 3.8.2019 (JW); Turkey Carpet, 21 & 28.6.2019 (SF); Harwood Dale Forest, 22.6 & 25.8.2019 (RWo, SF); Broxa, 28.6 & 12.7.2019 (GF); Bickley Gate, 30.6.2019 (AR, JHo); Moorsholm, 2 & 17.7.2019 (SF); Clay Bank Plantation, 10.7.2019 (SF).

64. Brimham Rocks, 21.6.2019 (CHF et al.); Colt Park, 24.6.2019 (TMW, KA, JHa); Dob Park, 18, 22 & 29.7.2019 (CGH); Grass Wood, 3.8.2019 (PMi); Bastow Wood, 6.8.2019 (PMi).

70.116 Blomer's Rivulet *V. blomeri* (Curtis)

A reduction in numbers in 2019 after two record years. All records from the usual areas.

62. Raincliffe Woods, 17.6.2019 (AR, JHo); Broxa Forest, 18.7.2019 (AR, JHo); Forge Valley, 30.7.2019 (AR, JHo).

64. Hackfall Woods, 1.6.2019 (CHF); Ellington Banks (MOD), 8 & 22.7.2019 (CHF, JCW, SMP, AWh).

70.118 Brown Scallop *Philereme vetulata* ([Denis & Schiffermüller])

A good year for this rather drab buckthorn-feeding species with records from typical areas. Nosterfield

NR is a new site and it is good to record it again at Askham Bog after a gap of over 100 years.
63. Brockadale NR, 18.7.2019 (P&JS, DWi).
64. Askham Bog, 8 & 25.7.2019 (AF, TJC, PMa et al.); Bellflask, 23.7.2019 (BM).
65. Nosterfield NR, 4.7.2019 (CHF, JCW); High Batts NR, 12.7.2019 (CHF, TMW, DMS et al.).

70.119 Dark Umber *P. transversata* (Hufnagel)
Scattered records of this buckthorn-feeding species. Most records were from the usual areas
however three records from Spurn are most unusual as it has never been seen there before and the
nearest known colonies are many miles away.
61. Spurn, 6, 9 & 24.7.2019 (JHF).
63. Brockadale NR, 18.7.2019 (DWi); Went Hills, 20.7.2019 (DWi).
64. Bellflask, 23 & 30.7.2019 (BM).
65. High Batts NR, 12.7.2019 (CHF, TMW, DMS et al.).

70.120 Argent and Sable *Rheumaptera hastata* (Linnaeus)
A lot of recorders caught up with this day-flying species in 2019 at its main haunt at Bishop Wood
with a maximum count of 21 moths. There were no records from the Boltby Forest site. The flight
time has become earlier in recent years. In the past, sunny days in mid-June were the time to look
for this moth, but the best time now is the last week in May.
64. Bishop Wood, 22.5 to 2.6.2019 (SB, IM, AR, TAB, PMa, TJC, CM, PLe).

70.121 Scallop Shell *R. undulata* (Linnaeus)
A poor year, with scattered records from lowland areas of the county.
61. North Cliffe Wood, 5.7.2019 (IM, ADN); Market Weighton, 9.7.2019 (PA).
62. Fen Bog, 16.7.2019 (TAM).
63. Austerfield, 23.6.2019 (SB); Wintersett Country Park, 24.6.2019 (PSm et al.); Owston, 29.7.2019 (MaP).
64. Askham Bog, 8.7.2019 (AF, TJC, PMa et al.).
65. Hutton Conyers, 2.7.2019 (CHF); Foxglove Covert, 9.7.2019 (FCMT).

70.123 Tissue *Triphosa dubitata* (Linnaeus)
The over-wintering populations in the Dales remain healthy. Maximum numbers in the main cave at
each end of the year were 162 in February and 160 in October. Unusually there were several moths
caught at light in all five VCs including five new sites.
61. Lund, 13.5.2019 (DA).
62. Ravenscar Tunnel (over-wintering), 13.1.2019 (NAd).
63. Thornton (Bradford), 22.4.2019 (MaP).
64. Various caves in the limestone Dales (over-wintering) (DHo, N&DF, PMi, MCu, DFe, ARh et al);
Yockenthwaite, 30.4.2019 (PMi, ARh, N&DF, C&FH); Bellflask, 14.5.2019 (BM); Grass Wood (larvae),
10 & 12.6.2019 (PMi, DFe, DWa, MWa); Burley-in-Wharfedale, 25.7.2019 (P&AR).
65. Foxglove Covert, 1.5.2019 (FCMT); Hutton Conyers, 8.5.2019 (CHF).

70.128 Pretty Chalk Carpet *Melanthia procellata* ([Denis & Schiffermüller])
A single moth from its only site in the county.
63. Brockadale NR, 18.7.2019 (DWi).

70.129 Dentated Pug *Anticollix sparsata* (Treitschke)
An encouraging number of records from its most regular site. These are the first records in the
county since 2013. Askham Bog is the most northerly site in the country for this moth of wet
woodland, the larvae feeding on yellow loosestrife.
64. Askham Bog, 24.5, 1.6, 8.7 & 3.8.2019 (AF, TJC, PMa et al).

70.134 Barred Rivulet *Perizoma bifaciata* (Haworth)
What on earth has happened to Barred Rivulet? Numbers have been low for a few years but never to
this extent. This is the lowest total since 1973 and there are twenty-five times more total records this
year than there were back then. Its food plant red bartsia is not uncommon in the county.
61. Spurn, 14.8.2019 (JCr).

70.135 Heath Rivulet *P. minorata* (Treitschke)
Two moths seen by day at a site where it was first seen in 2016. This elusive species is confined in
England to the upper Wharfedale area and one site in Cumbria – as far as we know! It still occurs at
several sites in Scotland and in the Burren in Ireland. All of our records are of moths seen by day. If you

are searching for this moth, and we hope that you will do, it behaves like a miniature Twin-spot Carpet.
64. Arncliffe, Sleets Gill, 15.8.2019 (PMi, ARh, DFe).

70.137 Grass Rivulet *P. albulata* ([Denis & Schiffermüller])
Another poor year with only 19 individual moths seen, after record numbers in 2016 and 17. There are few records from the western half of the county despite its food plant, yellow rattle, being common.
61. Easington (Spurn), 31.5 & 17.6.2019 (MFS); Spurn, 15.6.2019 (JHF).
62. Newtondale, 17.6.2019 (SF); Skinningrove, 7.7.2019 (DM); South Gare, 14.7.2019 (DM); Scarborough, 22.7.2019 (L&JW).
63. Brockadale NR, 23.5 & 6.6.2019 (P&JS, DWi); Kirk Smeaton, 29.5.2019 (DWi); Rotherham, 31.5.2019 (MSm); Owston, 1.6 & 4.7.2019 (MaP).

70.139 Barred Carpet *Martania taeniata* (Stephens)
This local species of damp woodland is doing well. Wykeham Causeway is another new site in its main area in the east of VC62 but it is also doing well at Grass Wood. In a national context, our populations are very important.
62. Goathland, 13.7.2019 (WN); Lealholm, 16 & 27.7.2019 (GF); Forge Valley, 30.7.2019 (AR, JHo); Wykeham Causeway, 2.8.2019 (SF).
64. Grass Wood area, 3 & 6.8.2019 (PMi).

70.043 Chalk Carpet Flamborough VC61 Mike Pearson   70.120 Argent & Sable Bishop Wood VC64 Allan Rodda.

Pugs (*Eupithecia* and related species)
We get the impression that you might all be getting a bit better at identifying Pugs and not guessing quite so wildly. Perhaps you all have a copy of Brian Hancock's *Pug Moths of North West England* or even Riley and Prior's *British and Irish Pug Moths*. Quite a few of you are finding that dissection isn't quite as difficult as you thought. We can still spot some of your errors when we look at flight times. Brindled Pugs in July and Slender Pugs in May are often reported but are unlikely to be correct, and some of the rarer Pugs in the wrong sort of habitat ring alarm bells. We're a bit sceptical about some records of Triple-spotted Pug in your gardens well away from damp areas, and some of you confuse Toadflax and Foxglove Pugs, but in general, standards of Pug spotting are improving. Some words of warning. Don't ever try to identify worn individuals. They are hard enough when fresh but we can't identify a lot of worn Pugs from photos. Green Pug fooled a lot of people this year, as when it has been on the wing for a while it tends to lose the green colour and look like something else. Never try to identify melanic Pugs to species level. Many species have melanic forms and they all need dissection. Be wary of some identifications when you post pictures on social media. We have seen a lot of very confident suggestions for moths which we really feel should be dissected. If in doubt, don't record it or let it fly away accidently! A really good way to find some of the rarer species is to go out at dusk with a torch and net and target the food plant. Several species can be found much more easily that way than by operating a light trap.

70.143 Sloe Pug *Pasiphila chloerata* (Mabille)
Despite blackthorn being widespread across the county, we receive few records of this species which may be more common than we think. Dusking around overgrown blackthorn hedges in June might be a good way to find it. It is easy to confuse it with Green Pug, especially when worn, as the green colouration tends to fade. Fresh specimens however should be identifiable by paying attention to the shape of the outer cross line and looking for the salmon-pink band at the base of the abdomen.

61. Muston, 8.6.2019 (PQW); Kilnwick, 22.6.2019 (MCo).

70.145 Bilberry Pug *P. debiliata* (Hübner)
First found in the county in 2016, these are our third and fourth records and are from new sites. Although the two moths at Guisecliffe came to light, it is more often found at dusk by targeting open woodland areas, preferably with scots pine and an understory of bilberry. At this stage it is difficult to tell whether it has moved into the county or is an overlooked long-standing resident. It is highly likely that it occurs at other sites and may well occur in VC62, but it does need actively looking for.
63. Wadsley and Loxley Commons, 24.6.2019 (AS).
64. Guisecliffe (Yorke's Folly), 19.7.2019 (CHF, JCW).

70.146 Haworth's Pug *Eupithecia haworthiata* (Doubleday)
As its food plant, traveller's joy, is uncommon in the county, we receive few records of this diminutive Pug. If you want to find it, either look for it at dusk, or put your moth trap very close to the food plant as it tends not to wander very far. Fresh specimens are easy to identify due to the tiny size (the same as Maple and Slender Pugs) and the reddish band at the base of the abdomen.
63. Potteric Carr NR, 5.7.2019 (RI&JCH, HEB).
65. High Batts NR, 12.7.2019 (CHF, TMW, DMS et al.).

70.147 Slender Pug *E. tenuiata* (Hübner)
53 records of 106 moths from 28 sites is a healthy total. Peak flight time was as usual the last week in July. Take care with moths caught much earlier or later. It will wander to gardens but is far commoner in damp areas with willows. The tiny size and the flight time are the biggest pointers.

70.148 Maple Pug *E. inturbata* (Hübner)
The second very healthy year in a row for this species, the third of the tiny late-flying Pugs, with 34 records of 42 moths from 11 sites across VC61, 64 and 65. It can look remarkably similar to Slender Pug, especially when worn, and it flies at the same time, so it might be a good idea to dissect it if you are not sure. There were several records from new sites and it is not obvious whether it really is becoming more common or whether we are becoming better at identifying it. Again, dusking around field maple is a good way to find it.

70.150 Toadflax Pug *E. linariata* ([Denis & Schiffermüller])
A reduction in numbers this year. This is a smaller, neater version of the commoner Foxglove Pug and some people confuse the two. If in doubt, it is probably Foxglove Pug, especially early in the year.
61. Easington (Spurn), 3.6, 23.7, 23 & 27.8.2019 (MFS); Skidby, 10.7.2019 (ADN); Tophill Low NR, 12.7.2019 (MHo, DF); Spurn, 10 & 12.9.2019 (JCr, MA).
62. Wilton (Teesside), 25.7.2019 (RWo); Skelton Castle, 3.8.2019 (DM); York, 9.9.2019 (AF).
63. Cudworth, 24.8.2019 (CP).
64. Little Preston, 14 & 29.8.2019 (JMa).

70.154 Marsh Pug *E. pygmaeata* (Hübner)
This elusive species may be more common than the few records suggest. It is a moth of wet meadows where its food plant, field mouse-ear grows and is usually seen by day, though we do occasionally get records of moths at light. We had a healthy spread of records this year, and the VC63 and 64 records were from new sites.
61. Muston, 31.5 & 8.6.2019 (PQW); Flamborough, 27.6.2019 (AAl).
62. Walmgate Stray, York, 21.5.2019 (PMa).
63. Moorlands Farm (Calderdale), 22.6.2019 (DSu); Withens Head, 22.6.2019 (DSu).
64. Rodley NR, 12.5.2019 (JG).

70.158 Juniper Pug *E. pusillata* ([Denis & Schiffermüller])
This species is now quite rare in the county and is commonest around native junipers rather than those in gardens. Numbers peaked in the 1990s and have gradually declined since then.
62. York, 12.7.2019 (AF); Strensall Village, 22.7.2019 (YB); Strensall Common, 22.8.2019 (YB).
64. West Bradford, 16 & 18.7.2019 (BH); Ribblehead Quarry, 18.7.2019 (TMW); Moughton, 23.7.2019 (TMW).

70.162 Dwarf Pug *E. tantillaria* (Boisduval)
This species would prove to be a lot more common if more people trapped in spruce plantations. Six sites were new this year. A well-marked distinctive species when fresh. Not our smallest Pug

despite the name.

61. Tophill Low NR, 23.5.2019 (MHo, DF).

62. Low Dalby, 30.5.2019 (JW); York, 30.5.2019 (AF); Dalby Forest, 31.5.2019 (AR, JHo); Haxby, 1.6.2019 (TJC); Harwood Dale Forest, 22.6.2019 (RWo, SF).

64. Wharfedale Caravan Site (Threshfield), 17.5.2019 (N&MT); Stainburn Forest, 31.5.2019 (CHF); Coniston Cold, 1, 22 & 24.6, 4.7.2019 (ARh); Askham Bog, 25.7.2019 (AF, TJC, YB, NH).

70.163 Larch Pug *E. lariciata* (Freyer)

A good spread of records across the county with the exception of VC63. Look out for the white spot on the metathorax which makes it a little easier to identify.

61. Tophill Low NR, 12.7.2019 (MHo, DF).

62. Guisborough, 19.5.2019 (PWF); Skelton, 5.6 & 26.7.2019 (SF); Low Dalby, 9 & 7.6, 11, 24 & 29.7.2019 (JW); Turkey Carpet, 21 & 28.6.2019 (SF); Harwood Dale Forest, 22.6.2019 (RWo, SF); Broxa, 28.6 & 12.7.2019 (GF); Moorsholm, 2.7.2019 (SF); Clay Bank Plantation, 10.7.2019 (SF); York, 23.7.2019 (AF); Dalby Forest, 31.7.2019 (SF).

64. Coniston Cold, several dates 10.5 to 18.7.2019 (ARh); Stainburn Forest, 16.7.2019 (CHF); Burley-in-Wharfedale, 25.7.2019 (P&AR).

65. Semerwater SSSI, 26.7.2019 (CHF, JCW, DMS, TMW).

70.165 Pimpinel Pug *E. pimpinellata* (Hübner)

Records from two regular sites plus a new site at Semerwater, well away from any known populations. The larvae apparently feed on Burnet Saxifrage at Muston and Greater Burnet Saxifrage at Hutton Conyers, and targeting these food plants at dusk would no doubt add more sites.

61. Muston Wold, 12.9.2019 (PQW).

65. Hutton Conyers, 14, 17 & 24.7.2019 (CHF); Semerwater SSSI, 26.7.2019 (CHF, JCW, DMS, TMW).

70.166 Plain Pug *E. simpliciata* (Haworth)

Numbers of this large Pug have tailed off a little in recent years and we have tended to list all records, so it is encouraging to report 45 records of 51 moths from 21 sites across lowland parts of all five vice counties. The majority of records as usual were from VC61.

70.169 Angle-barred Pug *E. innotata* (Hufnagel)

A recovery at Spurn following the very low numbers of 2018. The Spurn moths feed on sea buckthorn whilst those in western parts of the county (previously called Ash Pug) feed on Ash. It is rare in other parts of the county and we often find that claimed records are of other species.

61. Spurn area, 20 records of 25 moths from 1.6 to 20.8.2019 (MFS, JHF, MA).

64. Coniston Cold, 1 & 22.6, 22 & 24.7.2019 (ARh); Burley-in-Wharfedale, 1 & 2.8.2019 (P&AR); Thornton-in-Craven, 9/8/2019 (DIS).

70.171 Ochreous Pug *E. indigata* (Hübner)

A good year for this moth of scots pine woodland. A rather plain-looking little pug which occasionally wanders away from pines and visits gardens. It has a characteristic posture with slightly "swept back" wings.

61. North Ferriby, 19 & 20.5.2019 (IM); Elvington, 25.5.2019 (JSm).

62. Haxby, 1.6.2019 (TJC); Scarborough, 29 & 30.6.2019 (L&JW).

64. Tadcaster, 15.5.2019 (DBa); Ellington Banks (MOD), 22.5.2019 (CHF); Bellflask, 26.5 & 1.6.2019 (BM); Coniston Cold, 1.6.2019 (ARh); Colt Park, 24.6.2019 (TMW, KA, JHa).

70.172 Thyme Pug *E. distinctaria* (Herrich-Schäffer)

A very local and infrequently recorded species with all recent records from the western Dales. Our only record this year is from a new location considerably to the east of the core area.

64. Duck Street Quarry (Greenhow), 17.7.2019 (PMi, ARh, PR, DFe et al.).

70.174 Pinion-spotted Pug *E. insigniata* (Hübner)

A single moth from Coniston Cold where it has now been recorded three years in a row. This is the only known site in the north of England for this very distinctive species.

64. Coniston Cold, 15.5.2019 (ARh).

70.175 Triple-spotted Pug *E. trisignaria* (Herrich-Schäffer)

A very poor year for this moth of damp woodland and marshy areas. Its food plant, wild angelica, is widespread and in the past this species has been recorded all across the county, so perhaps it is being overlooked.

62. York, 21.7.2019 (AF).

63. Kirk Smeaton, 24.6.2019 (P&JS).

65. Foxglove Covert, 23.8.2019 (CHF, JCW, DMS et al.).

70.177 Satyr Pug *E. satyrata* **(Hübner)**

An average year for this uncommon Pug of heathland and calcareous areas. This species is often disturbed by day, and this was the case with all of the Strensall records.

61. Lund, 31.5.2019 (MCo).

62. Strensall Common, 1, 4, 14 & 15.7.2019 (PMa).

64. Moughton, 23.7.2019 (TMW); Askham Bog, 25.7.2019 (AF, TJC, YB, NH).

70.181 Valerian Pug *E. valerianata* **(Hübner)**

We receive few records of this species which really ought to be more common in damp woodland where common valerian grows. Again targeted searching by dusking would be a good way of finding it.

61. Wheldrake, 10.7.2019 (JOHS).

70.186 Yarrow Pug *E. millefoliata* **(Rössler)**

Following its arrival in the county in 2018, it is good to report more moths at the same site. This species is spreading slowly across the country and we are likely to see it at other sites in the next few years.

63. Austerfield, 24 & 29.7.2019 (SB).

70.188 Bordered Pug *E. succenturiata* **(Linnaeus)**

A big drop in numbers this year means that we should list all records. This is another moth of disturbed ground which is doing badly across the country.

61. Market Weighton, 18.6.2019 (PA); Spurn, 2, 10, 22, 24 & 27.7.2019 (JHF); Lower Derwent Valley, 23.8.2019 (CSR).

62. Haxby, 3 & 5.8.2019 (TJC); Saltburn, 27.8.2019 (IE).

63. Sprotbrough, 18.7.2019 (DBo); Austerfield, 24.7.2019 (SB); Wakefield, 26.7.2019 (JD); Doncaster, 29.7.2019 (NB); Carlton Marsh NR, 5.8.2019 (HEB, CG et al.); West Melton, 28.8.2019 (HEB).

64. Dob Park, 22 & 29.7.2019 (CGH); Sharow, 29.7.2019 (JCW); Little Preston, 1.8.2019 (JMa); Askham Bryan, 4.8.2019 (DLa).

70.189 Shaded Pug *E. subumbrata* **([Denis & Schiffermüller])**

Another healthy spread of records from the site where it was discovered last year. These are the only records in the county since 2001.

63. Austerfield, 5, 23 & 29.6, 29.7.2019 (SB).

70.148 Maple Pug David Baker

70.166 Plain Pug David Baker

70.192 Treble-bar *Aplocera plagiata* **(Linnaeus)**

This is not a common species in the county. Most records come from eastern parts of VC63 and from the west of VC64 and 65. Records from other parts of Yorkshire often turn out to be Lesser Treble-bar which is much more common in our area. Separating these two species by relying on the shape of the basal cross band is fraught with difficulty and it is much more reliable to look at the underside of the tip of the abdomen (in males). This is easy if you put the moth in a clear container and use the pictures in Waring and Townsend's field guide – page 134 in the third edition. Lesser Treble-bar was widespread across lowland parts of the county in 2019 with 114 records of 561 moths from 28 sites.

widespread across lowland parts of the county in 2019 with 114 records of 561 moths from 28 sites.
63. Went Hills, 13.5.2019 (LD); Austerfield, 14.5.2019 (SB); Potteric Carr NR, 1.6.2019 (RI&JCH, HEB); Sprotbrough, 25.7.2019 (DBo); Balby, 3.8.2019 (PG), Swinefleet, 26 & 27.8.2019 (RP).

70.195 Streak *Chesias legatella* ([Denis & Schiffermüller])
A very poor year for this broom-feeding species with records from only one site.
63. Austerfield, 6, 11, 15 & 18.10, 1.11.2019 (SB).

70.198 Seraphim *Lobophora halterata* (Hufnagel)
An average year for this rather variable moth of woodland with aspen and other poplars. Records were scattered across all lowland parts of the county.
61. Tophill Low NR, 24 & 31.5.2019 (MHo, DF); North Cliffe Wood, 31.5.2019 (IM, ADN); Lund, 2.6.2019 (MCo); North Ferriby, 4.6.2019 (IM).
62. York, 30.5.2019 (AF).
63. Austerfield, 17, 24 & 31.5, 1.6.2019 (SB); Rodley, 25.5.2019 (JWC); Potteric Carr NR, 25.5.2019 (RI&JCH, HEB); Pledwick, Wakefield, 26.5.2019 (MHe); Rotherham, 31.5.2019 (MSm).
64. Menston, 14.5.2019 (CGH); High Batts NR, 26.5.2019 (CHF, LR, PT).
65. Hutton Conyers, 30.4, 13, 18, 19, 23 & 24.5, 3.6.2019 (CHF); Beverley Wood, Great Smeaton, 30.5.2019 (JE); Ainderby Steeple, 1.6.2019 (JE).

70.201 Barred Tooth-striped *Trichopteryx polycommata* ([Denis & Schiffermüller])
Recorded from its usual site at Grass Wood and also at the Littondale site where it was first discovered in 2018. Records at both sites were of moths attracted to both actinic light and to pheromone lures.
64. Grass Wood area, 9 & 16.4.2019 (PMi) and larvae on both privet and ash on 12.6.2009 (PMi, DFe, DWa, MWa); Littondale, 18.4.2019 (PMi, N&DF).

70.203 Orange Underwing *Archiearis parthenias* (Linnaeus)
32 records of 79 moths from 23 sites so there were too many to list individually this year. There were no records from VC61 or 65 but in the other three vice counties, moths were reported widely flying by day in open wooded areas with birch in March and April. Generally, numbers reported are proportional to the amount of fine sunny weather at this time of year.

70.206 Clouded Magpie *Abraxas sylvata* (Scopoli)
A big drop in numbers with records from only three sites. This moth of elm-rich woodland is commonest in VC62 and 64 but remains rather local.
62. Broxa Forest, 18.7.2019 (AR, JHo).
64. Hackfall Woods, 1.6.2019 (CHF); Fewston Reservoir, 9.6.2019 (N&DF).

70.208 Scorched Carpet *Ligdia adustata* ([Denis & Schiffermüller])
Most records as usual from the central magnesian limestone belt where its food plant, spindle, is commonest, but also a more unusual record from Lund – only the second for VC61.
61. Lund, 3.6.2019 (DA).
63. Sprotbrough, 24.5.2019 (DBo); Balby, 30.5, 1.6 & 27.8.2019 (PG); Austerfield, 1.6.2019 (SB).
64. Bellflask, 2.6 & 5.7.2019 (BM).
65. Hutton Conyers, 4.7.2019 (CHF).

70.211 Peacock Moth *Macaria notata* (Linnaeus)
These are the first records of Peacock Moth in the county since 2008. The Wykeham Causeway moth was only the second for VC62, and it was a new species at Spurn. It is easy to mistake for Sharp-angled Peacock but both records were submitted with clear photos. Fresh specimens should be fairly easy to identify. Look for the lack of a grey cross band running through the "paw print" and the continuous line on the edge of the hindwing. Other features are listed in the usual field guides.
61. Easington (Spurn), 28.7.2019 (MFS).
62. Wykeham Causeway, 5.8.2019 (AWr).

70.212 Sharp-angled Peacock *M. alternata* (Denis & Schiffermüller)
A return to more normal numbers after a very bad year in 2018.
61. Spurn area, 42 records of 50 moths from 1.5 to 30.8.2019 (MFS, JFH, JCr, MCo).

70.215 V-Moth *M. wauaria* (Linnaeus)
Records were received from just three sites, all north of Ripon. It has disappeared from large areas of the country for reasons which are not easy to identify. This area is the most reliable part of the county

64. Grewelthorpe, 13, 16, 17 & 19.7.2019 (MH); Ellington Banks (MOD), 22.7.2019 (CHF, JCW, SMP, AWh).
65. High Batts NR, 12.7.2019 (CHF, TMW, DMS et al.).

70.223 Barred Umber *Plagodis pulveraria* (Linnaeus)
This is another late spring moth of broad-leaved woodland which did very badly in 2019. Records as usual were from wooded upland fringes in the northern half of the county.
62. Moorsholm, 13.5.2019 (SF); Douthwaitedale (Kirkbymoorside), 15.5.2019 (SN); Broxa Forest, 16.5.2019 (AR, JHo); Low Dalby, 19.5.2019 (JW).
65. Foxglove Covert, 14.5.2019 (FCMT).

70.227 Bordered Beauty *Epione repandaria* (Hufnagel)
Numbers of this attractive moth of damp woodland were down a little in 2019. Records as usual were scattered across lowland parts of the county.
61. Tophill Low NR, 12 & 27.7, 2 & 8.8.2019 (MHo, DF); Wheldrake, 22 & 25.7, 8.8.2019 (JOHS).
62. Great Smeaton, 25.7.2019 (JE); Haxby, 28.7.2019 (TJC); Brafferton Spring Wood, 3 & 4.8.2019 (TAB); Low North Camp, 23.8.2019 (RWo, GF, AR, JHo).
63. Hatfield Moors, 16.7.2019 (HEB); Haw Park, 25.7.2019 (PSm et al.); Potteric Carr NR, 24.8.2019 (RI&JCH, HEB), Swinefleet, 22.7.2019 (MJP); Blacktoft Sands, 26.7.2019 (MJP).
64. Bellflask, 19 & 30.7, 4.8.2019 (BM); Little Preston, 2.8.2019 (JMa); Askham Bog, 3.8.2019 (AF).
65. High Batts NR, 12.7.2019 (CHF, TMW, DMS et al.); Hutton Conyers, 23.7 & 26.8.2019 (CHF).

70.228 Dark Bordered Beauty *E. vespertaria* (Linnaeus)
Following three years of recovery thanks to the efforts of the conservation team, 2019 was a very sobering year on the Strensall monitoring transect. The flight season was very short (just eight days from first to last records, a drop of 65%), the peak count was just nine moths (a drop of 71%), only 15 moths were counted over the season (a drop of 88%), and the mean count was less than 4 moths (a drop of 68%). There was no strong indication of why this drop occurred, but nonetheless a working party in September has established further grazing protection for existing Creeping Willows in one of the main areas along the monitoring transect and also carried out weeding around established plants inside some of the exclosures. Whilst there were no records of Dark Bordered Beauty this year from the Yorkshire Wildlife Trust reserve, it was reassuring that moths were seen at three other closely-linked locations in the live firing zone, where numbers appeared more normal. We hope for a rapid recovery of the moth in 2020.

70.229 Speckled Yellow *Pseudopanthera macularia* (Linnaeus)
Records of this day-flying species came from the usual upland open wooded areas in the west of VC64 and 65, where the larvae feed on wood sage.
64. Grass Wood/Bastow Wood area, 12, 14 & 20.5.2019 (PMi, IP, N&MT, TJC); Coniston Cold, 15.5.2019 (ARh).
65. Whaw, 6.6.2019 (UR).

70.231 Lilac Beauty *Apeira syringaria* (Linnaeus)
A very poor year for this attractive woodland moth with records from typical sites.
61. Wheldrake, 4.7.2019 (JOHS); Tophill Low NR, 5 & 19.7.2019 (MHo, DF); Lower Derwent Valley, 9.7.2019 (NC, SC).
62. Brafferton Spring Wood, 28.6.2019 (TAB); York, 29.6.2019 (AF).
64. Askham Bog, 8 & 25.7.2019 (AF, TJC, PMa et al.); Bellflask, 15.7.2019 (BM).

70.232 Large Thorn *Ennomos autumnaria* (Werneburg)
All recent records have come from this site which is its northernmost outpost in the country. This is the fourth year in a row it has been recorded there.
61. Easington (Spurn), 5 & 9.9.2019 (MFS).

70.233 August Thorn *E. quercinaria* (Hufnagel)
A further reduction in reported sightings this year. Most records tend to come from the south and east of the county but this year we have had some records further west. Take care not to confuse this species with September Thorn which flies at the same time and has paler plainer wings which it holds at a steeper angle than August Thorn. The kink in the outer cross line of August Thorn can sometimes be difficult to judge and should not be used as the only distinguishing feature.
61. North Ferriby, 23.7.2019 (IM); Muston, 3, 4 & 23.8.2019 (PQW); Lower Derwent Valley, 13.8.2019

61. North Ferriby, 23.7.2019 (IM); Muston, 3, 4 & 23.8.2019 (PQW); Lower Derwent Valley, 13.8.2019 (CSR); Easington (Spurn), 27.8.2019 (MFS).
62. Strensall Common, 16.7.2019 (YB); Strensall Village, 5.8.2019 (YB); Forge Valley, 30.7.2019 (AR, JHo); Tollerton, 4.8.2019 (MBe); Scarborough, 7.8.2019 (L&JW).
63. Austerfield, 24.7.2019 (SB); Rotherham, 27.7.2019 (MSm); Sprotbrough, 4.8.2019 (DBo).
64. Alwoodley, 6.8.2019 (PRM); Coniston Cold, 26.8.2019 (ARh).

70.236 September Thorn *E. erosaria* ([Denis & Schiffermüller])
Numbers of this and the previous species always used to be similar in the county, but in recent years August Thorn seems to have declined whilst September Thorn has increased. This has not been mirrored nationally as September Thorn is reputed to be in greater decline across the country. September Thorn is commonest over most of the county apart from the south east though there are parts of the county in the centre and south where both species occur. This year there were 77 records of 140 moths from 32 sites, so a healthy total.

70.238 Lunar Thorn *Selenia lunularia* (Hübner)
This species has disappeared from lowland Yorkshire and is now a moth of upland wooded areas in the north of the county. Along with many late spring woodland moths, numbers were down this year.
62. Nawton, 1.6.2019 (UR).
64. Yockenthwaite, 30.4.2019 (PMi, ARh, N&DF, C&FH); Skyreholme, 27.5.2019 (PMi); Ingleborough NR, 1.6.2019 (TMW).
65. Healey, 24.5.2019 (DMS, IW); Foxglove Covert, 4 & 18.6.2019 (FCMT).

70.248 Brindled Beauty *Lycia hirtaria* (Clerck)
Another good year for this woodland moth and with record numbers, this is the first year we have not listed all sightings. There were 31 records of 56 moths from 11 sites across VC62, 63 and 64. These included two unusual sites in the west of the county – Keighley Moor and Littondale which are not normally areas associated with this species, but both records were accompanied by good photographs. Nationally, numbers have been falling in recent years.

70.253 Spring Usher *Agriopis leucophaearia* (Denis & Schiffermüller)
This is another species where we normally list all records but there were unprecedented numbers across the county this year with 51 records of 298 moths from 22 sites, several being from new areas. There were some big catches, and 54 at Austerfield on 6th February is the most ever caught on one night in the county. These totals were largely due to unseasonably warm weather in February which tempted moths to fly and tempted moth recorders to get their traps out of the shed a little earlier than usual.

70.254 Scarce Umber *A. aurantiaria* (Hübner)
43 records of 73 moths from 23 sites across all five vice-counties is a healthy total and whilst not up to the record numbers of 2018, it still means there are too many to list individually. This is another species whose numbers have dropped nationally but is doing fairly well in Yorkshire.

70.264 Satin Beauty *Deileptenia ribeata* (Clerck)
This species should be more common than these records suggest. Perhaps few people trap in coniferous woodland in the summer or mistake it for Willow or Mottled Beauty. Dark or obscurely marked forms are quite common but it should be recognisable by the feathery antennae of the male and the broader, more rounded wing shape. It seems to be less common in VC63.
62. Moorsholm, 2.7.2019 (SF); Great Smeaton, 6.7.2019 (JE); Broxa, 12.7.2019 (GF); Low Dalby, 16 & 24.7.2019 (JW).
64. Ellington Banks (MOD), 8 & 22.7.2019 (CHF, JCW, SMP, AWh); Coniston Cold, 11.7.2019 (ARh); Stainburn Forest, 16.7.2019 (CHF); Tadcaster, 18.7.2019 (DBa); Guisecliffe (Yorke's Folly), 19.7.2019 (CHF, JCW); Malham Tarn, 22.7.2019 (DCGB); Coniston Cold, 28.7.2019 (ARh).

70.268 Pale Oak Beauty *Hypomecis punctinalis* (Scopoli)
Two records from its most regular site where it was first found in 2016.
63. Thorne Moors, 5 & 9.6.2019 (RM).

70.274 Grey Birch *Aethalura punctulata* ([Denis & Schiffermüller])
A big drop in numbers, but again this seemed typical for most late-spring woodland moths this year.
62. Pilmoor Wood, 21.4.2019 (TAB); Strensall Common, 24 & 29.4, 10.5.2019 (YB); Strensall Village, 1.5.2019 (YB); Broxa Forest, 16.5.2019 (AR, JHo); Low Dalby, 30.5.2019 (JW).
63. Potteric Carr NR, 6 & 24.4.2019 (RI&JCH, HEB); Thorne Moors, 18, 22 & 29.5.2019 (RM).

64. Askham Bog, 24.5.2019 (AF, TJC); Bellflask, 24.5.2019 (BM).

65. Beverley Wood, Great Smeaton, 30.5.2019 (JE).

70.287 Annulet *Charissa obscurata* ([Denis & Schiffermüller])

This is the biggest number of records since 2001. Most recent moths have come from the Flamborough area so it is encouraging to see it recorded again at some of its old haunts in coastal VC62. There were no records from the small population in the Dales.

61. Flamborough, 24.7, 1.8 & 11.9.2019 (MiP, AAl).

62. Wilton (Teesside), 25.7.2019 (RWo); Scarborough, 1.8.2019 (AR, JHo); Saltburn, 2 & 5.8.2019 (IE); Skelton Castle, 3.8.2019 (DM).

70.292 Grey Scalloped Bar *Dyscia fagaria* (Thunberg)

Another good year for this moth of heather moorland. Like last year, several records were from new sites far from apparently suitable habitat. For a moth which is meant to be in national decline, our populations appear to be doing well. Another surprise is that it is many years since it has been recorded from any of our lowland heaths.

62. Lealholm, 25.5.2019 (GF).

63. Keighley Moor, 24.5.2019 (IHa).

64. Ellington Banks (MOD), 22.5.2019 (CHF); Coniston Cold, 26.5.2019 (ARh); Grewelthorpe, 2.6.2019 (MH); Guisecliffe (Yorke's Folly), 19.7.2019 (CHF, JCW).

65. Healey, 24 & 31.5.2019 (DMS, IW); High Batts NR, 26.5.2019 (CHF, LR, PT).

70.295 Grass Wave *Perconia strigillaria* (Hübner)

As usual, all our records were of day-flying moths from lowland heaths and from upland areas in the east of VC62.

62. Strensall Common, several records from 25.5 to 22.6.2019 (PMa, TJC, DWa, YB); Jugger Beck, 18.6.2019 (GF); Black Dyke Moor, 22.6.2019 (WN).

70.297 Grass Emerald *Pseudoterpna pruinata* (Hufnagel)

A rather local moth in the county; the larvae feeding on gorse and broom. All records were from known sites this year.

62. Strensall Common, 7.7.2019 (YB).

63. Austerfield, 24 & 25.7.2019 (SB).

65. Foxglove Covert, 9.7.2019 (FCMT).

70.300 Blotched Emerald *Comibaena bajularia* ([Denis & Schiffermüller])

A healthy number of records from typical sites in the centre of the county. This moth of oak woodland is at its northern limit in Yorkshire though there is a small population in south Cumbria. Our numbers appear to be stable though nationally it is in decline.

61. North Cliffe Wood, 29.6 & 5.7.2019 (DA, IM, ADN); Lower Derwent Valley, 30.6.2019 (CSR).

63. Austerfield, several dates, 17.6 to 11.7.2019 (SB); Fishlake, several dates, 22.6 to 4.7.2019 (RP); Owston, 24 & 28.6.2019 (MaP).

64. Askham Bog, 17.6 & 8.7.2019 (AF, TJC, PMa et al.).

70.303 Little Emerald *Jodis lactearia* (Linnaeus)

This moth of scrubby birch heathland and open woodland is rather local in areas of central and north-east Yorkshire. We never receive many records and this is a typical year, though Wykeham Causeway and Brompton are new sites.

62. Haxby, 1.6.2019 (TJC); Newtondale, 17.6.2019 (SF); Wykeham Causeway, 14.7.2019 (AR, JHo); Brompton, 26.7.2019 (AR, JHo).

NOCTUOIDEA
NOTODONTIDAE

71.001 Oak Processionary *Thaumetopoea processionea* (Linnaeus)

This is the third record for the county. A larval web was found on a recently planted oak. It was reported to the Forestry Commission and the tree was destroyed. It is likely that despite control measures, we are fighting a losing battle against this species.

61. University of Hull, 16.7.2019 (FC). NEW VC RECORD.

71.003 Puss Moth *Cerura vinula* **(Linnaeus)**
Another poor year for this spectacular moth, though there were records from several new sites. All adults unless stated.
61. Muston, 5.7.2019 (PQW); Flamborough, 7.7.2019 (MiP).
63. Halifax, 18.5.2019 (DSu); Balby, 20.5.2019 (PG); Thorne Moors, larva, 9.7.2019 (MWa et al.); Austerfield, 10.7.2019 (SB); Thornton (Bradford), 29.6.2019 (MaP); Kimberworth (Rotherham), larva, 15.7.2019 (UR).
64. High Farnhill, 28.4.2019 (NS); West Bradford, 30.4.2019 (BH); Selby, 29.6.2019 (UR); Coniston Cold, 4.7.2019 (ARh).
65. Brompton-on-Swale, 15.5.2019 (BW).

71.006 Alder Kitten *Furcula bicpis* **(Borkhausen)**

71.007 Poplar Kitten and 71.006 Sallow Kitten 6 July 2019 Flamborough VC61 Mike Pearson.

These are both new sites. They continue the trend of scattered records from the western fringes of the county. This species is commoner over the border in Lancashire and south Cumbria.
63. Thurlstone, 23.5.2019 (CB); Barnsley, 28.5.2018 (JWi).

71.007 Poplar Kitten *F. bifida* **(Brahm)**
Take care not to confuse this species with the much commoner Sallow Kitten which is smaller with shorter wings.
61. Flamborough, 6.7.2019 (MiP).
62. Stokesley, 29.6.2019 (SW); Skelton, 8.7.2019 (SF).
64. Bellflask, 25.5.2019 (BM); Brayton, 2.6.2019 (PT); Alwoodley, 3.6.2019 (PRM).
65. Foxglove Covert, 24.7.2019 (FCMT).

71.010 Marbled Brown *Drymonia dodonaea* **([Denis & Schiffermüller])**
A rather local moth of central Yorkshire. Only two records so a very poor year.
62. Strensall Common, 25.5.2019 (YB); Haxby, 3.6.2019 (TJC).

71.011 Lunar Marbled Brown *D. ruficornis* **(Hufnagel)**
Another record year for this species and a spectacular recovery following a population crash in 2012 when we only had two records. 65 records were received of 142 moths from 38 sites across all five vice-counties including several new sites. Some people confuse this with the previous species but it flies at least a month earlier, and it is at the very end of its flight time when Marbled Brown is flying.

71.023 Scarce Prominent *Odontosia carmelita* **(Esper)**
This rather local moth of birch woodland tends to fly earlier than some of the other "Prominents" and is single-brooded. It was recorded from typical sites in VC62 and also at Austerfield in the south east of VC63. The small population in this area is contiguous with records in Nottinghamshire.
62. Brafferton Spring Wood, 19.4.2019 (TAB); Low North Camp, 19.4.2019 (AR, JHo); Broxa Forest, 20 & 24.4.2019 (AR, JHo); Pilmoor Wood, 21.4.2019 (TAB); Low Dalby, 24.4.2019 (JW).
63. Austerfield, 1.5.2019 (SB).

71.027 Chocolate-tip *Clostera curtula* **(Linnaeus)**
Since recolonising the county in 2009, this species has slowly moved northwards and become more common. We received records from 11 sites, the most ever, and many of these were on the periphery of its range. Only one record was from the second brood which is common in the south of England.
61. Market Weighton, 12.5.2019 (PA); Spurn, 21 & 24.5.2019 (JHF, MA); Lund, 31.5 (MCo) & 18.8.2019 (DA).
63. West Melton, 20.4.2019 (HEB); Potteric Carr NR, 22.4.2019 (RI&JCH, HEB); Austerfield, 30.4, 1 & 14.5.2019 (SB); Owston, 15 & 19.5.2019 (MaP); Kirk Smeaton, 27.5 & 5.6.2019 (DWi); Thorne Moors, 29.5.2019 (RM).

71.028 Small Chocolate-tip *C. pigra* **(Hufnagel)**
Larvae were found again at its main site. There were no records from Allerthorpe Common this year.
62. Strensall Common area, 5 & 19.7.2019 (PMa).

EREBIDAE

72.007 Beautiful Snout *Hypena crassalis* (Fabricius)

A very good year for this recent colonist with record numbers seen, and many sites in VC62 and 64 recording it for the first time. It is no surprise that it has now spilled over into VC61 so we have now had records from all five vice-counties.

61. Muston, 13.7.2019 (PQW). NEW VC RECORD
62. Newtondale, 17.6.2019 (SF); Turkey Carpet, 21 & 28.6.2019 (SF); Harwood Dale Forest, 22.6.2019 (RWo, SF); Rosedale, 27.6.2019 (SN); Broxa, 28.6, 12 & 18.7.2019 (GF, AR, JHo); Rievaulx Moor, 29.6.2019 (RWo); Low Dalby, 29 & 30.6.2019 (JW); Malton, 14.7.2019 (UR).

70.025 Scarlet Tiger Burley (Leeds) 22 June 19
first for Yorkshire photographer unknown.

64. Ilkley, 1 & 14.6, 8 & 13.7.2019 (P&JB); Burley-in-Wharfedale, 22.6.2019 (P&AR); Menston, 22.6.2019 (CGH); Coniston Cold, 29.6.2019 (ARh); Guisecliffe (Yorke's Folly), 19.7.2019 (CHF, JCW).

72.010 Black Arches *Lymantria monacha* (Linnaeus)

The best year yet for this oak-feeding species which recolonised the county in 2004 after a long absence. Four of the six sites were new so there has been a significant expansion of range this year.

61. North Frodingham, 25.7.2019 (AAl); Wawne, 30.7.2019 (BD).
63. Lindholme, 16.7.2019 (P&JS, MP, HEB); Rotherham, 23.7.2019 (MSm); Austerfield, 25.7.2019 (SB).
64. Askham Bog, 25.7.2019 (AF, TJC, YB, NH).

72.018 Scarce Vapourer *Orgyia recens* (Hübner)

Records of larvae from its most regular site.

63. Thorne Moors, 7, 21, & 22.5, 2 & 10.6.2019 (MWa et al.).

72.023 Clouded Buff *Diacrisia sannio* (Linnaeus)

We expect records from lowland heaths and upland areas so two at Spurn were unusual. They were the first there since 1947 and were a long way from any known colonies. There were no records from the west of the county this year.

61. Easington (Spurn), 7 & 9.6.2019 (MFS).
62. Strensall Common, 24.6, 4 & 7.7.2019 (YB, PMa); Birk Nab (Pockley Moor), 2.7.2019 (MRB).

72.025 Wood Tiger *Parasemia plantaginis* (Linnaeus)

Typical records from moorland and scrubby areas including several from new sites.

61. Wharram Quarry, 1.7.2019 (MNe).
62. Danby Low Moor, 9.6.2019 (WN); Dalby Forest, 18.6.2019 (LW); Fen Bog, 28.6.2019 (GF).
63. Hollins Hall, 4.7.2019 (HCSG).
64. Kilnsey, 29.6.2019 (PMi); Bastow Wood, 4.7.2019 (IPow); Barden Moor, 6.7.2019 (UR).
65. Great Pinseat, 11.7.2019 (UR).

72.029 Scarlet Tiger *Callimorpha dominula* (Linnaeus)

A moth was seen flying by day and photographed by an unknown recorder near Leeds. This species has undergone considerable expansion in the last few years and it is not entirely unexpected that it should turn up in Yorkshire.

64. Burley, Leeds, 22.6.2019 (UR). NEW COUNTY RECORD

72.037 Round-winged Muslin *Thumatha senex* (Hübner)

A fall in numbers which is mainly due to few being caught at Spurn this year, but otherwise this moth of lichens in damp places is doing well in the county. It appeared at several new sites this year. One at Semerwater was interesting as there are few records from the Dales.

61. Spurn, 6 & 9.7.2019 (MFS, JCr); Wheldrake, 13 & 16.7.2019 (JOHS); Easington (Spurn), 17.7.2019 (MFS).
62. Haxby, 8.7.2019 (TJC); York, 9.7.2019 (AF); Strensall Village, 9.7.2019 (YB); Strensall Common, 11.7.2019 (YB).
63. Potteric Carr NR, 5.7.2019 (RI&JCH, HEB); Austerfield, 9, 11, 24 & 25.7.2019 (SB); Hatfield Moors, 16.7.2019 (HEB, DWi); Lindholme, 16.7.2019 (MP, P&JS); Thorpe Marsh NR, 22.7.2019 (DWi, MaP).

64. Askham Bog, 8 & 25.7.2019 (AF, TJC, PMa et al.); Bishopthorpe, 15.7.2019 (JT).
65. Semerwater SSSI, 26.7.2019 (CHF, JCW, DMS, TMW).

72.038 Four-dotted Footman *Cybosia mesomella* (Linnaeus)
Records from the usual central areas of the county. This is a rather local moth of heathy areas but it can wander at times and one turned up at Fishlake for the first time this year.
61. Skipwith Common, 17.7.2019 (NC, SC).
62. Strensall Village, 6, 14, 17 & 19.6.2019 (YB); Strensall Common, 9 & 29.6, 8 & 11.7.2019 (YB, TJC, PMa); Haxby, 6 & 7.7.2019 (TJC).
63. Fishlake, 6.7.2019 (RP); Thorne Moors, 8 & 10.7.2019 (MWa et al.); Crowle Moor, 11.7.2019 (DWi).

72.042 Red-necked Footman *Atolmis rubricollis* (Linnaeus)
After several years of increasing records, there has been a marked drop in numbers this year. Perhaps this is part of the normal fluctuations as its parasitoids catch up with it after a period of rapid expansion. Despite this it was seen at four new sites and is colonising new areas now, such as Skipwith Common and Askham Bog. It remains commonest in VC62 in coniferous woodland.
61. North Ferriby, 10.7.2019 (IM); Skipwith Common, 12.9.2019 (PA).
62. Wykeham Forest, 16.6.2019 (KL); Scawton, 17.6.2019 (DBa); Cropton Forest, 21.6.2019 (LW); Stape, 22.6.2019 (LW); Broxa, 28.6.2019 (GF); Low Dalby, 29 & 30.6.2019 (JW); Rievaulx Moor, 29.6.2019 (RWo); Guisborough, 29.6.2019 (RWo); Wykeham Causeway, 29.6.2019 (AR, JHo).
63. Lindholme, 15.8.2019 (P&JS).
64. Burley-in-Wharfedale, 5.7.2019 (P&AR); Otley, 6.7.2019 (JWi); Askham Bog, 8.7.2019 (AF, TJC, PMa et al.).

72.046 Scarce Footman *Eilema complana* (Linnaeus)
It is worth noting that this species is continuing its steady march north-west across the county. It was noted from 85 sites, 13 of which were new. Nine of these were from the periphery of its range and we now have records from the west of VC63, half way across VC64 and several from the south-east of VC65. One moth in the very west of VC65 is likely to have come from the expanding population in the Morecambe Bay area.

72.049 Orange Footman *E. sororcula* (Hufnagel)
A fall in numbers following several years of expansion, but this is a late-spring woodland species and they all did badly in 2019, so perhaps numbers are more stable than they appear. Beware of "Orange Footman" in July. They are usually the orange form of Buff or Dingy Footman.
61. Kilnwick, 25, 30 & 31.5.2019 (MCo); North Cliffe Wood, 31.5.2019 (IM, ADN); Stillingfleet Lodge, 1.6.2019 (DBa); Easington (Spurn), 3.6.2019 (MFS).
62. Low Dalby, 30.5.2019 (JW); Wykeham Causeway, 30.5.2019 (AR, JHo); Haxby, 3.6.2019 (TJC).
63. Austerfield, 14, 22, 26 & 31.5, 1.6.2019 (SB); Potteric Carr NR, 18 & 25.5, 1.6.2019 (RI&JCH, HEB); Fishlake, 1.6.2019 (RP).
64. Hackfall Woods, 1.6.2019 (CHF).
65. Beverley Wood, Great Smeaton, 23.4.2019 (JE).

72.0501 Nine-spotted *Amata phegea* (Linnaeus)
This was the most unexpected record of the year. One was seen flying by day and photographed. This showed the hindwings well enough to exclude the other possible *Amata* species which could possibly occur. The only previous British records are one in 1872 in Kent and one in 2000 in Essex. It is resident in central and southern Europe and is not normally known as a migrant. The larvae feed on a variety of herbaceous plants.
63. Near Wentbridge, 14.7.2019 (UR). NEW COUNTY RECORD.

72.060 Marsh Oblique-barred *Hypenodes humidalis* (Doubleday)
The only previous county records have all come from the west of VC64, these moths being part of the south Cumbria/north Lancashire population. It is a major surprise therefore to find it at Strensall Common. As one of our smallest macros, this undistinguished-looking species of boggy moorland

72.0501 Nine-spotted 14 July 19 photographer unknown first for Yorkshire, third for the UK.

and heathland has probably been lurking undetected in this area for some time.
62. Moorside campsite, Strensall, 28.7.2019 (RD). NEW VC RECORD.

72.066 Waved Black *Parascotia fuliginaria* (Linnaeus)

This elusive species of boggy woodland is rarely reported, in fact we only have eight previous records. It is quite exceptional therefore to have four records from three sites this year. It is likely that it is not strongly attracted to light.
61. Easington (Spurn), 4.8.2019 (MFS).
63. Austerfield, 20 & 24.7.2019 (SB); Carlton Marsh NR, 23.8.2019 (HEB, CG et al.).

72.073 Small Marbled Tadcaster 13 July 19
David Baker

72.067 Small Purple-barred *Phytometra viridaria* (Clerck)

This declining day-flying species was noted from typical areas in VC62. There were no records from our lowland heaths again this year. Unusually the Skelton record was attracted to light.
62. Hawnby, 15.5.2019 (DWa); Skelton, 1.6.2019 (SF); Fen Bog, 1 & 6.6 (GF) and 12.7.2019 (PMa).

72.069 Beautiful Hook-tip *Laspeyria flexula* ([Denis & Schiffermüller])

At some point, numbers of this attractive moth will dip as its parasitoids catch up with it after a period of rapid expansion. There is no sign of this yet however and although numbers stabilised a little this year (356 records of 606 moths), there was evidence of further range expansion in the north and west of the county. Of 85 sites reporting this species, 16 were new. It is now only absent from parts of northern VC64 and large areas of VC65. 11 records in September were from the second brood which is evidently becoming more common.

72.073 Small Marbled *Eublemma parva* (Hübner)

A small influx of this species into the country in July brought four moths to Yorkshire. We have had only five previous records, four of these coming from the influx of 2015.
61. Easington (Spurn), 9.7.2019 (MFS); Hunmanby Gap, 10.7.2019 (KC); Spurn, 12.7.2019 (JHF).
64. Tadcaster, 13.7.2019 (DBa). NEW VC RECORD.

72.074 Beautiful Marbled *E. purpurina* ([Denis & Schiffermüller])

Another unexpected migrant moth. This is the second county record; the first being at Spurn in 2017. This is a relatively recent migrant to the UK having first been seen at Portland in 2001.
63. Cudworth, 25.7.2019 (CG). NEW VC RECORD.

72.076 Clifden Nonpareil *Catocala fraxini* (Linnaeus)

For some, the fabled Blue Underwing is the Holy Grail of moth trapping. This was the 12th county record and the fifth for VC61. There were rumours of another seen in VC61 but no record was

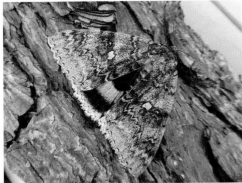
72.076 Clifden Nonpareil, Flamborough 30 Aug 19
Allan Rodda

72.074 Beautiful Marbled, Cudworth 25 July 19
Cliff Gorman VC63 record and second for Yorkshire.

received. This was the first record since 2007.

61. Flamborough, 30.8.2019 (AR, JHo).

72.081 Dark Crimson Underwing *C. sponsa* **(Linnaeus)**
This attractive species is resident in woodland in Hampshire and Wiltshire but records elsewhere are of migrants. A small influx brought one to Yorkshire. This is our second record; the first being at the same site in 2017.

61. Spurn, 1.8.2019 (JHF).

72.083 Burnet Companion *Euclidia glyphica* **(Linnaeus)**
Rather low numbers again of this moth of calcareous flower-rich grassy areas. An encouraging record from Skipton Quarry was well away from any known sites.

61. Enthorpe, 16.6.2019 (AA); Wharram Quarry, 9.7.2019 (JG).
62. Ellerburn Bank, 15.6.2019 (UR); Heckdale Quarry, 16.6.2019 (UR); Dalby Forest, 22.6.2019 (UR).
63. Thorne Moors, 3, 4 & 6.6.2019 (MWa et al.); Barrow Colliery site, Worsbrough, 18.6.2019 (UR).
64. Skipton Quarry, 24.5.2019 (ARh).

72.084 Mother Shipton *E. mi* **(Clerck)**
A very encouraging total of 43 records of 83 moths from 35 sites means that unusually there are too many to list individually. Reported widely across the county from flower-rich grassy areas. It was recorded at Spurn where it used to be common, after an absence of four years. It was also noted from upper Teesdale for the first time.

NOCTUIDAE

73.008 Golden Twin-spot *Chrysodeixis chalcites* **(Esper)**
The nineteenth county record of this migrant species, and the first since 2011.

61. Catwick, 1.8.2019 (JM).

73.014 Golden Plusia *Polychrysia moneta* **(Fabricius)**
Another poor year for this species which is doing badly across the country. Are we growing fewer Delphiniums in our gardens or are there other factors at work?

61. Rudston, 19.7.2019 (HEB).
62. York, 17 & 18.7.2019 (AF).
63. West Melton, 6 & 16.7.2019 (HEB); Rotherham, 22.7.2019 (MSm).
64. Burley-in-Wharfedale, 13.7.2019 (P&AR).

73.018 Gold Spangle *Autographa bractea* **([Denis & Schiffermüller])**
This is the lowest total of moths since 2007 so unusually we are listing all records. This species is now much rarer in the lowlands than it used to be and is one of several species which appear to be adapting to climatic change by moving to higher ground.

61. Lund, 29.7.2019 (MCo).
62. Lealholm, 23.7.2019 (GF); Marske Beach, 28.7.2019 (DM); Scarborough, 28.7 & 1.8.2019 (BR, AR, JHo); Beast Cliff, 3.8.2019 (SN); Errington Copse, New Marske, 8.8.2019 (DM).
63. Thornton (Bradford); 16 & 27.7.2019 (MaP).
64. Ribblehead Quarry NR, 18.7.2019 (TMW); Malham Tarn, 22.7.2019 (DCGB); Coniston Cold, 25 & 29.7.2019 (ARh); Little Preston, 28.7.2019 (JMa); Bellflask, 30.7.2019 (BM); Burley-in-Wharfedale, 3.8.2019 (P&AR); Giggleswick, 3 & 29.8.2019 (RW); West Bradford, 7.8.2019 (BH); Yockenthwaite, 14.8.2019 (PMi, ARh, DFe).
65. Constable Burton Hall, 29.6.2019 (RWi); Foxglove Covert, 24.7.2019 (FCMT); Lartington, 24.7.2019 (PWe); Semerwater SSSI, 26.7.2019 (CHF, JCW, DMS, TMW); Hutton Conyers, 5 & 7.8.2019 (CHF).

73.021 Scarce Silver Y *Syngrapha interrogationis* **(Linnaeus)**
An average year with records from the usual upland areas.

63. Golcar, 25.7.2019 (CSR); Keighley Moor, 29.7, 1, 2, 5 & 7.8.2019 (IHa); Halifax, 17.8.2019 (DSu).
64. Guisecliffe Wood, 19.7.2019 (CHF, JCW); Coniston Cold, 22.7.2019 (ARh); Skyreholme, 23.7 & 1.8.2019 (PMi); Burley-in-Wharfedale, 25.7.2019 (P&AR); Ilkley, 31.7.2019 (P&JB); West End, 1.8.2019 (CGH); Yockenthwaite, 14.8.2019 (PMi, ARh, DFe).
65. Marrick Moor, 27.6.2019 (PCo); Semerwater SSSI, 26.7.2019 (CHF, JCW, DMS, TMW); Foxglove Covert, 23.8.2019 (CHF, JCW, DMS et al.).

73.026 Silver Hook *Deltote uncula* **(Clerck)**
As usual, all of our records came from Strensall Common.

62. Strensall Common, several records, 24.5 to 16.7.2019 (YB, TJC, PMa).

73.032 Nut-tree Tussock *Colocasia coryli* (Linnaeus)

All of our records came from the east of VC62 where this species can be locally common in broadleaved woodland. It is rare in other parts of the county.

62. Broxa Forest, 24.4 & 16.5.2019 (AR, JHo); Sutherbruff Rigg, 19 & 30.5.2019 (JW); Low Dalby, 24 & 30.5, 6, 7 & 17.6.2019 (JW).

73.033 Figure of Eight *Diloba caeruleocephala* (Linnaeus)

A declining species across the country and this is the lowest total of records we have ever had. Reasons for the decline are not obvious.

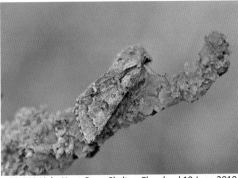

73.042 Light Knot Grass Skelton Cleveland 19 June 2019 Damian Money

62. Nunthorpe, 23.10.2019 (EG); Great Smeaton, 23.10.2019 (JE).
64. Otley, 11 & 19.10.2019 (M&JC).

73.036 Alder Moth *Acronicta alni* (Linnaeus)

A big drop in numbers, typical of most May/June woodland moths in 2019.

61. Skidby, 30.5.2019 (ADN); Tophill Low NR, 9.8.2019 (MHo, DF).
62. Lealholm, 24.6.2019 (GF).
63. Potteric Carr NR, 25.5 & 1.6.2019 (RI&JCH, HEB); Rodley, 1.6.2019 (JWC).
64. Coniston Cold, 29.5.2019 (ARh); Little Preston, 30.5.2019 (JMa); Bellflask, 31.5.2019 (BM); Hackfall Woods, 1.6.2019 (CHF); Colt Park, 24.6.2019 (TMW, KA, JHa); Menston, 28.6.2019 (CGH).
65. High Batts NR, 26.5.2019 (CHF, LR, PT).

73.039 Sycamore *A. aceris* (Linnaeus)

A drop in numbers following the big totals of 2018. There was no evidence of northerly movement this year, though there was spread to some new sites in the west of VC63.

61. Spurn, 8.7.2019 (JHF); Catwick, 10 & 25.7.2019 (JM); Easington (Spurn), 23.7.2019 (MFS); Withernsea, 23.7.2019 (MCF); North Ferriby, 24.7.2019 (IM).
63. Bramley (Rotherham), 20.5.2019 (UR); Rodley, 31.5.2019 (JWC); Sheffield Area, 7.6, 7 & 8.7.2019 (PMe, AG); Austerfield, 29.6, 4 & 9.7.2019 (SB); Dewsbury, 29.6.2019 (PD); Cudworth, 5.7.2019 (CG); Oughtibridge, 6.7.2019 (PBu); West Melton, 17, 21, 25 & 27.7.2019 (HEB); Sprotbrough, 21.7.2019 (DBo); Carlton, 24.7.2019 (DSm); West Tong, 22.9.2019 (UR).
64. Cookridge, 8.7.2019 (PL).

73.042 Light Knot Grass *A. menyanthidis* (Esper)

The best year ever for this moth of moorland and heathland, with records from several new sites. Two unusual records in VC61 and one in the east of VC63 were on lower ground well away from any suitable habitat. These coincided with two very strange records in Nottinghamshire on 24th May and Leicestershire on 25th May. This sounds like a coordinated arrival of a moth which is not usually thought of as a migrant.

61. Long Riston, 24.5.2019 (MI); Goxhill, 1.7.2019 (MI).
62. Great Smeaton, 24.5.2019 (JE); Skelton, 18.6.2019 (DM).
63. Keighley Moor, 21 & 30.4, 14, 15, 22 & 24,5, & 9.6.2019 (IHa), plus a larva at this site on 27.8.2019 (IHa); Austerfield, 25.5.2019 (SB); Thornton (Bradford), 21.4.2019 (MaP).
64. Ingleborough NR, 1.6.2019 (TMW); West Bradford, 24.6.2019 (BH).
65. Lartington, 5.7.2019 (PWe).

73.047 Coronet *Craniophora ligustri* ([Denis & Schiffermüller])

The old population in the western half of VC64 and 65 remains stable with 16 records from 11 sites this year. The new invaders which arrived at Spurn in 2010 continue to advance slowly north and west, in the manner of Vikings but without the raping and pillaging. This population provided 83 records, all in VC61 and 63, and there were several new sites at the periphery of the range. At this rate of progress, our Anglo-Saxon natives are safe for several more years.

73.048 Small Yellow Underwing *Panemeria tenebrata* (Scopoli)

It is encouraging to report that there were too many records of this day-flying moth of flower-rich grassland to report this year. 33 records of 221 moths from 16 sites is a good total. There appears to be a particularly healthy population at Walmgate Stray in York where about 20 were recorded on several dates in May (PMa). This species really ought to be called "Small Yellow Typo" as we receive a lot of records of moths caught at light in July and August. These are all other "Yellow Underwings".

73.048 Small Yellow Underwing Walmgate Stray York
13 May 2019 Peter Mayhew

73.050 Wormwood *Cucullia absinthii* (Linnaeus)

This species is still hanging on in the south of VC63 but numbers have dropped dramatically across the country. If we could persuade the authorities not to tidy up and build on brownfield sites and to leave stands of wormwood, mugwort and other flowering plants, species like this would do a lot better.
63. West Melton, 29.7.2019 (HEB); Hayfield, 19.8.2019 (UR).

73.052 Shark *C. umbratica* (Linnaeus)

A good recovery after two very poor years with records scattered across four vice-counties.
61. Lower Derwent Valley, 25.6, 9, 23, 24 & 25.7.2019 (CSR, LM, NC, SC); Catwick, 27.6 & 10.7.2019 (JM); Hunmanby Gap, 5.7.2019 (KC); North Frodingham, 9.7.2019 (AAl); Muston, 21.7.2019 (PQW); Elvington, 27.7.2019 (JSm).
62. Saltburn, 4.7.2019 (IE); Guisborough, 4 & 9.7.2019 (RWo); Skelton, 19.7 & 3.8.2019 (DM); Marske Beach, 28.7.2019 (DM); Strensall Village, 8.8.2019 (YB).
63. Austerfield, 20.5.2019 (SB); Rotherham, 9.7 & 5.8.2019 (MSm); Fishlake, 10.7.2019 (RP); West Melton, 13, 14, 18 & 31.7.2019 (HEB); Sheffield, 25.7.2019 (UR).
64. Tadcaster, 28.7.2019 (DBa).

73.053 Chamomile Shark *C. chamomillae* ([Denis & Schiffermüller])

More records than last year but numbers are still much lower than they were 20 years ago, probably due to changing farming practices and a lack of agricultural weeds. Apart from Spurn, all the other records were from new sites.
61. Spurn, 5 & 24.5, 5.6.2019 (MA, JHF); Kilnwick, 24.5.2019 (MCo); East Cottingwith, 3.6.2019 (RFor).
63. Thornton (Bradford), 1.6.2019 (MaP).
64. Alwoodley, 2.4.2019 (RWi).
65. Nosterfield NR, 17.5.2019 (CHF).

73.055 Star-wort *C. asteris* ([Denis & Schiffermüller])

Numbers at Spurn are stable but much reduced from the totals seen 20 years ago.
61. Spurn, ten records, all of single moths, from 20.6 to 28.7.2019 (JHF, JCr, MA).

73.058 Mullein *C. verbasci* (Linnaeus)

67 records from 41 sites is by far the biggest total ever received so there are too many to list individually. These were spread all over the county with the exception of the western fringes. 23 records were of the distinctive larvae – usually on mulleins but sometimes on figwort. This is usually the easiest way to record the moth and it is surprising how many plants have larvae when checked.

73.061 Anomalous *Stilbia anomala* (Haworth)

Typical records from upland parts of VC62 and from the west of the county, but numbers are down in recent years and it remains rather local.
62. Skelton, 23 & 28.8.2019 (DM); Harwood Dale, 25.8.2019 (SF); Lealholm, 27.8.2019 (GF); Rievaulx Moor, 29.8.2019 (RWo).
63. Keighley, 25.8.2019 (IHa).
64. Moughton, 23.7.2019 (TMW); High Bentham, 23.8.2019 (RF).

73.070 Bordered Sallow *Pyrrhia umbra* (Hufnagel)

A second year of very low numbers, particularly at Spurn where the population seems to have crashed quite dramatically.

61. Flamborough, 9.6 & 8.7.2019 (MiP); Muston, 18.6.2019 (PQW); Wharram Quarry, 21.6.2019 (AM); Hunmanby Gap, 25 & 28.6.2019 (KC); Easington (Spurn), 8.7.2019 (MFS).
62. Guisborough, 29.6.2019 (RWo).
64. Askham Bog, 8.7.2019 (AF, TJC, PMa et al.).

73.072 Marbled Clover *Heliothis viriplaca* (Hufnagel)

These are the fourth and fifth county records, and the first since 1968. This species is resident in East Anglia and Wiltshire; records elsewhere are migrants.

73.082 Tree-lichen Beauty Swinefleet 25 July 19 Mike Pilsworth VC63 record.

A small influx in early August brought moths to Yorkshire and up into Northumberland. The Beverley moth came to a light trap and the Ripon moth was seen by day. Both were photographed.

61. Beverley, 1.8.2019 (KW).
64. Ripon, 2.8.2019 (R&PR). NEW VC RECORD.

73.074 Bordered Straw *H. peltigera* ([Denis & Schiffermüller])

There were only two records of this migrant species. The Asenby moth in March was the earliest ever recorded in the county; southerly winds and warm weather brought several unexpected migrants to the country in late February and early March.

61. Flamborough, 29.7.2019 (MiP).
65. Asenby, 3.3.2019 (K&DH).

73.076 Scarce Bordered Straw *Helicoverpa armigera* (Hübner)

A good year for this migrant which despite the name tends to be commoner than Bordered Straw in most years.

61. Spurn area, 22.8, 4, 5, 6 & 7.9.2019 (MFS, JCr); Muston, 5 & 9.10.2019 (PQW).
64. Coniston Cold, 28.7.2019 (ARh); Mickley, 23.9.2019 (CHF, JCW, JH, FC).
65. Hutton Conyers, 24.9.2019 (CHF).

73.082 Tree-lichen Beauty *Cryphia algae* (Fabricius)

Following its first appearance in the county in 2018, this species had a remarkable year with many more records in the Spurn area, northward spread to Flamborough and westward spread to Swine-fleet. The most likely scenario is that this spread will continue over the next few years, though in some species we see a period of consolidation before further expansion.

61. Spurn area, 11 records of 12 moths from 23.7 to 20.8.2019 (MFS, JHF); Flamborough, 23.8.2019 (IM, MP, LB).
63. Swinefleet, 25.7.2019 (MPi). NEW VC RECORD.

73.086 Shining Marbled *Pseudeustrotia candidula* ([Denis & Schiffermüller])

A rare and quite unexpected migrant. There have only been a handful of British records since the first in 2006.

61. Easington (Spurn), 28.7.2019 (MFS). NEW COUNTY RECORD.

73.087 Small Mottled Willow *Spodoptera exigua* (Hübner)

A good year for this migrant species. The January record was of a moth found alive inside a yellow pepper from a supermarket in Otley. The pepper is thought to have come from Spain. There was a similar record in 2014 inside a red pepper from a Pontefract supermarket. The two February records are unprecedented and were part of a very early invasion of migrants in an unseasonable warm spell with southerly winds.

61. Lund, 16.2.2019 (MCo).
63. Owston, 15.7.2019 (MaP).
64. Otley, 11.1.2019 (CGH); Ingleton, 23.2.2019 (JP); Coniston Cold, 11.7.2019 (ARh).

73.105 Bird's Wing *Dypterygia scabriuscula* (Linnaeus)

The two records from VC62 were the first since 2015 and the Wykeham Causeway moth was the most northerly in the country this century. Good numbers were reported from two sites in the east

of VC63 but despite these encouraging signs, it remains rare in the county and is probably declining.
62. Wykeham Causeway, 23.6.2019 (AR, JHo); Strensall Common, 11.7.2019 (YB).
63. Austerfield, 18 records of 23 moths in an extended single brood from 18.5 to 2.8.2019 (SB); Doncaster, 14, 22 & 25.7.2019 (NB).

73.118 Haworth's Minor *Celaena haworthii* (Curtis)
This moth of boggy moorland with cottongrass should really be confined to upland areas and lowland heaths, but it has a tendency to wander and appear in odd places miles from its food plant. There were few records this year.
61. North Ferriby, 21 & 24.7.2019 (IM).
62. Helwath, 29.8.2019 (GF).
63. Lindholme, 16.7.2019 (MP).
64. Malham Tarn, 22.7.2019 (DCGB); Moughton, 23.7.2019 (TMW); Syningthwaite Farm, 3.8.2019 (JCW); Dob Park, 23.8.2019 (CGH); New Laithe Farm, 24.8.2019 (MB); Cookridge, 26.8.2019 (PL); High Bentham, 23.8.2019 (RF).
65. Hutton Conyers, 27.8.2019 (CHF).

73.124 Butterbur *Hydraecia petasitis* (Doubleday)
This rather local moth was recorded from an encouraging ten sites though in smaller numbers than last year and on each occasion just one moth was caught. We receive few records from VC63 and the Brockadale record was far from any known sites.
61. Hunmanby Gap, 4.8.2019 (KC).
62. Low Dalby, 23 & 26.8.2019 (JW); Forge Valley, 25.8.2019 (AR, JHo); Scarborough, 26.8.2019 (L&JW); Haxby, 28.8.2019 (TJC).
63. Brockadale NR, 2.9.2019 (DWi).
64. Coniston Cold, 31.7.2019 (ARh); Bellflask, 25.8.2019 (BM); Sharow, 29.8.2019 (JCW).
65. Hutton Conyers, 30.8.2019 (CHF).

73.126 - 9 The "Ear" moths *Amphipoea* spp.
The exact distribution of these four species within the county still requires some work. We received 125 records of "Ear Moth agg." from 47 sites all across the county. This is of course the correct way to record undissected moths, but it would be nice to be able to identify these down to species level a bit more often. Please do send us some of these moths for dissection, especially from new sites, as it would make our distribution maps look more exciting. Perhaps you could even try to dissect some yourself. The males are really quite easy, apart from separating Saltern Ear and Large Ear, but this is normally only a problem on the coast. Saltern Ear can occasionally fool us and turn up inland, and it probably hybridises with Large Ear, but this is not common. As there are no reliable features to separate any of these species, the following records are of dissected moths:

73.126 Saltern Ear *A. fucosa* (Freyer)
Many coastal moths were probably this species but we can only be sure of this one.
61. Catwick, 27.8.2019 (JM).

73.127 Large Ear *A. lucens* (Freyer)
This is the commonest species in Yorkshire, especially in the north and west.
63. Hatfield Moors, 15.8 & 27.9.2019 (HEB).
64. Mickley, 25.8.2019 (CHF, JCW, FC, JH).
65. Hutton Conyers, 6 & 26.8.2019 (CHF); Foxglove Covert, 23.8.2019 (CHF, JCW, DMS et al.).

73.128 Ear Moth *A. oculea* (Linnaeus)
Widespread across the county with a south-easterly bias. Rare in VC62.
63. West Melton, 4.8.2019 (HEB).
64. Hartwith, 27.7.2019 (CHF).

73.129 Crinan Ear *A. crinanensis* (Burrows)
Very much a moth of the north-west quarter of the county.
64. Yockenthwaite, 14.8.2019 (PMi, ARh, DFe); Scar Close NNR, 21.9.2019 (TMW).
65. Hutton Conyers, 6.8.2019 (CHF).

73.138 Lyme Grass *Longalatedes elymi* (Treitschke)
This species is said to be doing well on a national basis but the situation in Yorkshire is more worrying as this is the lowest total of records ever received. There were no records from the Flamborough area this year.

61. Spurn area, 11 records, all of single moths, from 31.5 to 27.7.2019 (MFS, JHF, JCr).
62. Marske Beach, 28.7 & 2.8.2019 (DM).

73.139 Twin-spotted Wainscot *Lenisa geminipuncta* (Haworth)
45 records of 50 moths from 26 sites is a reduction from last year's record numbers but it is still a healthy total. It is still absent from many northern and western parts of the county and further spread is limited by a lack of suitable reed beds in these areas. It does however tend to wander locally and was found at five new sites.

73.141 Brown-veined Wainscot *Archanara dissoluta* (Treitschke)
Another reed bed species but much more thinly distributed. Very few records this year.
61. Tophill Low NR, 1.8.2019 (MHo, DF).
63. Potteric Carr NR, 24.7 & 7.8.2019 (RI&JCH, HEB).
65. Hutton Conyers, 25.7.2019 (CHF).

73.142 Small Rufous *Coenobia rufa* (Haworth)
A reduction from last year's big totals but still too many to list individually. 34 records of 51 moths from 20 sites spread across low-lying parts of the county.

73.145 Mere Wainscot *Photedes fluxa* (Hübner)
This moth of wet woodland is very local in the county. Yorkshire is the most northerly outpost of this species.
61. Wheldrake, 24.7.2019 (JOHS).
63. Austerfield, 3.8.2019 (SB).

73.146 Least Minor *Photedes captiuncula* (Treitschke)
This elusive species of limestone grassland is restricted to the west of VC64 and across into south Cumbria. It is one of our most important moths. All records as usual were of moths seen by day.
64. Arncliffe, 29.6.2019 (PMi); Kilnsey, 8 & 17.7.2019 (PMi, ARh).

73.157 Large Nutmeg *Apamea anceps* ([Denis & Schiffermüller])
This species has a toe hold in the very south of the county since it reappeared in 2012 after a gap of 16 years.
61. Spurn, 5.7.2019 (MFS).
63. Austerfield, 24.5.2019 (SB).

73.161 Crescent Striped *A. oblonga* (Haworth)
A slight recovery following a low point of only two records in 2017. Nationally it has been doing poorly in recent years.
61. Spurn area, 11 records of 15 moths from 6.7 to 7.8.2019 (MFS, JHF, JCr).

73.165 Confused *A. furva* ([Denis & Schiffermüller])
Records as usual from upland western parts of the county. There were no records from the coastal population at Flamborough this year. Take care not to confuse it with the rather similar form of Dusky Brocade which is common and widespread across the county.
64. Coniston Cold, 3, 11, 18, 24 & 31.7, 7, 8 & 22.8.2019 (ARh); Skyreholme, 25 & 27.8.2019 (PMi).

73.179 Orange Sallow *Tiliacea citrago* (Linnaeus)
An average year for this moth of lime woodland. Unusually there were no records from VC61.
62. Great Smeaton, 27.8.2019 (JE); York, 3, 5 & 7.9.2019 (AF).
63. Halifax, 19.7.2019 (DSu); Bramley, 27.8 & 14.9.2019 (JWC); Doncaster, 31.8.2019 (RM); Pledwick, Wakefield, 8.9.2019 (MHe); Sprotbrough, 11.9.2019 (DBo).
64. Mickley, 25.8.2019 (CHF, JCW, FC, JH); Little Preston, 26.8.2019 (JMa); Coniston Cold, 1.9.2019 (ARh); West Bradford, 4.9.2019 (BH); Giggleswick, 5 & 14.9.2019 (RW); Dob Park, 8.9.2019 (CGH); Bishopthorpe, 8.9.2019 (JT); Tadcaster, 11.9.2019 (DBa).
65. Hutton Conyers, 2.9.2019 (CHF); Asenby, 28.9.2019 (K&DH).

73.183 Dusky-lemon Sallow *Cirrhia gilvago* ([Denis & Schiffermüller])
A very poor year with just eight records, all of single moths and all from the eastern half of the county.
61. Easington (Spurn), 10 & 24.9, 5.10.2019 (MFS); Lund, 19.9.2019 (MCo); Catwick, 21.9.2019 (JM); North Ferriby, 6.10.2019 (IM).
62. Haxby, 15.9.2019 (TJC).
63. Austerfield, 26.9.2019 (SB).

73.184 Pale-lemon Sallow *C. ocellaris* (Borkhausen)
The rarest of the "Sallows". This is the third county record following single moths in 2006 and 2012.

This species is resident in parts of eastern and south-eastern England and moths outside these areas are usually classed as migrants though some may be wanderers from the core area.
61. North Ferriby, 5.10.2019 (IM).

73.188 Flounced Chestnut *Agrochola helvola* (Linnaeus)
An average year for this moth of upland wooded areas which occasionally wanders to the lowlands. Nationally, numbers have dropped considerably. Encouragingly, five of these records are from new sites.
62. Helwath, 29.8.2019 (GF); Broxa Forest, 19.9.2019 (AR, JHo).
63. Keighley Moor, 15 & 22.9.2019 (IHa); Rishworth, 4.10.2019 (EE); Thornton (Bradford), 23.9.2019 (MaP).
64. Little Preston, 21.9.2019 (JMa); High Farnhill, 22.9.2019 (NS).
65. Healey, 14.9.2019 (DMS, IW).

73.200 Tawny Pinion *Lithophane semibrunnea* (Haworth)
A poor year for this over-wintering ash-feeding species and there were no records of moths in the autumn. Again all records were of single moths and scattered across the county. All except for the Haxby records were from new sites. This is typical for this species which seems to be able to pop up anywhere. It may not be strongly attracted to light. Occasionally people confuse it with the much commoner Pale Pinion (44 records from 27 sites in 2019).
61. Beverley, 24.3.2019 (DT).
62. Haxby, 19 & 27.3.2019 (TJC).
63. Halifax, 29.3.2019 (DSu).
64. West Bradford, 24.4.2019 (BH).

73.207 Golden-rod Brindle *Xylena solidaginis* (Hübner)
Typical records from upland areas with heather.
62. Harwood Dale, 25.8.2019 (SF); Rievaulx Moor, 29.8.2019 (RWo).
63. Keighley Moor, 2, 22 & 23.8.2019 (IHa); Pateley Bridge, 1.8.2019 (T&PB).
64. Ilkley, 10 & 25.8.2019 (P&JB).

73.209 Red Sword-grass *X. vetusta* (Hübner)
An average year for this moth of damp areas, particularly in upland parts of the county.
61. Hunmanby Gap, 22.3.2019 (KC); Elloughton, 3.4.2019 (MPa); Wheldrake, 4.4.2019 (JOHS).
62. Broxa Forest, 12.1 & 20.3.2019 (AR, JHo); Grinkle Park, 22.2.2019 (SF).
64. Coniston Cold, several dates 24.1 to 26.11.2019 (ARh); Grass Wood, 24.2.2019 (PMi); Summerbridge, 2.3.2019 (MAR); Littondale, 26.3.2019 (PMi, N&DF); Sharow, 15 & 20.4.2019 (JCW); Ripon, 21.4.2019 (CNe); Giggleswick, 23.10.2019 (RW); Burley-in-Wharfedale, 24.10.2019 (P&AR); Ingleton, 25.10.2019 (RN); Skyreholme, 26.11.2019 (PMi).
65. Cotherstone, 7.4.2019 (PWe).

73.211 Angle-striped Sallow *Enargia paleacea* (Esper)
Another good year for this birch-feeding species with 54 records of 76 moths from 36 sites across all parts of the county except for the north-western third and the east of VC61 where it does not occur. Our population is nationally important as it has a restricted distribution in the UK.

73.212 Double Kidney *Ipimorpha retusa* (Linnaeus)
This is the only population in the north of England where it is resident in a small area of damp woodland north of Ripon on the VC64/5 border. Numbers were good this year and moths wandered as far as Sharow which is a new site.
64. Bellflask, 18 records of 131 moths from 5.7 to 26.8.2019 (BM); Sharow, 21 & 29.7.2019 (JCW).
65. High Batts NR, 12.7.2019 (CHF, TMW, DMS et al.); Hutton Conyers, 23 & 28.7.2019 (CHF).

73.213 Olive *I. subtusa* ([Denis & Schiffermüller])
This species appears to be less common than it was 20 years ago though the distribution has not altered. A drop in records this year with most again coming from VC61.
61. Spurn, 8.7.2019 (JHF); Lund, 16, 21 & 25.7, 3.8.2019 (MCo); Tophill Low NR, 18, 21, 22 & 26.7, 1 & 2.8.2019 (MHo, DF); North Ferriby, 24.7.2019 (IM); Kilnwick, 25.7.2019 (MCo).
62. York, 24.7.2019 (AF); Haxby, 24.7.2019 (TJC); Low Dalby, 23.8.2019 (JW); Great Smeaton, 27.8.2019 (JE).
63. Sprotbrough, 25.7.2019 (DBo).
64. Ripon, 12.7.2019 (CNe); Burley-in-Wharfedale, 31.7.2019 (P&AR); West End, 1 & 24.8.2019 (CGH); Mickley, 25.8.2019 (CHF, JCW, JH, FC).
65. High Batts NR, 12.7.2019 (CHF, TMW, DMS et al.); Hutton Conyers, 25.7.2019 (CHF).

73.215 Lesser-spotted Pinion *Cosmia affinis* (Linnaeus)

Just one record of this elm-feeding species which is usually found down the centre of the county along the magnesian limestone belt.

63. Austerfield, 12.7.2019 (SB).

73.220 Minor Shoulder-knot *Brachylomia viminalis* (Fabricius)

This very local willow-feeding moth of damp woodland was, as usual, reported from few sites. At some locations however it is evidently doing well for example. 51 caught at Ellington Banks on a warm night on 22.7.2019 was the biggest total ever caught in the county.

62. Aislaby, 23.7.2019 (WE); Robin Hood's Bay, 24.8.2019 (AR, JHo); Harwood Dale, 25.8.2019 (SF); Helwath, 29.8.2019 (GF).

64. Ellington Banks (MOD), 8 & 22.7.2019 (CHF, JCW, SMP, AWh); Sharow, 31.7 & 9.8.2019 (JCW); Syningthwaite Farm, 3.8.2019 (JCW).

73.221 Suspected *Parastichtis suspecta* (Hübner)

We usually list all records of this species but 32 records of 49 moths from 21 sites means there are too many to list individually. Records were mostly from scrubby birch-rich areas in the centre of the county.

73.228 Grey Chi *Antitype chi* (Linnaeus)

A return to normal levels following the big numbers seen in 2018. This species has appeared to have retreated to higher ground in recent years in response to climatic change.

62. Goathland, 1.8.2019 (WN); York, 22.8.2019 (MWal); Brompton, 26.8.2019 (SBo); Aislaby, 27.8.2019 (WE).

63. Nether Edge, 1.8.2019 (GA); Golcar, 5.8.2019 (CSR); Halifax, 6.8.2019 (DSu); Bramley, 12.8.2019 (JWC); Keighley Moor, 12, 25, 29 & 30.8.2019 (IHa); Thornton (Bradford), 4.8.2019 (MaP).

64. Cookridge, 4.7.2019 (PL); Giggleswick, 22.7, 3, 16, 20, 26 & 30.8.2019 (RW); Grass Wood, 3.8.2019 (PMi); Ingleton, 21 & 24.8.2019 (RN); Dob Park, 23.8.2019 (CGH); West End, 24.8.2019 (CGH); High Farnhill, 24.8.2019 (NS); Skyreholme, 25.8.2019 (PMi); Pateley Bridge, 24.8.2019 (T&PB).

65. Hutton Conyers, 24.8.2019 (CHF).

73.232 Northern Deep-brown Dart *Aporophyla lueneburgensis* (Freyer)

It remains unclear whether Northern Deep-brown Dart and Deep-brown Dart are two species, and whether we have both in the county. The new *Atlas of Britain and Ireland's Larger* Moths maps them separately in most of the county, however the two appear to be indistinguishable on wing pattern or genitalia, so until someone tells us how to separate them, we will continue to list them all as Northern Deep-brown Dart. It remains local in the south and the north of the county.

62. Saltburn, 14.9.2019 (IE).

63. Austerfield, 21, 25 & 26.9, 4, 6 & 11.10.2019 (SB); Kirk Smeaton, 28 & 30.9.2019 (DWi).

64. Little Preston, 4, 7 & 11.10.2019 (JMa).

73.234 Brindled Ochre *Dasypolia templi* (Thunberg)

A healthy spread of records of this over-wintering species from uplands in the west, and from rocky coastal areas, with several new sites.

61. Flamborough, 17, 23 & 25.10, 8.11.2019 (AAl, IM, MiP).

62. Sneaton, 29.10.2019 (N&MT).

63. Keighley Moor, 15.9.2019 (IHa).

64. Skyreholme, 16.4.2019 (PMi); Coniston Cold, 30.9.2019 (ARh); Grimwith Reservoir, 2.10.2019 (ADN); Colt Park, 9.10.2019 (JP, JHa, CNe).

65. Bishopdale, 24.3.2019 (JT).

73.235 Feathered Ranunculus *Polymixis lichenea* (Hübner)

Like last year, there were no records from any of our small inland colonies. In coastal areas there were 86 records of 122 moths from 13 sites so it is evidently doing well.

73.246 Lead-coloured Drab *Orthosia populeti* (Fabricius)

Most photographs of Lead-coloured Drab that we receive turn out to be the "lead-coloured" form of Clouded Drab. Have a good look at the antennae which are much more feathery (or bipectinate if you want to be scientific) in the males than those of Clouded Drab. Females are harder but few of these come to light anyway. This is a local moth which doesn't stray far from aspens and poplars.

61. Tophill Low NR, 9, 10, 14, 15, 21, 22 & 28.3.2019 (MHo, DF); Wheldrake, 22.3.2019 (JOHS).

62. Clay Bank Plantation, 23.5.2019 (SF).

63. Austerfield, 18, 19 & 21.3.2019 (SB); Kirk Smeaton, 21.3.2019 (P&JS); Potteric Carr NR, 21.3.2019 (RI&JCH, HEB).

64. Bellflask, 24, 27 & 30.3, 5, 6 & 23.4.2019 (BM).

65. Brompton-on-Swale, 21.3.2019 (TCo); Hutton Conyers, 6.4.2019 (CHF); Nosterfield NR, 7.4.2019 (CHF, JCW).

73.252 Hedge Rustic *Tholera cespitis* ([Denis & Schiffermüller])

This rather local moth of open grassy areas is in decline nationally. It still occurs in several places in Yorkshire and this was a good year.

62. Strensall Common, 22 & 27.8, 10.9.2019 (YB); Strensall Village, 23.8.2019 (YB); Harwood Dale, 24.8.2019 (AR, JHo).

63. Austerfield, 8 records of 29 moths from 21.8 to 8.9.2019 (SB).

65. Foxglove Covert, 23.8 & 29.9.2019 (CHF, JCW, DMS et al.).

73.257 Beautiful Yellow Underwing *Anarta myrtilli* (Linnaeus)

This species is sometimes attracted to light but is more often seen flying by day. All these records were of day-flying moths and were from, or near, typical heathery sites – lowland heaths and upland areas.

61. Lower Derwent Valley, 13 & 20.5.2019 (CSR); Wheldrake Bank Island, 13.5.2019 (CSR); Skipwith Common NNR, 12.9.2019 (PA).

62. Danby Beacon, 13.5.2019 (SF); Strensall Common, 31.5.2019 (DWa); Goathland Moor, 16.7.2019 (AGar, TAM); Tranmire Bog, 23.7.2019 (PA).

63. Thorne Moors, 1, 2 & 29.7.2019 (MWa et al.); Keighley Moor, 22.7.2019 (IHa).

73.266 Dog's Tooth *Lacanobia suasa* ([Denis & Schiffermüller])

This species appears to be in a slow and steady decline and this was a poor year, the only records coming from the Spurn area.

61. Spurn area, 12 records of 12 moths from 30.5 to 19.8.2019 (JHF, MFS).

73.272 Glaucous Shears *Papestra biren* (Goeze)

Healthy totals this year, especially on Keighley Moor where it seems that this species is thriving. Away from upland moorland, individuals can wander several miles on warm nights. Records from our lowland heaths are rare, though one at Haxby may have been a wanderer from Strensall Common.

62. Great Smeaton, 24.5.2019 (JE); Haxby, 30.5.2019 (TJC).

63. Keighley Moor, ten records of 78 moths from 21.4 to 26.5.2019 (IHa); Thornton (Bradford), 12.5.2019 (MaP); Rodley, 26 & 29.5.2019 (JWC).

64. Menston, 24.4.2019 (CGH); Hawkswick, 30.4.2019 (PMi, ARh, N&DF, C&FH); Colt Park, 15.5.2019 (JP); Ingleton, 17.5 (JP) and 18.5.2019 (RN); Burley-in-Wharfedale, 18.5.2019 (P&AR); Wetherby, 21.5.2019 (DJR); Colt Park, 23.5.2019 (JP); Ingleborough NR, 1.6.2019 (TMW).

73.275 White Colon *Sideridis turbida* (Esper)

This species has decreased severely in numbers and distribution across the country in recent years. Our figures mirror this, however this year there was a modest increase in numbers at Spurn.

61. Spurn area, nine records, all of single moths, from 30.5 to 23.7.2019 (MFS, JHF, JCr).

73.279 Broad-barred White *Hecatera bicolorata* (Hufnagel)

A very poor year for this declining moth of flower-rich calcareous grassy areas.

61. Market Weighton, 24.6.2019 (PA).

63. Rawcliffe Bridge, 22.5.2019 (RM); Austerfield, 29.5, 2.6 & 10.7.2019 (SB); Doncaster, 30.5.2019 (RM); Sprotbrough, 24.8.2019 (DBo).

64. West Bradford, 24.6.2019 (BH).

73.280 Small Ranunculus *H. dysodea* ([Denis & Schiffermüller])

A slight decrease in number of records. Its advance across the county is not proving to be as rapid as some people expected, and there were no records in the York area this year. There was however some increase of territory into more western parts of VC63.

61. Easington (Spurn), 22.7.2019 (MFS); Spurn, 5.9.2019 (MA).

63. Wakefield, 28.6.2019 (JD); Austerfield, 24.7.2019 (SB); Outam Wood, 23.8.2019 (UR); Rotherham, 6.9.2019 (MSm); Wombwell, 5, 9 & 13.7, 22.9.2019 (HBe); Mirfield, 12.7.2019 (LJa).

73.295 Delicate Flamborough VC61 Mike Pearson
A rare migrant.

64. Burley, 10.9.2019 (UR).

73.282 (2170) Varied Coronet *Hadena compta* (Denis & Schiffermüller)
It is interesting to monitor the spread of this species. There was an increase in numbers this year to 72 records of 79 moths from 42 sites, but not much expansion in range. There has been a little encroachment into more westerly parts of VC63 and mid-VC64, but it remains rare in VC62 and shows no inclination at present to fly across the border into VC65.

73.283 Marbled Coronet *H. confusa* (Hufnagel)
Low numbers as usual. The new Atlas points out that it has been lost from many inland sites, and it is interesting that all of our records in the last two years have been from coastal areas.

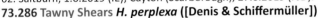

73.297 White-point, Austerfield 9 July 19 Samantha Batty.

61. Muston, 27.5.2019 (PQW).
62. Saltburn, 1.6.2019 (IE); Cayton (Scarborough), 27.6.2019 (PJD).

73.286 Tawny Shears *H. perplexa* ([Denis & Schiffermüller])
Another declining species of flower-rich calcareous grassland which is rather local in the county. Several claimed records turned out to be other species this year.
61. Catwick, 3.6.2019 (JM); Easington (Spurn), 27.7.2019 (MFS).
62. York, 28.7.2019 (AF).
63. Balby, 22.7.2019 (PG).

73.289 Striped Wainscot *Mythimna pudorina* ([Denis & Schiffermüller])
This moth of marshes and heathland is very local in the county but where it does occur it can be common. A poor year.
62. Strensall Common, 29.6 & 5.7.2019 (YB).
63. Hatfield Moors, 16.7.2019 (HEB, DWi).

73.295 Delicate *M. vitellina* (Hübner)
A fairly good year for this sporadic migrant.
61. Muston, 3, 4, 9, 24 & 31.10.2019 (PQW); Flamborough, 11.10.2019 (MiP).
62. Haxby, 22.9.2019 (TJC).

73.297 White-point *M. albipuncta* ([Denis & Schiffermüller])
This species is moving slowly north and west so it is no surprise that we now have a record for VC63. We find that a lot of claimed records turn out to be Clay, so be cautious if you catch this species out of its usual area.
61. Spurn area, 22.6, 1, 8 & 19.8.2019 (JHF, MFS).
63. Austerfield, 9.7.2019 (SB). NEW VC RECORD.

73.299 Shore Wainscot *M. litoralis* (Curtis)
Numbers appear to be stable at Spurn and this species remains uncommon in the Teesside area.
61. Spurn area, 17 records of 21 moths from 19.6 to 24.7.2019 (MFS, JHF, JCr).
62. Marske Beach, 28.7.2019 (DM).

73.302 Obscure Wainscot *Leucania obsoleta* (Hübner)
This species continues to do well with 43 records of 202 moths from 16 sites. Most records were in VC61 however moths were seen at several new sites further north and west and it is worth looking for now in any reed beds in the county.

73.299 Shore Wainscot Marske Cleveland VC62 28th July 19 Damian Money

73.307 Pearly Underwing *Peridroma saucia* (Hübner)

An average year for this migrant after only two records in 2018.

61. Spurn area, 28 & 29.9, 16 & 21.10.2019 (JHF, MFS); Muston, 6.10.2019 (PQW); North Ferriby, 7.10.2019 (IM); Flamborough, 13.10.2019 (MiP).
62. Saltburn, 2.8.2019 (IE).
63. Kirk Smeaton, 31.5.2019 (P&JS).

73.320 Heart and Club *Agrotis clavis* (Hufnagel)

This species is commonest in coastal areas and on calcareous grassland where it can be locally common, for example 47 at Ellington Banks on 8th July. Away from these areas it is much rarer and we find that it is sometimes confused with the much commoner Turnip Moth. There were 33 records of 108 moths from 19 sites this year.

73.322 Archer's Dart *A. vestigialis* (Hufnagel)

A slightly better year at Spurn following the very low totals in 2018. This species is much rarer inland, so it was encouraging to receive a record from the Lower Derwent Valley.

61. Spurn area, 12 records of 15 moths from 31.7 to 28.8.2019 (JHF, MFS, MA, JCr); Lower Derwent Valley, 28.6.2019 (NC, SC).
62. Marske Beach, 28.7 & 2.8.2019 (DM).

73.323 Sand Dart *A. ripae* (Hübner)

A good recovery following the low point of only six moths in 2018. Numbers remain low however compared to ten years ago. It is good to see two records in the Teesside area where it was first found in 2015.

61. Spurn area, 78 records of 118 moths from 23.5 to 19.8 (JHF, MFS, JCr, MA).
62. Marske Beach, 28.7 & 2.8 (DM).

73.327 Dark Sword-grass *A. ipsilon* (Hufnagel)

A fairly poor year for this migrant species with 149 records of 167 moths from 49 sites. The bulk of the records were in VC61 and 64.

73.331 Barred Chestnut *Diarsia dahlii* (Hübner)

Another good year for this moth of broadleaved woodland in upland areas where it can be locally common.

62. Goathland, 21.7.2019 (WN); Guisborough, 3.8.2019 (RWo); Low North Camp, 23.8.2019 (RWo, GF, AR, JHo); Littlebeck, 24.8.2019 (MN); Saltburn, 28.8.2019 (IE); Helwath, 29.8.2019 (GF); Rievaulx Moor, 29.8 & 6.9.2019 (RWo); Wykeham, 30.8.2019 (IM, MP, LB).
63. Marsden, 8.8.2019 (AB); Greno Wood, 8.8.2019 (MBr).
64. Sawley, 20.8.2019 (CHF); Dob Park, 12, 23 & 29.8, 8 & 11.9.2019 (CGH); West End, 24.8.2019 (CGH); Mickley, 25.8.2019 (CHF, JCW, JH, FC).
65. Foxglove Covert, 23.8.2019 (CHF, JCW, DMS et al.).

73.335 Fen Square-spot *D. florida* (Schmidt)

A slight drop in numbers this year. This species, as most people now realise, is a larger, paler, univoltine and (usually) upland version of Small Square-spot. It is at its peak between the two broods of Small Square-spot. These however are continuous with no proper gap. They reached a low point this year in the second week of July, so by this time, the first brood would look worn and tatty, and any second brood moths on the wing should be obvious by appearing smaller and darker than the first brood. Take care not to over-diagnose this moth. It is usually fairly obvious when you see it. Surprisingly we have no records from VC63 though it is likely to be present in some upland areas in the west.

61. Muston, 5, 7 & 8.6.2019 (PQW).
64. Coniston Cold, 18, 24 & 29.6, 4.7.2019 (ARh); Skyreholme, 23.7.2019 (PMi); Malham Tarn, 25.7.2019 (DCGB).
65. Nosterfield NR, 27.6.2019 (JCW).

73.337 White-marked *Cerastis leucographa* ([Denis & Schiffermüller])

A poor year with records from only three sites. It is locally common in a small area north of Ripon and less common in VC62. Shandy Hall was a new site.

62. Shandy Hall, Coxwold, 30.3.2019 (PW).
64. Bellflask, 22 records of 55 moths from 18.3 to 24.4.2019 (BM).
65. Hutton Conyers, 6 records of 6 moths from 20.3 to 5.4.2019 (CHF).

73.341 Northern Rustic *Standfussiana lucernea* (Linnaeus)

This moth of rocky upland areas is rather local, with most records coming from the west of the county.

64. Duck Street Quarry (Greenhow), 17.7.2019 (PMi, ARh, PR, DFe et al.); Ribblehead Quarry NR, 18.7.2019 (TMW); Moughton, 23.7.2019 (TMW); Malham Tarn, 25.7.2019 (DCGB).

73.354 Square-spotted Clay *Xestia stigmatica* **(Hübner)**
A rather local moth of broadleaved woodland, usually in upland areas in the north of the county, and locally common in parts of the northern Dales. There were records from several new sites this year and the first from Strensall Common for many years.
62. Saltburn, 16.7.2019 (IE); Goathland, 27.7.2019 (WN); Strensall Common, 20.8.2019 (YB).
64. Bellflask, 4, 8 & 25.8.2019 (BM).
65. Semerwater SSSI, 26.7.2019 (CHF, JCW, DMS, TMW); Hayberries, 1.8.2019 (PWe); Marrick Moor, 27.8.2019 (PCo).

73.355 Neglected Rustic *X. castanea* **(Esper)**
A healthy spread of records from heathery upland areas but also from Strensall Common where it had not been recorded for several years and where it seems to be more common than we realised.
62. Strensall Common, 20, 22 & 27.8, 10.9.2019 (YB); Strensall Village, 3.9.2019 (YB); Robin Hood's Bay, 24.8.2019 (AR, JHo); Great Barugh, 26.8.2019 (PC); Guisborough, 29.8.2019 (RWo); Rievaulx Moor, 29.8 & 6.9.2019 (RWo); Helmsley, 26 & 30.8.2019 (DIS).
63. Keighley Moor, 22, 23 & 25.8.2019 (IHa).
64. Yockenthwaite, 14.8.2019 (PMi, ARh, DFe); Coniston Cold, 21 & 26.8.2019 (ARh); New Laithe Farm, 24.8.2019 (MB); Skyreholme, 25 & 27.8.2019 (PMi); High Farnhill, 26.8.2019 (NS); Giggleswick, 2.9.2019 (RW).

73.356 Heath Rustic *X. agathina* **(Duponchel)**
This heather-feeding species is locally common in moorland areas and it also occurs on our lowland heaths. It wanders widely at times to the lowlands and has a habit of turning up in unusual places. Five of the 20 sites this year were new. Several records were of the distinctive striped larva.
61. Allerthorpe Common (larvae), 18.4.2019 (DA); Skipwith Common (larvae), 23.4.2019 (DA); Lower Derwent Valley, 23.8.2019 (CSR); Wheldrake, 27.8.2019 (JOHS); North Ferriby, 3 & 5.9.2019 (IM); Lund, 3.9.2019 (DA).
62. Robin Hood's Bay, 24.8.2019 (AR, JHo); Strensall Common, 27.8 & 10.9.2019 (YB); Rievaulx Moor, 29.8.2019 (RWo); Tollerton, 30.8.2019 (MBe); Fen Bog, 14.9.2019 (JW).
63. Keighley Moor, 21.5 & 1.6.2019 (larvae) and 22, 23, 25.8.2019 (IHa); Fishlake, 27 & 30.8.2019 (RP); West Melton, 28.8.2019 (HEB); Low Moor (Bradford), 30.8.2019 (MVP).
64. Askham Bryan, 25.8.2019 (DLa); Dob Park, 29.8.2019 (CGH); Coniston Cold, 3.9.2019 (ARh).
65. Foxglove Covert, 23.8.2019 (CHF, JCW, DMS et al.).

73.366 Plain Clay *Eugnorisma depuncta* **(Linnaeus)**
Reduced numbers following the record totals of 2018. There were 47 records of 110 moths, all from the core area in the north/centre of the county between Harrogate and Richmond. Almost all of its English population is now confined to this area apart from scattered records in the south-west. The Grewelthorpe trap again attracted the biggest single counts.

NOLIDAE

74.002 Kent Black Arches *Meganola albula* **([Denis & Schiffermüller])**
A big reduction this year with just 10 records, all of single moths. This species has been slowly extending its range over the last 40 years but the expansion seems to have reached a halt recently, and for the second year in a row, it was not recorded any further north than North Ferriby.
61. Spurn area, 8 records of 8 moths from 18.7 to 25.9.2019 (JHF, JCr, MFS); North Ferriby, 29.7 & 2.8.2019 (IM).

74.007 Scarce Silver-lines *Bena bicolorana* **(Fuessly)**
It is nice to report a return to normality for this attractive species after some poor years. 37 records of 40 moths from 27 sites across all five vice-counties means that there are too many to list individually. Over 90% of records on our database are of single moths.

74.009 Oak Nycteoline *Nycteola revayana* **(Scopoli)**
For the third year in a row there are too many records to list individually. 32 records of 37 moths from 17 sites spread across lowland parts of all five vice-counties. This over-wintering species has been seen in every month of the year in Yorkshire except for December. Take care not to mistake it for an *Acleris* species in particular *A. cristana* and *A. hastiana* which are smaller and do not have such broad wings.

74.011 Cream-bordered Green Pea *Earias clorana* **(Linnaeus)**
61 records of 87 moths from 22 sites – the biggest numbers yet recorded, so too many to list individually. There was no expansion in range however and most records were from the south-eastern quarter of the county.

CONTACTS
Yorkshire Lepidoptera Recording Team Address List 2020

Chair, BC Yorkshire: Acting Chair Les Driffield contact details on BCY website:
www.yorkshirebutterflies.org.uk
Chair, YNU Lepidoptera Group: Ian Marshall (Mr): 19 Ferriby High Road, North Ferriby, East Yorkshire, HU14 3LD. ☎ 01482 627446 | ✆ recording.fbo@outlook.com

LepNET Yorkshire: Butterfly Conservation Yorkshire, and the YNU Lepidoptera Group joint recording scheme. Joint Project Co-ordinators:
County Micro-moth Recorder: Harry E Beaumont (Mr): 37 Melton Green, West Melton, Rotherham, S63 6AA. Holds the county micro-moth database.
County Macro-moth Recorder: Charles H Fletcher (Dr): The Forge, Hutton Conyers, Ripon, N Yorks, HG4 5EB. ☎ 01765 600586 | ✆ chfletcher@btinternet.com Holds the county macro-moth database.
County Butterfly Recorder: David RR Smith (Dr): 56 South Street, Cottingham, HU16 4AT. ☎ 07906 160447 | ✆ davidsmith.butterflies@gmail.com Holds the county butterfly database.
Annual Report General Editor: Penny A Relf: Brock House, St Helens Square, Barmby Moor, YO42 4HH. ☎ 01759 307943 | ✆ pennyrelf59@gmail.com
Butterfly Recording VC Co-ordinators:
VC61: Sean Clough (Mr): 51 Thoresby St, Hull, HU5 3RA. ☎ 01482 448088 | ✆ sean@51thor.karoo.co.uk
VC62: Dave O'Brien (Mr): 42 Pritchett Road, Middlesbrough, TS3 ONG. ☎ 07521 802282 | ✆ dobrien6@virginmedia.com
VC63: David RR Smith (Dr): 56 South Street, Cottingham, HU16 4AT. ☎ 07906 160447 | ✆ davidsmith.butterflies@gmail.com
VC64: Dave Ramsden (Mr): 3 Burnham Court, Wetherby, Leeds, LS22 6XJ. ☎ 01937 520919 | ✆ dave.ramsden@outlook.com
VC65: Paul Millard (Dr): Ghyll House, Skyreholme, Skipton, N Yorks, BD23 6DE. ☎ 01756 720490 | ✆ butterfly.millard@btinternet.com
Moth Recording Co-ordinators:
VC61: Ian Marshall: 19 Ferriby High Road, North Ferriby, East Yorkshire, HU14 3LD. ☎ 01482 627446 | ✆ recording.fbo@outlook.com
VC62: Robert Woods: 19 Thirlby Way, Guisborough, Cleveland, TA14 6GN. ☎ 01287 631901 | ✆ rwoods1163@aol.com
VC63: Mike Couling: 'High Up', Binns Lane, Holmfirth, HD9 3BJ. ☎ 01484 685286 | ✆ mike_couling@yahoo.co.uk
VC64/65: Charles H Fletcher (Dr): The Forge, Hutton Conyers, Ripon, N Yorks, HG4 5EB. ☎ 01765 600586 ✆ chfletcher@btinternet.com
Butterfly Species Co-ordinators (who write up the indicated species in the annual report):
Philip Brook (Mr): *Large Skipper, Meadow Brown* 194 Leeds Road, Kippax, Leeds, LS25 7EL. ☎ 0113 2867235 | ✆ prbandsue@superb19.plus.com
Nyree Fearnley (Mrs): *Brimstone, Green Hairstreak* 2 St. Helena's Caravan Park, Otley Old Road, Horsforth, W. Yorkshire, LS18 5HZ. ☎ 0113 2843540 | ✆ david.nyree@btinternet.com
Paul Fletcher (Mr): *Small White* 38 Heslington Lane, York, YO10 4LX. ☎ 01904 631585 | ✆ pazfletcher@yahoo.com
Mark Hasson: *Large White* Westfield House, Grewelthorpe, Ripon, North Yorkshire, G4 3BS. ✆ markhasson1972@gmail.com
Dave Hatton (Mr): *Small Skipper* 29 Merton Drive, Farsley, Pudsey, LS28 5EB. ☎ 01132 552807 | ✆ dh.computers@ntlworld.com
Lizzie Ingram: *Comma* 12 Coxwold View, Wetherby, W Yorks, LS22 7PU. ☎ 07904 595798 | ✆ bs08ei@hotmail.co.uk
Steve Mattock (Mr): *Wall* 8 Malvern Ave, York, YO26 5SG. ☎ 01904 786022 | ✆ mattock99@sky.com

Ron Moat (Mr): *Large Heath* 39 Zetland Rd, Town Moor, Doncaster, S. Yorks, DN2 5EQ. ☎ 01302 327880 | ⌁ ronmoat@btinternet.com

Peter Mayhew (Dr): *Common Blue* 41 Keble Park South, Bishopthorpe, York, YO23 2SU. ☎ 07519 877922 | ⌁ peter.mayhew@york.ac.uk

Callum Macgregor (Dr): *Ringlet* 44 West Green Drive, Pocklington, York, YO42 2YZ. ☎ 07886 149722 | ⌁ callumjmacgregor@gmail.com

Dave O'Brien (Mr): *White-letter & Purple Hairstreak & Grayling* address details above ⌁ d.obrien6@ntlworld.com

Robert Parks (Mr): *Duke of Burgundy* 'Rosehill', Dovenby, Cockermouth, Cumbria, CA13 0PN. ☎ 01900 828607 | ⌁ r.parks13@yahoo.com

Martin Partridge (Mr): *Brown Argus & Northern Brown Argus* Balgownie, Manor Drive, Hilton, TS15 9LE. ☎ 07729 328691 | ⌁ martingpartridge@gmail.com

Dave Ramsden (Mr): *Holly Blue* address details above ⌁ dave.ramsden@outlook.com

Paul & Joyce Simmons: *Clouded Yellow, Gatekeeper, Small Heath* 16 Springfield Crescent, Kirk Smeaton, Pontefract, WF8 3LE. ☎ 01977 620725 | ⌁ paul or joyce@gentian.plus.com

David R R Smith (Dr): *Essex Skipper, Small Copper plus rarities, exotics and any unlisted species* address details above ⌁ davidsmith.butterflies@gmail.com

Jennifer A Smith (Dr): *Marbled White* 56 South Street, Cottingham, East Yorkshire, HU16 4AT. ⌁ jennifer.smith4000@yahoo.co.uk

Andrew Suggitt (Dr): *Orange-tip, Speckled Wood* . ⌁ andrew.suggitt@northumbria.ac.uk

Emily Summer: *Small Tortoiseshell* 30 Wood Lane, Beverley, HU17 8BS. ☎ 01482 860921 | ⌁ emilysummer2508@gmail.com

Dave Wainwright (Dr): *Pearl-bordered Fritillary* c/o Butterfly Conservation, Low Barns, Witton-le-Wear, Bishop Auckland, Co. Durham, DL14 0AG. ☎ 01388 488428 or 07709 278407 | ⌁ dwainwright@butterfly-conservation.org

Jennifer Watts: *Dingy Skipper* 16 Denton Street, Beverley, HU17 0PX. ☎ 07930 841601 | ⌁ me@jenniewatts.co.uk

Jax Westmoreland (Mrs): *Green-veined White, Painted Lady* 1 Glynndale Drive, Newby, Scarborough, YO12 5SQ. ☎01723 341 193 | ⌁ jaxw@btinternet.com

Lee Westmoreland (Mr): *Red Admiral* as for Jax Westmoreland except ⌁ leew@btinternet.com

Terry Whitaker (Dr): *Small Pearl-bordered Fritillary, Dark Green Fritillary* 4 Crowtrees, Low Bentham, Lancaster, LA2 7EE. ☎ 01524 262269 | ⌁ t.whitaker1@btinternet.com

David Woodmansey: *Peacock* East Lea, Back St, Langtoft, Driffield, YO25 0TG. ☎ 01377 267694 | ⌁ dwoodmansey@hotmail.co.uk

Derek Parkinson (Dr): *Lepidoptera Parasitoid Recorder* 11 Crow Tree Close, Baildon, Shipley, West Yorkshire, BD17 6JH. ☎ 01274 595185 | ⌁ derekparkinson@icloud.com

Dave Ramsden (Mr): *Weather Statistics Co-ordinators* address details above ⌁ dave.ramsden@outlook.com

Orange Swift *Hepialus sylvina* Loftus N Yorks John Money

Marbled Clover Ripon 2 August 2019
Ray and Pat Rumbold VC64 record

CONTRIBUTORS 2019

This Annual Report is a team effort involving a large number of people. Records are initially sent in before the end of the year to our 9 VC Co-ordinators who enter them into the Levana database for butterflies or a MapMate database for moths. In the case of butterflies, the data is re-arranged into species lists and sent to the Species Co-ordinators during December to be analysed and written up by early January. The various reports are then collated and put together by the Butterfly County Recorder. For the moths, the Co-ordinators edit the data and select the most interesting and relevant records to include out of many tens of thousands submitted. All the material is then passed to the Editor who brings together the several hundred files of texts and photos, and lays out the contents page by page ready for the printer by the summer.

The majority of 2019 contributors who provide their sightings direct to the VC recorders are listed below, except for those who have passed their records on via one of the many nature reserves, societies or recording groups which submit records. Then, in most cases, only the group name is included. Some names are repeated in different groupings because they have contributed to those different groupings. Where people have contributed their records through iRecord, Wider Countryside Survey, Migrant Watch etc it has not always been possible to include their names because of reasons of space. Where contributor names have been credited with initials in the text, those initials are added immediately after the name to which they refer. We are most grateful to everyone concerned, and apologise if any names have been missed out. The large size of the current input means that a few names will almost inevitably go astray for one reason or another. Last minute editing can also lead to some names slipping out of alphabetical order! Rest assured that even if your name has been missed, your contributions are still much appreciated. Thanks!!

VC61 Butterflies (123+ contributors) Chris Abbott, Phyl Abbott, Paul Adams, Roy Ainley, Pauline Allenby, Judith Allinson, Rob Andrews, David Ashton, Paul Ashton, Andrew Ashworth, David Ashworth, Robert Atkinson, Derek Bailey, Dennis Baker, Llewellyn Baker, Alan Bakewell, Martin Bland, Jesika Bone, David F Boocock, Stephen Booth, Audrey Bowland, Polly Bradley, Dave Britton, Neil Brown, Molly Bruce, Pauline Bursell, Alan Burnham, Colin Bushell, Brian Cain, Margaret Carus, Mike Clarke, Sean Clough, Tim Collins, Pam Cook, Ben Coulson, Lynda Cox, Terry Crawford, Stewart Crouch, Jan Crowther, Julie Davies, Trevor Davies, Paul Davison, James Dodd, Ray Edgar, Howard English, Edward Everingham, Jonnie Fisk, Christine Frost, Howard Frost, Andrew Gibson, Lina Girling, Robert Goodison, Mitchell Graham, Steve Green, Barry Greenacre, Sheelagh Halsey, Marion Hannaford, Mike Hayes, John Hesslewood, John Hewitt, Peter Hinks, David Howson, Tony Hull, Evie Hunt, Adrian Johnson, Alan Josephs, Lawrie King, Paul Leyland, Derek Longe, Jill Lucas, Rebecca Lynam, Edgar Mail, Ian Marshall, Andy Mason, Peter Mayhew, Ian McDonald, Bill McLaren, Ann Mettam, David Miller, Michael Mitchell, Phil Morgan, Roger Neale, Patricia Nobbs, Stephen Parkes, Ewan Parry, Philippa Pearson, David Penny, Susan Platter, Penny Relf, Rosemary Roach, Carole Robinson, Ainley Roy, Yvonne Ryan, Richard Shillaker, David Smith, Jenny Smith, A Slade, Mike Small, Richard Southwell, Barry R Spence, Lauren Spencer, Spurn Bird Observatory, Claire Starbuck, Paul Stark, N Stephenson, Mark Stoyle, Martin Stoyle, Peter Summers, Peter Swallow, Alice Thompson, Paul Townsend, David Turner, Nicky Vernon, Alan Wain, Robert Waldron, Peter Waterton, Charles Wheelwright, Terry Whitaker, Derek Whiteley, Ron Wild, Brian Wilson, Maggie Wingfield, David H Woodmansey, Rob Young.

VC62 Butterflies (61 contributors) Ian Armitage, Ian Austin, Mike Barnham, Tony Butler, Terry Crawford, Carol Dickinson, John Edwards, Wendy English, Rolf Farrell, Graham Featherstone, David Phillips, Charles Fletcher, Howard & Christine Frost, Tim Furness, Anne & Rodney German, Kenneth Hale, Dee Hanson, Ian & Janet Heppenstall, Nigel Heptinstall, Peter Hinks, Julie Hogg, Wendy Holliday, Paul Ingham, Peter Izzard, Stephen Kirtley, Peter Liddle, Paul & Denise Martin, Sue & Steve Mattock, Peter Mayhew, Alan Miller, Damian Money, Phil Mountain, Wilf Norman, Dave O'Brien, Geoff Oxford, Lynda Parkes, Robert Parks, Martin Partridge, Pauline & Ian Popely, Dave Ramsden, Andrew Rhodes, Richard Scruton, Paul & Joyce Simmons, Ed Snell, David & Janet Tighe, Maureen & Malcolm Thompson, Paul Townsend, Dave Wainwright, Emma Walters, Mike Walton, Lee & Jax Westmoreland.

VC63 Butterflies (115 contributors) Norman Alvin, Garrod Ange, Ian Armitage, Keith Bannister, Mike Barnham, Pete Bibby, Ian & Barbara Blomfield, James Bradbury, Steve Branch, Margaret Brett, John Burdall, Peter Burgin, Tony Butler, Geoff M Carr, Sylvia Cooke, Les Corrall, Terry Crawford, Howard Crossley, Dennis Dell, Geoff Dibb, James Dickinson, Jim Dignan, David Dodsworth, John Dove, Leslie Driffield, Barry Evans, Vivien Fairhurst, Tom Fincham, D Firth, Barry Foster, Richard Freestone, P Gilbert, Stephen Gordon, Cliff Gorman, Louise Green, Sue Griffiths, Peter Gurney, P M Haigh, Nick Hall, Elaine & Dave Hatton, Edward Hawes, Arthur Hellewell, Ian Hey, Ralph Hibbert, James Hinchcliffe, Dudley Hind, Steve Hiner, Peter Hinks, John Hitchcock, Julie Hogg, Steve Holliday, Dave Holmes, Jim Horsfall, Philip Ireson, J Ingram, Luke & David Jackson, David & Les Johnson, L Johnson, Helen Kirk, Richard Laverack, G Y Leach, R Leighton, Paul Leonard, John Matthews, D McMahon, Ron Moat, Diana Monahan, T Morrill, P Morris, Eric Murphy, Chris Parkin, David Parkin, R Parsons, M Paul, K Pearson, J Pickering, David Plews, Martyn Priestley, M Pullan, G Rickers, Ion

Riley, Martin Roper, Roger Shaw, Stephen & Norah Schonhut, P & J Simmons, Mike Smethurst, David Smith, Dave M Smith, Bill Smyllie, S R Sowden, Susan Stead, Christine Stonier, John A Thickitt, Richard Thomas, Gerry Thornton, A Tiffany, Alwyn Timms, Mick Townsend, Paul Townsend, Diane Wardley, Martin Warne, Ian & Kath Weeks, Derek Whiteley, John A Wilkinson, Graeme Williams, David Williamson, Kay Woodward, Darren Wozencroft, Chris Yeates.

VC64 Butterflies (335+ contributors) Andrea Addyman, Christine Albone, Chris Alder, Josie Aldridge, Pauline Allenby, David & Joan Alred, Kay Andrews, Chloe Archer, Ian Armitage, Andrew Ashworth, Philip Askew, Caz Austen, David & Ann Austin, Ray Baker, Dave Balding, Peter Bancroft, Mike Barnham, Beth Barron, Susan Barton, Rick Batterbee, Geoff Blakesley, Martin Bland, Cathy Bleakley, Ian & Barbara Blomfield, Daniel Blyton, Rebecca Bolster, David Bond, Mick Borroff, J Brierley, Giles Brockman, Philip Brook, Simon Bryant, Karen Bullimore, Cian Burke-Brown, Peter & Janet Burns, Dick & Heather Burrows, Catherine Burton, Claire Burton, Heather Campbell, Michael Cardus, Joe Carmichael, Alan Chambers, Vicki Chew, Kay Child, Mike Clark, Jill Clarke, Edwina Clements, Mike & Joyce Clerk, Jerry Clough, Sean Clough, P G Coates, Frances Cole, David Cook, Derek Cook, Charlotte Copley, Ian Court, Mandy Cox, Stella Craven, Terry Crawford, Jim Cresswell, Ginni Darbyshire, Sally Davey, Martin Davies, M D Dawson, James Dickinson, Jenny Dixon, Jeremy Dunford, Paul Dutton, East Dales RG, Paul Eccles, John Edwards, Fairburn Ings RSPB, Amanda Fall, Richard Falls, Ali Fawcett, David & Nyree Fearnley, D Firth, David Firth, Aimee Fletcher, Charles Fletcher, Paul Fletcher, Charlotte Fox, Pam Francis, Alice Franks, John Galloway, Chris Garbutt, Steve Garland, Tony Garnett, John Gavaghan, A German, Christopher Gleeson, Barry Graham, Fran Graham, Linda Graham, Audrey Gramshaw, Ian Grange, Jeannie Grant, Barbara Greenwood, Melvin Grey, P Griff, Andrew Griffiths, Sue Griffiths, Robyn Guppy, Mark Gurney, Peter Gurney, P M Haigh, Nick Hall, Sheelagh Halsey, Jon Hamnett, Lori Handley, Marie Harbour, Corrie Hardaker, Mark Hardaker, Karen Hargreave, Jen Harley, Harrogate & District Naturalists Society Via J.E.A, Rachael Haw, Gordon Haycock, Alison Hayward, John Healey, John Heap, Ian Heard, Nigel Heptinstall, Margaret Heselton, Mark Hewitt, Gillian Higgins, Peter Hinks, Mark Hockey, Julie Hogg, Sue Holden, Mary Holland, Gordon Holmes, Martin Holmes, Paul Holmes, Robert Homan, Judith Hooper, Cathy Hopley, F & C Horner, Peter Howe, David Howson, Phil Howson, Peter Hughes, Natalie Hunt, Kath Hunter, R Hunton, Kelli Imms, J Ingram, Diana Jakeways, Rosy Jamieson, Linda Jenkinson, Andrew Jennings-Giles, Neera Johnson, A E Jones, Carolyne Jones, Andy Jowett, Julia Kay, Andrew Kelly, Dave Kelly, Rebecca Kennedy, Gordon Kidd, John Kilner, Steve Kirtley, Julia Kozlowska, Kyriacos & Janet Kyriakides, Mick Lambert, Michael P. Laycock, G Y Leach, David Leather, R Leighton, J Lewis, Gerald Light, Ros Lilley, Ken Limb, Margaret Longden, Liz & Steve Lonsdale, Denis Lord, Callum Macgregor, Jennifer Marshall, Christine Martin, J Martin, Steve Mathers, P Matt, Steve & Sue Mattock, Peter Mayhew, Maurice Maynard, Hilary McGuire, Terry McKenzie, D McMahon, Dave McMahon, Amelia McNair, Avis Meades, Mike Meakin, Neil Messenger, Ann Mettam, Jon Middleton, Carina Milburn, Andy Millard, Paul Millard, Peter Miller, Lawrence Moores, Caroline Moorhouse, Terry Morgan, T Morrill, Diane Morris, P Morris, Ray Morris, Kerry Morrison, Chris Morton, Roger Neale, Colin Newlands, Nidderdale AONB Blog, Belinda Nixie, Andrew & Sharon Nobel, Cecile Nock, Stephen North, Becky Norville, Denis O'Connor, G Orr, David Owen, Caroline Page, Rosalind Parkes, Steve Parkes, R Parsons, Rob Parsons, Martin Partridge, M Paul, Sophie Payne, Ruth Paynter, Mark Penny, Jessica Penrose, John Perry, David Philips, David Pickens, J Pickering, Bob Pickthall, Jim Pierce, Angela Ponsford, Ian Powell, Charles & Fiona Prest, David Preston, M Pullan, Paul Purvis, Tim Quantrill, Dave Ramsden, Dave & Ros Ramsey, Hannah Read, Andrew Rhodes, Julia Ribbons, Will Rich, Scruton Richard, G Rickers, Stephen Rigden, Peter & Anne Riley, Frank Roberts, Martin Roberts, Stephen Root, Terry Rowe, Jenny Rydzewski, Ruth Rymer, J Saville, Ernie Scarfe, Janice Scott, Judith Scott, Richard Scruton, Malcolm Secrett, Helen Sergeant, Karen Shackleton, John Shillcock, Brian & Elizabeth Shorrock, Graham Short, Maggie Shutt, D Singleton, Elizabeth Slingsby, Kelvin Smith, Melanie Smith, N Smith, Bruce Speed, Susan Stead, Tam Stewart, John & Sue Stidworthy, P Storie, Margaret Stringer, Andrew Sturmey, Elizabeth Sullivan, Andrew Sumnall, Andy Sumnall, Alistair Taylor, Angela Taylor, Marian Taylor, Julia Tetley, Andrew Thompson, Bill Thorne, Maeve Thwaites, A Tiffany, Alison Tribe, N & M Tuck, Rachael Tulloch, Janet Turnbull, Susan Turner, Bob Upton, G Vause, David Wadding, Vladislava Waley, Lindsey Walker, Anna Wallin, P Walton, Teresa Warbrick, Susan Ward, Patrick Wardle, Roger Wareing, David Warr, Jill Warwick, Simon Warwick, Jenny Watson, Sam Watson, Graham Weaver, Colin Welch, Leigh Weston, Phillip Whelpdale, Rachael Wherry, Alex Whitaker, Terry Whitaker, Joanne Wiggins, Samantha Wignall, Chris Wild, Royanne Wilding, Steve Wilkinson, Thomas Willis, Richard Wilson, Lee Wiseman, Jo Wolforth, Clive Wood, Steve Worwood, Jim Wright, Paul Young.

VC65 Butterflies (97+ contributors) Carolyn Bailey, Ray Baker, Mike Barnham, D Bellamy, David Belshaw, Cathy Bergs, D Bilton, Martin Bland, Mick Borroff, Nige Brummie, Andrew Bunce, Brian Cain, David Claxton, David Coltman, Pauline Cordner, Ian Court, Terry Crawford, Genevieve Dalley, Geoff Dibb, David Doodle, East Dales RG, Mike Eccles, John Edwards, Robert Elliott, Dave Fearnley, Nyree Fearnley, Charles Fletcher, Mike Gibson, Steve Green, David Hargreave, Karen Hargreave, Alison Harris, Jean Helm, Tim Helps, Martin Henstock, Nigel Heptinstall, Mark Hewitt, Simon Hodgson, Paul Holmes, Mike Horn, Peter Hughes, Patricia Illingworth, Carolyn Inskipp, Catherine Jones, Stephen Jones, Ben Keywood, Emma King, Paul Kipling,

Stephen Kirtley, Michaela Lambert, Susan Le Brocy, Ken Limb, Steve Lonsdale, Liz Lonsdale, John Luck, Keith Marshall, Andrew McMullon, Naomi Meredith, Paul Millard, Alan Miller, Nick Morgan, Andrew Murray, D Nath, Pat Nevison, David Oldham, Adam Parker, Jane Paul, Robert Pennington, Pauline Percival, David Phillips, David Pickens, David Raffle, Dave Ramsden, Andrew Rhodes, Marie Robinson, Arnold Robson, Tim Scott, Richard Scruton, Alison Shepherd, Diane Smiley, John Smith, Richard Southwell, Michael Spensley, Valerie Standen, Andrew Steele, Upper Wharfedale Field Society, Jill Warwick, Simon Warwick, Christine Weaver, David Wedd, Terry Whitaker, Jennie White, Royanne Wilding, Kevin Wilkes, Lorna Winstanley, Clive Wood, Steve Worwood.

Moths (484 contributors)

Chris Acomb, Robert Adams, Theresa Adams, Nick Addey-NAd, Chris Alder, Tracy Allen, Andrew Allport-AAl, Judith Allinson, Gina Allnatt-GA, Ken Alston, Norman Alvin-NAA, Robert Amos, Ian Andrews-IA, Kay Andrews-KA, Mark Andrews-MA, Paul Andrews, India Ashfield-IAs, Dave Ashton-DA, Gail Ashton, Paul Ashton-PA, Andrew Ashworth-AA, Mike Bailey, David Baker-DBa, Richard Baker, Trevor & Pam Baker-T&PB, Adam Bakewell, Chris Barlow, Dave Barlow, Mike Barnham-MRB, Kate Bartram, D Bastow, Samantha Batty-SB, Harry Beaumont-HEB, Amanda Beck, Roger Bell, Sandra Bell, D Bellamy, Heather Bennett-HBe, Michele Beverley-MBe, David Bickerton, K Bilon, D Bilton, Roger Bird, Tim Birkinshaw, Andrew Bissitt, Kit Beard, Chris Blanco-CB, Christopher Blakey, I&B Blomfield, Sue Boal-SBo, Barbara Boize-BB, Ian Bond, David Booth-DBo, Yves Bouvet-YB, Richard Borrett, L Bowes, Terry Box-TAB, Nora Boyle-NB, Alex Bozman-AB, Rex Bradshaw-RB, Mark Breaks-MB, Andrew Brown, Bruce Brown, David Brown-DCGB, Vin Browne, Lenora Bruce-LB, Marion Bryce-MBr, Sam Buckton, Karen Bullimore, Christine Burgin, Peter Burgin-PBu, Peter & Janet Burns-P&JB, Diane Burton-DBu, Roger Butterfield-RBu, Roger Campbell, Mike Cardus, Bryony Carling, Joe Carmichael, Nick Carter-NC, Sandra Carter-SC, Imogen Cavadino, David Chambers, Ron & Helen Chambers-R&HC, Paul Chapman-PC, Stuart Churchill, Julian Clarke, Keith Clarkson-KC, Norman Clarkson-NCl, B P Clayton, Mike and Joyce Clerk-M&JC, Jerry Clough, Frances Cole-FC, Simon Conyers, John Cooper-JWC, Tony Cooper-TCo, Pauline Cordner-PCo, Peter Corry, Robin Costello, Mike Couling, Kerry Coupe-KCo, Ian Court, Mike Coverdale-MCo, Terry Crawford-TJC, Jonathan Cridford, Jan Crowther-JCr, Mark Cubitt-MCu, Andrew Culshaw, Ian Cunliffe, Jill Cunningham, Phil Cutt, Genevieve Dalley, Stuart Davies, Richard Dawson, Richard Dennison-RD, Richard Dillon, Paul Disken-PD, Thomas Dixon, David Dodsworth, John Dove-JD, Alan Draper-AD, Les Driffield-LD, Sally Driscoll, Bryn Duffill-BD, Peter Dunn-PJD, Jessica Dylan, Helen Earnshaw, Ian Edgar-IE, John Edwards-JE, Matthew Ellison, Wendy English-WE, Edward Evans-EE, Doug Fairweather-DF, Amanda Fall, Richard Falls, Steve Farish-SF, Graham Farmer, Jo Fauvet, Nyree and David Fearnley-N&DF, Graham Featherstone-GF, Pete Feetham, David Fisher, Jonnie Fisk-JHF, Alastair Fitter-AF, Charles Fletcher-CHF, Ian Fletcher, Forestry Commission-FC, Ron Forrester-RFor, Paul Forster, M&A Forsythe, Mike Forty, Rob Foster, Keith Fowler, Charlotte Fox, June Fox, Foxglove Covert Moth Team-FCMT, Mick Francis, Georgia French-GFr, Chris Frost-MCF, Rebecca Frost-RF, R Fuller, Steve Gallis, John Galloway, Andy Gardiner-AGar, Ange Garrod, S Garvey, Helen Gaunt, John Gavaghan-JG, Eric Gendle-EG, D Gillespie, Nigel Gilligan, Keith Gittens-KG, Africa Gomez, Cliff Gorman-CG, Audrey Gramshaw, David Greaves-DMG, Peter Greaves-PG, Gillian Gribbin, Robyn Guppy, Nick Hall-NH, Robert Hall-RHa Jon Hamnett-JHa, Wendy Handford, Hardcastle Crags Survey Group-HCSG, Karen & David Hargreave-K&DH, Ian Hargreaves-IHa, Colin Harrison-CGH, Ian Hartley-IRH, Martin Harvey, Mark Hasson-MH, Dave Hatton-DH, Linden Hawthorne, Gordon Haycock, Martyn Hayes-MHy, Mark & Zach Haynes-M&ZH, Alison Hayward, Ian Heard, Rachel Heath, Tim Helps, Mick Hemingway-MHe, Ian & Janet Heppenstall-RI&JCH, Maggie Heselton, Tom Hibbert, High Batts NR Log, Gillian Higgins, Dave Higginson-Tranter, High Batts NR log, David Hill, James Hinchliffe, Martin Hodges-MHo, David Hodgson-DHo, Simon Hodgson, Julie Hogg, Pauline Hogg, Jackie Holder-JHo, Mary Holland, Gordon Holmes, Paul Holmes-PH, Robert Homan, Bill Honeywell-BH, Andrew Hood, Judith Hooper, Mike Horn, Carmen & Fred Horner-C&FH, David Howdon, Paul Hughes, Peter Hughes, Anthony Hurd, L Hutton, Mike Ibbotson-MI, Patricia Illingworth, Carol Inskipp, Luke Jackson-LJa, Diana Jakeways, Amy James-AJ, Angus Jennings, Jim Jobe, Les Johnson, Les & David Johnson, Carole Johnston, Catherine Jones, Jennifer Jones, Rebecca Jones, Ben Keywood, Gordon Kidd, John Kilner, Emma King, Lawrie King-LK, Helen Kirk-HRK, Steve Kirtley, David Knight, Victor Kolodziejczyk, Julia Kozlowska, Michaela Lambert, Karen Landimore, Peter Larner-PL, Andrew Lassey, Brian Latty, David Laughlin-DLa, Claire Lavery, David Leather, Phil Lee-PLe, Mike Leonard, Pete Leonard, J&J Lewis-J&JL, Paula Lightfoot, Ralph Lilley, Ken Limb-KL, Craig Linford, Emma Lomas, Dan Lombard, Toby Long, Norman Lowe-NL, John Luck, Ken McCann, Anthony McDonald, Hilary McGuire, Neal McKenna, Steve McWilliam, Brian MacGregor-BMc, Callum MacGregor-CM, Antony Marriott-AM, Ian Marshall-IM, John Martin-JMa, Mike Martin, Andrew Mason, Stephen Mason, David Mather, Steve Mathers, Lara Mayhew-LFM, Peter Mayhew-PMa, Pete Mella-PMe, Colin Menston, Jon Middleton, Paul Millard-PMi, Alan Millar-AM, Rob Miller, Ellen Milner, James Minchin, Ron Moat-RM, Damian Money-DM, John Money-JMon, Tracey Money-TAM, Jim Morgan-JM, Nick Morgan, Phil Morgan, Brian Morland-

BM, Diane Morris, Jack Morris, Paul Morris-PRM, Janice Morritt, Tony Moverley, John Mowbray, Lucy Murgatroyd-LM, Danny Murphy, Peter Murphy-PM, Susan Murphy, Andrew Murray, Roger Neale-RN, Toby Needs, Dave Nesham, Mervin Nethercoat-MNe, Amanda Newham, Colin Newlands-CNe, Sam Newton-SN, Debbie Nicholson-DN, Claire Nixon-CNi, Simon Noble, Wilf Norman-WN, Becky Norville, Mark Nowers-MN, Andy Nunn-ADN, Denis O'Connor- Gaby O'Toole, Stuart Ogilvy, Graham Oliver, Mik Ostapjuk, Geoff Oxford, Steve Palmer-SMP, Stuart Panton, Adam Parker, Chris Parkin-CP, Derek Parkinson-DPa, Roger Parrish, Ewan Parry, Paul Parsons, Ailsa Peace, Mark Pearson-MaP, Mike Pearson-MiP, Philippa Pearson, John Perry-JP, Michael Perry, Anna Pethen, David Phillips, David Pickens, Matt Pilkington, Mike Pilsworth-MJP, Sophie Pinder, Connah Platt, Angela Ponsford, Ian & Pauline Popely, Pauline Popely, Tessa Potter, Ian Powell-IPow, David and Janine Preston, Martyn Priestley-MVP, Ray Priestley-RP, Margaret Prior-MaP, Jonathan Proud, Mike Pryal, David Pye, Calum Rae, Craig Ralston-CSR, Dave Ramsden-DJR, John Rawcliffe, Laurie Reed-LR, Penny Relf-PRe, Colin Rew-CSR, Andrew Rhodes-ARh, Brett Richards, Paul Richards, M Richardson-MAR, Stephen Rigden, Peter and Ann Riley-P&AR, Hannah Risser, Martin Roberts, Belinda Robson-BR, Allan Rodda-AR, Simon Rolph, Adam Rowe, Suzanne Rowe, Eddie Ruddock, R&P Rumbold-R&PR, Ken Rutter, David Sales-DIS, Mike Samworth-MSa, Jane Sanders, Mark Sargent, Deb Schild, Will Scott, Helen Sergeant, David Shenton-DSh, Megan Shepherd, Sorrel Sheridan, Richard Shillaker, Victoria Shone, Paul Simmons-PSi, Paul and Joyce Simmons-P&JS, David Slade, Colin Slator, Julian Small-JOHS, Mike Smethurst-MSm, Diane Smiley-DMS, Alan Smith-AS, Dave Smith-DSm, Jan Smith-JSm, Peter Smith-PSm, Richard Southwell, Stephen Sowden, Barry Spence, Alison Stead, Nancy Stedman-NS, Mick Stoyle-MFS, Charlie Streets-CS, David Sutcliffe-DSu, Janice Sutton, David & Helen Tanner-D&HT, Peter Tannett-PT, Sandra Tate, Freddie Taylor, Marian Taylor, Jane Thomas-JT, Pandora Thoresby-PT, Alwyn Timms, Marta Alfara Tirado, Richard Tite, Mick Townsend-MT, Paul Townsend, Norman and Margery Tuck-N&MT, David Turner-DT, Elizabeth Turner, Jack & Ruth Upsall, Dave Wainwright-DWa, Christine Walker, Michael Walton-MWal, Sarah Ward, Lindsay Wardell-LW, Martin Warne-MWa, Lynn Warrington, Jill Warwick-JCW, Simon Warwick, Andrew Watchorn, George Watola, Ashley Watson, Jenny & Alistair Watson, John Wearmouth-JW, Peter Webb-PWe, Graham Wenman, Lee & Jax Westmoreland-L&JW, Alan Wheeldon-AWh, Philip Whelpdale, Terry Whitaker-TMW, Derek Whiteley, DWh, Dan Whitley, Ian Whittaker-IW, John Wilcox–JWi, Patrick Wildgust-PW, Royanne Wilding-RW, Raye Wilkinson-RWi, Brian Williams-BW, Karen Williams-KW, Dave Williamson-DWi, Jane Willis, Richard Wilson-RWi, Steve Wilson, Philip Winter-PQW, Lee Wiseman-LWi, Harry Witts-HW, Robert Woods-RWo, Jennifer Woollin, Rachel Wray, Anthony Wren-AWr, Tricia Wright-TWr, Paul Young, Stefan Young.

Narrow-bordered Five-spot Burnets, Strensall Common, 5 July 2019 Peter Mayhew

Julia *Dryas iulia* with Comma Hornsea, 9 Sept 2019 Graham Lowe